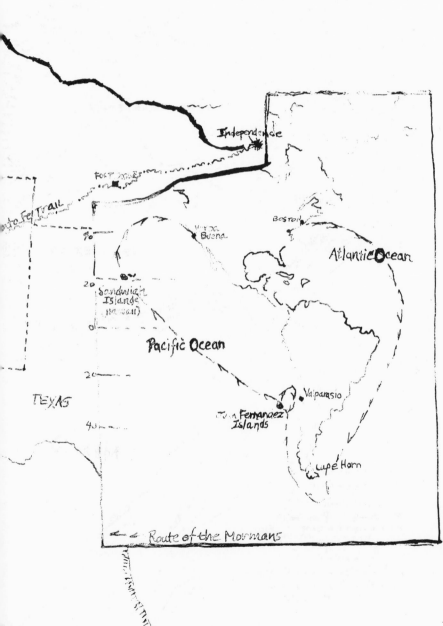

Independence

FORT LOOB

Santa Fe Trail

Vista Buena

Boston

Atlantic Ocean

Sandwich Islands (Hawaii)

Pacific Ocean

TEXAS

Valparaiso

Juan Fernandez Islands

Cape Horn

Route of the Mormans

Mexico City

Daughters of History

DAUGHTERS OF HISTORY

Centennial Memoirs of the Daughters of California Pioneers

Compiled and Edited by
Jane V. R. Bernasconi, Vera Freeman Felchlin, Mary Mason Friman,
Lorrainne Albach McLaughlin, Lucille Swasey Vinsant

Drawings and Maps by
Marion Poett Howard Hoekenga

BERKELEY HILLS BOOKS
BERKELEY, CALIFORNIA

Published by
Berkeley Hills Books
P. O. Box 9877
Berkeley, California 94709
(888) 848-7303
www.berkeleyhills.com

Comments on this book may also be addressed to: jpstroh@berkeleyhills.com

Cover design by Elysium, San Francisco.

Manufactured in the United States of America.

Library of Congress Cataloging-in-Publication Data

Daughters of history : centennial memoirs of the Daughters of California Pioneers /
compiled and edited by Jane V. R. Bernasconi ... [et al.] ; drawings and maps by Marion
Poett Howard Hoekenga.
        p. cm.
Includes bibliographical references and index.
ISBN 1-893163-31-8
    1. Women pioneers--California--Biography. 2. Pioneers--California--Biography. 3.
Frontier and pioneer life--California. 4. California--Biography. 5. Daughters of
California Pioneers--History. I. Bernasconi, Jane V. R. II. Hoekenga, Marion Poett
Howard.

F864.D24 2000
979.4'03'0922--dc21
[B]

Table of Contents

Part Eight: Manuscripts Written in 1917

Acknowledgements

We are grateful for the support of the many people who have contributed to the Daughters' active existence for the last one hundred years, leading up to, and culminating with, the compiling of this book. In appreciation we wish to recognize especially, among our members:

Laura Jacobs, who took over her mother's position as membership secretary, and kept the Daughters from fading away by writing personal notes to each member. She continues to keep track of all of us.

Lorrainne McLaughlin, Past President, whose inspiration initiated our project to assemble the history of the Daughters, along with biographies of our pioneer ancestors.

Jane Bernasconi, who started as a board member, then volunteered to do the newsletter and has been extensively involved with the putting together of this book.

Lucille Vinsant, a wonderful Recording Secretary and the third person who has been involved with the book since the beginning.

Mary Friman, several terms as President, who organized our documents which had lain dormant in storage for many years. She undertook to have the minutes of the past one hundred years professionally bound.

Janice Cline, who over the years has served us well on the board in many different capacities.

Patricia U'ren who keeps our mailing list up to date and supplies mailing labels for invitations and newsletters.

Eileen Callaghan, who took Patricia's list and produced the first membership directory in more than a few years.

Nancy Downey, who designed and donated the fine plate for our membership certificates.

Vivian Dane, who lends her calligraphy expertise to our certificates.

Nancy Powers, active attorney among us.

And the volunteers who, whenever asked, always help — Mary Baumann, Lucille Corcel, Nancy DeLara, Vera Felchlin, Barbara Macaire, and Marian Mohr.

And others:

Stephen Gallaway, historian, who has been in charge of the Daughters' scrapbooks, containing documents, newspaper clippings, photographs, and other archival materials, collected over the years.

Stanleigh Bry, Librarian at Pioneer Hall on McAllister Street, who initiated our quest in researching our family histories.

The Society of California Pioneers, for the use of Pioneer Hall for board meetings and social events during our one hundred years, for invitations to their social events, and the support of their members and staff — Herbert Garcia, Igor Blake, Susan Haas, Amy Boyd, Mercedes Divine, Gerry Gantner, Elizabeth Flynn, and Donald Bering.

The Women's Auxiliary, who have invited us to many of their activities.

And John Strohmeier, our Publisher, who has encouraged us from the early days of our project, convincing us that we had valuable stories to share. He gave us an outline of strategy, and a plan to lead us through the steps to completion and publication.

Introduction

Daughters of History was written to commemorate the one-hundred-year anniversary of the Daughters of California Pioneers. We have collected for this volume, from our members, sixty brief accounts of our pioneer ancestors, organized according to the time of their arrival in California. Following these accounts is a collection of eighteen biographical statements written in 1917 by founding members of our organization. The book's last section is a history of the Daughters taken from annual meeting minutes recorded over the past century.

Daughters of History tells of California's very earliest settlers of European descent and of their families. Traders and Yankees mingled with these Californios, and their stories are related here as well. Old California became a blending of cultures, and the population reflected both Spanish and American influences. By the 1840s California would no longer be a Mexican province, but a great mélange of many traditions from the entire world, a place where all were welcome to harvest the riches of the earth. The population exploded with the great migration of the 1849 gold discovery, and the Californios adapted to the influence of the newcomers to the West. The state of California was a reality, its future assured, and a new era had begun.

In discovering our stories we have sometimes had only scraps of information to work with. Some of us have hunted through old family records, legal documents, and history books in order to piece together a picture of the settling of the West and the role of our ancestors in this epic quest. Others have turned primarily to family memories, the oral histories told to us as children by a grandmother who heard it from her father or grandfather in fragments and anecdotes — cherished treasures handed down to us as family heirlooms.

The stories are told in various forms according to the sources that were available. Some are but brief sketches; others are taken from larger published works. In either case they are fascinating tales of pioneer adventure and courage. Our narratives are as accurate and truthful as possible, each written by a different individual according to her own viewpoint.

Following the requests of most of the authors that we "use this material any way you can" or "feel free to edit however appropriate," the editors have reviewed each manuscript carefully to ensure clarity and continuity in leading one story into the next.

Each of the accounts is marked by an icon indicating by what means its subject came to California (with a few exceptions, where the mode of transportation is not known). Travel by ship around the Horn is indicated by the image of a clipper ship; travel overland is denoted by a wagon; and those who came over the isthmus of Panama are marked by a man and burro.

Note also that most photos are from the collections of the authors. In those cases where they come from other sources, those sources are named.

Daughters of History is but a small sample of much more that lies hidden in the attics of all our families — lively tales waiting to be discovered.

THE DAUGHTERS OF CALIFORNIA PIONEERS
PAST PRESIDENTS

1900-01	Mrs. Mary V. H. Gurnett	1933-35	Mrs. Naniel G. Shannon
1902-03	Mrs. Alice McWilliams Morse	1935-36	Miss Irene Meussdorffer
1903-04	Mrs. Lucy F. Adams	1936-37	Mrs. Florence A. Farrell
1904-05	Mrs. Mary McWilliam Palmer	1937-39	Miss Ottilie Meussdorffer
1906-07	Mrs. Ernest A. Leigh	1939-40	Mrs. Alma C. Chisholm
1907-08	Miss Julia Neppert	1940-41	Mrs. Edgar M. Grant
1908-09	Miss Clara Adams	1941-42	Miss Elizabeth W. Latham
1909-10	Mrs. Emma T. MacGregor	1942-44	Mrs. Edgar M. Grant
1910-11	Mrs. Walter A. Scott	1944-48	Miss Elizabeth W. Latham
1911-12	Miss Lucy F. Adams	1948-50	Miss Irene Meussdorffer
1912-13	Miss Louise Nolan	1950-52	Mrs. Edgar L. Calhan
1913-14	Mrs. H. W. Rike	1952-53	Mrs. Francis Melka
1914-15	Mrs. Kathryn D. Boyns	1953-56	Mrs. Ida Mesquite
1915-16	Mrs. Idah May Pattison		Mrs. Antoinette Hobbs
1916-17	Mrs. Wm. A. Limbaugh		Letitia Oaks, M.D.
1917-18	Mrs. Millie Scott Biven		
1918-19	Mrs. Edgar M. Grant	1962-64	Mrs. H.J. Keville
1919-20	Mrs. E. R. Jewell	1964-65	Mrs. Wm. Anderson
1920-22	Mrs. Louise M. Bartels	1967-68	Mrs. Elliott Evans
1922-24	Madame C.E. Grosjean	1968-70	Mrs. Walter Gallatin
1924-25	Mrs. Alma Craig Chisholm	1970-74	Mrs. Richard Kelly
1925-26	Mrs. John Ahnden	1974-78	Mrs. Adrian Wahlander
1926	El. Mrs. John W. Classen	1978-81	Mrs. Robert D. Bullock
1926-27	Miss Irene Meussdorffer	1981	Miss Delphina Hill
1927-28	Miss Elizabeth W. Latham	1981-87	Miss Jovita Fitzgerald
1928-30	Mrs. Webb N. Pearce	1987-89	Mrs. Henry Kearns
1930-31	Mrs. Frank E. Daubenbess	1989-91	Mrs. Richard Kelly
1931	Pr. El. Miss Ophelia C. Levy	1991-93	Mrs. George D. Friman
1931-32	Miss Lucy F. Adams	1993-95	Ms. Lori A. Meyer
1932-33	Miss Mary F.L. Nolan	1995-97	Ms. Lorrainne A. McLaughlin
		1997-	Mrs. George D. Friman

17

THE DAUGHTERS OF CALIFORNIA PIONEERS
LIST OF MEMBERS
DECEMBER, 2000
WITH THE NAME OF THEIR PIONEER ANCESTOR

MEMBER	ANCESTOR	MEMBER	ANCESTOR
Ms. Ellen Leslie Adams	H. Osborn	Mrs. Gail Creveling	W. Steele
Mrs. Russell Adams, Jr.	H. Osborn	Ms. Paul Dane	J. I. Castro
Ms. Eunice Peña Alisea	M. de la Luz Verdugo	Mrs. Tada Lyons Darsie	W. H. Lyons
Ms. Cynthia Rogers Allison	S. J. S. Rogers	Mrs. Paul Davis	P. Marsicano
Mrs. Harold J. Anderson	J. Butterfield	Mrs. Nancy Dina DeLara	S. Moultrie
Audrey A. Arana	J. L. M. Moore	Ms. Deborah Ann Di Gangi	F. R. de Villar
Mrs. Michelle K. Aschwald	E. Nix	Ms. M. Terri Di Gangi	F. R. de Villar
Mrs. Suzanne Carol Auger	Lippencott	Mrs. Ralph L. Duncan	I. Corbett
Mrs. France de Sugny Bark	J. Parrott	Mrs. Jean Edwards	M. Mulcrevy
Mrs. Russell M. Bauer, Jr.	W. H. Hoburg	Ms. Florian C. Elliott	M. Mulcrevy
Mrs. Mary Baumann	P. de Cota	Mrs. Vale T. Feder	M. Levy
Ms. G. R. Beauchamp	M. Levy	Ms. Sarah A. Felchlin	D. S. Levy
Mrs. Karen Andrews Beebe		Mrs. Vera Felchlin	D. S. Levy
Mrs. Patricia Anne Bell	A. Von Schmidt	Mrs. Ilene Finn	L. C. Wittenmyer
Mrs. Peter G. Bentley	F. A. Bonner	Mrs. Rosemary Flamion	G. W. Oman
Mrs. Joyce Benton	J. Butterfield	Ms. Gabrielle Flavin	W. Money
Mrs. Jane V. R. Bernasconi	A. Russ	Mrs. Pamela Forbes	J. D. Ackerman, Sr.
Ms. Marcelline Abrego Blake	Abrego	Mrs. James C. Fowler	N. Hill
Ms. Diana Gaede Blatz	J. Irvine	Ms. Helene T. Frakes	J. M Aguirre
Mrs. Michael Boone	F. A. Bonnar	Ms. Ebe Frasse	M. Murphy
Ms. Patricia Pendleton Bragg	H. Coward	Miss Theresa A. Fregoso	J. A. Yorba
Mrs. Harold J. Broerman	Noriega	Mrs. Diane F. Friedlander	J. O'Brien, M.D.
Ruth B. Brown	C. C. Espinosa	Ms. Catherine E. Friman	J. A. Yorba
Mrs. James L. Browne	H. T. Graves	Mrs. George D. Friman	J. A. Yorba
Mrs. Robert D. Bullock	J. A. Rodriguez	Mrs. Howard Gaba	D. Harris
Ms. Channaine A. Burdell	J. Black	Ms. Tracey Gaede	J. Irvine
Ms. Vilolet Butler	J. Gregson	Mrs. Walter Gallatin	J. F. Pope
Eileen Carey Callaghan	D. Mahoney	Miss Linda Garrett	J. Butterfield
Mrs. Robert Carey	J. Palache	Mrs. Grace Fick Ghiselli	G. Borel
Mrs. Fred Cebola	A. Himmelman	Mrs. Ellina Marx Golub	D. S. Levy, Sr.
Ms. Susan Walker Christensen	J. F. Bekeart	Ms. Judith Marx Golub	D. S. Levy, Sr.
Mrs. Eleanor Roe Clark	R. Jordan	Mrs. Peter Grant	J. G. W. Schulte
Ms. Ninive Maria Clements	G. Schallenberger	Mrs. Maudee Graves	H. Green
Mrs Janice Cline	F. J. Tillman	Mrs. Susan Hackett Griffth	W. C. Abbay
Mrs. Marie Elaine Collins	K. H. Lippe	Ms. Maxine E. Grolier	Q. S. Sparks
Mrs. Janet Conley	J. Butterfield	Mrs. Susan Worn Grouell	J. Ross
Mrs. Mary Fairbanks Constant	W. B. Fairbanks	Ms. Lois Halliday	C. Holbrook
Mrs. Alison B. Cooper	J. de Fremery	Mrs. Roscoe M. Hamilton	Ortega
Mrs. Robert E. Corcel	P. A. Cota	Ms. Margaret Mason Hansen	W. C. Mason
Ms. Jeanine S. Cosden		Mrs. Joan Harter	C. R. Story
Ms. Mamie Craig	J. A. Yorba	Mrs. Kelly Slater Herman	D. Mahoney
Mrs. William J. Craig	J A. Yorba	Mrs. Virginia May Herndon	W . Hamel
Mrs. John D. Crane	M. S. Hudson	Mrs. Carolyn Hill	

MEMBER	ANCESTOR	MEMBER	ANCESTOR
Ms. Megan Clarke Hitchcock	Juan D. Rodriguez	Mrs. Jane Brennan McGovern	A. Harazthy
Ms. Patricia Kearns Hitchcock	Juan D. Rodriguez	Mrs. Marian E. McGuire	H. O. Waite
Ms. Marion Hoekenga	W. D. M. Howard	Laura Ann Settlemier McIntyre	G. R. Settlemier
Jessica D. Hladky	W. P. Harrington	Mrs. Katherine A. McKeever	T. A. O. Porter
Susan M. Hladky	W. P. Harrington	Mrs. Adrienne McKelvie	
Mrs. Constance K. Hopper	J. B. Kenny	Ms. Margaret D. McKelvie	
Diane Williams Langmack Howell	I. Williams	Ms. Lorraine A. McLaughlin	W. P. Harrington
Mrs. Amanda Leigh Howser		Miss Catherine Melone	R. B. Woodward
Mrs. Frederick R. Hudson, Jr.	J. G. Kennedy	Mrs. Margo Warnecke-Merck	J.O. Eldridge
Mrs. John H. Innes	R. Franklin	Ms. Christina M. Merlin	R. Tobin
Ms. Jorine Marin Irvine	J. Irvine	Mrs. Susan U. Methany	N. Beal
Mrs. Frank F. Jacobs	J. F. Bekeart	Mrs. Hugo Methman	E. B. Given
Dr. Laurel Powers Jacobson	M. Ayer	Ms. Lori Ann Meyer	D. Harris
Mrs. Barbara Hayes Jenks	T. Hayes	Mrs. Marguerite V. Meyer	G. H. Eggers
Mrs. Melvin Jones	E. Moore	Mrs. Robert G. Meyer	J. Clayton
Ms. Judith Lee Jordan	R. Hopkins	Ms. Francisca Middleton	Moran
Ms. Barbara Julian	J. C. Gummer	Ms. Joan Miles	E. Moore
Margaret Kautz	J. T. Lillard	Ms. Bernice Ybarra Miller	J. A. Navarro
Mrs. Henry Kearns	Rodriguez	Mrs. Julie Rianda Mitchell	I. Vallejo
Ms. Jennifer Joelle Kearns	Rodriquez	Mrs. Selby Mohr	J. P. Buckley
Mrs. Richard Kelly	S. Stivers	Mrs. Albert Monaco	Paravagna
Mrs. Peter Kerner	Castro	Ms. Louisa Jane Moore	J. Moore
Ms. Linda Lee Kerr	W. Craig	Ms. Sarah Moore	J. Moore
Mrs Vernon Korstad	E. Beard	Ms. Jayne Louise	Mordell
Ms. Marilyn Krieger	M. Levy	Mrs. Lincoln R. Morita	J. Edwards
Ms. Barbara B. Krusi	Lohse	Ms. Mollie M. Moroney	T. Cavanagh
Ms. Mary Ellen Kuhi	G. Haupt	Ms. Marie Morton	J. O'Farrell
Mrs. Betty La Course	N. Jones	Ms. Elena Gates Motlow	R W. Macondray
Mrs. Carl M. Larkin	J. Pryor	Mrs. Joan Moura	H. O. Waite
Ms. Constance Laventurier	J. T. Lillard	Mrs. Judy Louise Moyniham	E. T. Givens
Mrs. James Lawson	Rev. S. Grey	Mrs. Michael Murphy	Rev. S. Gray
Miss Kacie Lesky	J. A. Yorba	Mrs. Dwight Murray, Jr.	J. Potter
Mrs. Katherine Craig Lesky	J. A. Yorba	Ms. Christine Murray	J. Potter
Mrs. Frances G. Levy	J. F. Bekeart	Ms. Mary Wilson Neel	F. Talbot
Margaret Hart Lewis	Charles Blake	Mrs. Patricia A. Newman	J. Bolado
Ms. Diana Gullette-Lloyd	J. H. Moran	Mrs. Winifred Brady Noble	Hickman
Mrs. Eleanor Hamilton Lowengart	R. Clark	Mrs. Marilyn Kelly Ombaun	J. W. Clarke
Dr. Helyn Luechauer	M. D. Ritchie	Mrs. Robert G. Orr	J. King
Ms. Sharon J. Lutz	J. Gregson	Mrs. George Parson	Sutter
Mrs. Virginia S. Lynch	J. M. Estrada	Mrs. Norman Patterson	J. C. Churchman
Ms. Tara Lynch	J. M. Estrada	Mrs. Walter E. Paully	G. H. Malech
Barbara J. Macaire	W. P. Harrington	Ms. Sandra Perry	W. Hudson
Mrs. Susan K. Butler-Mapa	Butler	Ms. Wayne Peters	A. Farnsworth
Mrs. Richard Marino	C. L. Wiggin	Mrs. Dorothy E. Pflug	J. Anderson
Mrs. Gerald-Mason	J. Butterfield	Mrs. Marylyn Pickier	L. Hulin
Mrs. Sheila Sim Maze	Moore	Ms. Joni Theresa Podesta	C. F. Glein
Mrs. Terri McColloch	W. P. Harrington	Ms. Robin Poppers	J. Mathews
Kristin A. McColloch	W. P. Harrington	Ms. Eleanor K. Porter	D. Harris
Ms. Kathy McFarland	I.C.C. Lillard Russ	Ms. Mary Jane Porter	S. Mattingly
Miss Elizabeth McGinnis		Ms. Nancy L. Powers, Esq.	M. J. Ayer

MEMBER	ANCESTOR	MEMBER	ANCESTOR
Ms. Dorothy Ayer Powers	M. J. Ayer	Mrs. Adair Louise Tench	J. C. McCracken
Mrs. Mary Weir Pretlow	H. Byrne	Miss Adair Louise Tench	J. C. McCracken
Mrs. Anne Protopopoff	Y. M. Martinez	Miss Margaret Joan Tench	J. C. McCracken
Mrs. Terrence Quedens	W. Craig	Mrs. N. Terrill	T. E. Donahue
Mrs. Frederick T. Quiett	T. Rhoads	Mrs. Marianne Hobbs Thaeler Jr.	J. G. W. Schulte
Mrs. Kathleen B. Ransford	L. Chapman	Mrs. Dana Thayer	L. W. Moore
Mrs. Sue Rauzy	L. Binninger	Mrs. Richard Thieriot	N. Ortiz
Ms. Kathleen M. Rende	A. E. Ward	Mrs. Patricia W. Thompson	F. A. Bonner
Ms. Kori Ann Rianda	I. Vallejo	Mrs. Phyllis Adams Thompson	E. R. Stillman
Mrs. Harriett Paully Richards	M. F. G. Malech	Mrs. Frederick B. Thornburg	Critcher
Ms. Hope S. Rieden	C. Osuna	Ms. Patricia P. Tift	J. F. Pitcher
Ms. Mara Rieden	C. Osuna	Ms. Sharon Lee Tiret	D. Lewis
Mrs. Myles Ringle, Jr.	R. Nash	Mrs. John E. Turco	M. Murphy
Mrs. Carlos Adolpho Rodriguez	Potter	Ms. Beatrice C. Turner	J. Cantua
Ms. Hilda Louise Roe	C. Bertheau	Mrs. Raymond Twist	E, Moore
Mrs. Mary Kearns Rohe	M. Rodriguez	Ms. Mary Beth Uitti	J. F. Pope
Mrs. John Patrick Roney	J. A. Rodriguez	Mrs. Orville G. Uitti	J. F. Pope
Mrs. John Roth	E. Nix	Mrs. Honora Patricia U'ren	Soberanes
Mrs. David W. Russell	G. G. Gardner	Mrs. Bruce L. Van Alstyne	L. B. Clark
Mrs. Donald Sabatini	J. P. Clark	Ms. Leslie Van Orden	L. Van Orden
Ms. Mary Elizabeth Samson		Mrs. Maxine E. Vanderburg	H. Watson
Ms, Juana M. Schurman	J. Bandini	Ms. Marthanna E. Veblen	D. S. Austin
Mrs. Kathleen Nan Sciaroni	Cordero	Ms. Lucille S. Vinsant	E. McLean
Mrs. Jane Newman Scott	T. B. Miller	Ms. Luciel Walker	J. F. Bekeart
Ms. Virginia V. Seeger	N. Hamilton	Mrs. James A. Waterbury	Rev. S. Grey
Ms. Rita Clark Semple	J. Clark	Mrs. Betty J. Watts	J. I. Castro
Ms. Juliet G. Settlemier	G. R. Settlemier	Mrs. William T. Werschkull	G. Cook
Ms. Manon Ann Settlemier	G. R. Settlemier	Ms. Mele E. M. Wheaton	W. R. Wheaton
Mrs. Pilar Holmes Settlemier	G. R. Settlemier	Mrs. Bruce Whitten	C. C. Baker
Mrs. Carolyn Shachtman	Baker	Ms. Isabel Wiel	L. Sloss
Mrs. Anthony E, Siegman	W. D. M. Howard	Ms. Pamela Ward Wiley	S. M. Ward
Mrs. Stanley H. Sinton, Jr.	J. Morse, M.D.	Mrs. John E. Willi	Holland
Mrs. Dorris C. Slater	D. Mahoney	Ms. Elizabeth Anne Williams	W. H. Williams
Mrs. Alaister Smith	J. R. Estrada	Ms. Genevieve Williams	E. Nix
Mrs. Gloria B. Smith	Abrego	Mrs. Judie A. Williams	
Mrs. Linda Irvine Smith	J. Irvine	Ms. Monica J. Williams	W. H. Williams
Ms. Lisa Smith	W. G. Mason	Ms. Emelie Lyons Wilson	H. D. Lyons
Mrs. Roberta B. Spencer	C. Pedraita	Mrs. Joanne S. Wilson	C. E. Howard
Mrs. James B. Stapler	A. Beaman	Mrs. Terrence G. Wilson	C. Holbrook
Mrs. Laurence C. Stein	L. Sloss	Ms. Ann Witter	T. G. Phelps
Mrs. Joseph Stipinovich	Dennis	Ms. Gerry Wolff	L. Stone
Miss Loma Stipinovich	Dennis	Ms. Enid Wood	I. C. C. Russ
Ms. Carolyn A. Strand	E. Nix	Ms. Dorothy Wuss	Bernal
Ms. Susan M. Taylor	S. Mattingly	Ms. Jacqueline Van Rysselberghe	A. Russ

JUNIOR MEMBERS

MEMBER	ANCESTOR	MEMBER	ANCESTOR
Amelia Christine Anthony	W.P. Harrington	Natalie Rose MacLachlan	W. P. Harrington
Anastasia Rae Anthony	W.P. Harrington	Hilary McGinnis	J. Regaan
Maria Rose Anthony	W.P. Harrington	Danielle Ashley McLaughlin	W. P. Harrington
Elisabeth Marie Bernasconi	A. Russ	Jillian Alyse McLaughlin	W. P. Harrington
Marcela Bernasconi	A. Russ	Micaela Amber McLaughlin	W. P. Harrington
Irene Stivers Bonner	S. Stivers	Rachel Alyce McLaughlin	W. P. Harrington
Susanna Carson Bonner	S. Stivers	Trinity Lynn McLaughlin	W. P. Harrington
Carne Faye Godwin	W. Roberts	Kaili Rae Van Rysselberghe	A. Russ
Jessica Kimberly Godwin	W. Roberts	Marie Jolie Van Rysselberghe	A. Russ
Kelly Evelyn Korstad	E. L. Beard	Noelle Lily Van Rysselberghe	A. Russ
Andrea Michelle MacLachlan	W. P. Harrington		

WE GRATEFULLY DEDICATE THIS
BOOK TO PIONEER WOMEN

"Remarkable women in a remarkable time" best describes California pioneer women. They gave birth to and buried their children; they suffered illnesses with no medical assistance, often depending on Indian folk medicine, common sense, and courage.

They dutifully followed their husbands into unknown territory, establishing households while leaving behind families, treasures, and security. There was a spirit and hardiness in these pioneers who lived anonymously, leaving little record of their passing. Women's contributions have been minimized and rarely acknowledged. History has been read through the accomplishments of men. We recognize that courageous women were an integral part of the California heritage.

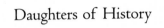

Daughters of History

Part One:
The Spanish-Mexican Period

We begin in the year 1776. While colonists on the east coast of North America were challenging Great Britain, the most powerful empire of the world, the Mexican-Spanish were quietly settling Alta California. It had taken many years since Hernan Cortes had conquered Mexico for European civilization to make its way northward to the vast western regions of what is now the United States. The settlers had made the long trip by ship and by land, and the presidios and pueblos were taming the wilderness at last. The Californios created the beginning of the great state of California. Some of their stories are the legacy of the Daughters of California Pioneers.

Missions, Presidios, and Pueblos

Early California was a province of Spain. In the vast wilderness bordering the Pacific Coast, isolation was probably the greatest danger, although transportation and communication were not far behind. It took a hardy kind of pioneer to brave the travel by ship, horse, mule, or foot to come north from Mexico to Alta California. These pioneers came as groups to settle the lands that Spain had acquired through the centuries. Their numbers were to be increased by the inclusion of the native population, who would be converted to Catholicism and trained in the ways of the Western World. The whole project would require organization and responsibility. The Spanish were well equipped for such an undertaking, and the project went forward. Spain would occupy California.

First came the soldiers, recruited and equipped by the government, accompanied always by a priest in charge of spreading the Gospel to the native population. The civilian settlers, including wives and children of the soldiers, would soon be included, and would require shelter and protection from the elements. The construction of buildings was the responsibility of the soldiers and work would start immediately when a likely site was selected.

The priests and their helpers were given vast tracts of land by the Spanish government, and with the help of the native population, as well as that of the settlers, the *mission* settlement took form. The soldiers, whose responsibility included fending off raids by the natives, required fortifications, and the *presidio* (or fort) came into being, usually close to the mission. The civilian population occupied areas close to the presidio, and their small settlement came to be known as the *pueblo,* or town. When all building had been completed, the new area included the three entities of mission, presidio, and pueblo. There was a mutually satisfactory relationship among these three as each supported the others, and the presidio became the center for business and seats of government.

Spain wanted to settle all her lands north of Mexico, in part to make sure that Russians from the North and British and American ships were not violating the embargo placed by Spain on those nations. Unfortunately, such embargoes meant not trading with sailing ships loaded with enticing embroidered shawls from China and beautiful furniture and silks. By the early 1800s, with government far south in Mexico, the laws were many times ignored, and the Spanish ladies were well supplied with luxury goods. The ships, in turn, accepted cow hides for delivery to the Boston shoe factories. It was a profitable business.

The Mexican Revolution in 1821 loosened the ties of California to the government in Mexico, and the vast lands of the missions were taken over by the Californios, the original settlers, and turned into *ranchos.* The money for support of the missions was gone, and a general decline of presidio and mission set in. The pueblos fared better, with San Jose becoming an important center after the Mexican-American War of 1846-48. Now the way was opened for American occupation of California, and by 1849, with the discovery of gold, the era of the mission, presidio, and pueblo was over.

The Spanish heritage of California would soon be diluted by immigrants from the eastern United States, as well as those from France, Germany, England, Peru, Chile, and everywhere else. Gold was an irresistible attraction, and with the new population that came in overwhelming numbers, the Mexican-Spanish influence merged with that of the newcomers, and the world of California would become "American."

Today many of the missions have been restored and are a visible and intriguing legacy of the old days. Place names and many a road sign proclaim the Spanish language. One goes from San Diego, through the missions of San Luis Obispo, and the pueblos of Los Angeles and San Jose, to end at the mission of Sonoma.

The Daughters of the California Pioneers are proud to proclaim their heritage from their Californio ancestors, and here present the stories of those early lives.

Mariano de la Luz Verdugo
Soldado de Cuero

BY EUNICE PENA ALISEA

 The Verdugo surname first appeared in *Nueva Espana* with the arrival of the conquistador Francisco Verdugo, when he accompanied Panfilo Narvaez in 1520. Verdugo later served as Captain of the Brigantine under Hernan Cortes, and from 1530 to 1532, he was one of Nuño de Guzman's captains in the conquest of *Nueva Galicia.*

In 1533, Francisco Verdugo Quetzalmamalintzin-Huetzin, descendant and heir of the Señores de San Juan de Teothihuacan, became *cacique* or *señorio* (Lordship) of Teotihuacan, site of the famous pyramids of Mexico. His wife was Ana Cortes Ixtlilxuchitl, daughter of Ixtlilxochitl, *tlatoani* or hereditary ruler of Texcoco. When the Verdugo family settled on the west coast of Mexico is unknown and what relationship, if any, they may have had to the above has not been ascertained.

The earliest known ancestors of the California Verdugos for whom we have a record are Blas Verdugo and his wife, Micaela de los Rios. They were residing at the Villa del Fuerte, Sinaloa, Mexico, in the early part of the eighteenth century when their son, Juan Diego Verdugo, was born.

Next, we find Juan Diego serving in the Spanish army at the Royal Presidio of Loreto, Baja California, where, circa 1742, he married María Ignacia de la Concepción Carrillo. She was the daughter of Juan Carrillo and Efigenia Millan.

Mariano de la Luz Verdugo, son of Juan Diego Verdugo and María Ignacia de la Concepción Carrillo, was born around 1746 at San Javier, Baja California. He enlisted in the Spanish army on

December 15, 1766 at the Presidio of Loreto and came to Alta California with Don Gaspar de Portola in the expedition of 1769. He served in the San Diego Company, and was made corporal on February 1, 1774. He was listed as *cabo* (corporal) on the San Diego garrison rosters of January 1, 1775, March 28, 1775, December 21, 1777, and January 1, 1780.

On December 12, 1778 Mariano appeared as a witness to a marriage at Mission San Juan Capistrano and was listed as *cabo de esta escolta* (corporal of the Mission Guard) in the record. He was promoted to sergeant and was transferred to the Monterey company where he served from 1781 to 1787. He was listed as sergeant on the Monterey garrison roster of July 31, 1782. Mariano served as *alcalde* (mayor) of Pueblo de Nuestra Señora de los Angeles from 1790 to 1793, and again in 1802.

According to most accounts, Mariano Verdugo was granted the Rancho de la Portezuelo in 1795. However, the noted authority of California land grants, W.W. Robinson, suggested that the concession was probably made as early as 1784, as it was mentioned in a letter from Governor Fages to the Commanding General, Jacobo Ugarte, on November 20, 1784, in which four provisional grants were listed. Site of modern-day Burbank and Universal City, the concession was named second on the 1795 report made to Governor Borica by Felipe Goycoechea, which listed the ranchos in the district. The Spanish grant consisted of four square leagues, but was abandoned as early as 1810.

Mariano de la Luz Verdugo married Maria Guadalupe Lugo at Mission San Carlos de Monterey on May 30, 1775. She was the daughter of Francisco Ginez de Lugo and Maria Gertrudis Armenta. She was born at Loreto, Baja California, circa 1758. They had one child, a daughter, Maria de la Concepción Verdugo, who was born at San Diego in 1778. Maria Guadalupe Lugo died in 1780 and was buried in the church of the Presidio of San Diego on April 15, 1780.

Mariano later married Maria Gertrudis Gregoria Espinosa, on November 26, 1778, at Mission San Gabriel. She was born circa 1760 at Villa de Sinaloa, Sinaloa, Mexico. She was the daughter of Bernardo Espinosa and Maria Isabel Acosta. Maria Gertrudis Gregoria Espinosa had come to Alta California with her first husband, Jose Pedro Lareto Salazar, a *soldado de cuero* of the Rivera y Moncada expedition. There were three children from that marriage: José Salazar, Maria Marta Salazar, and Maria Teodora Salazar.

Mariano de la Luz Verdugo died in 1822 and was buried at the Mission San Gabriel on September 26 of that year. Maria Gregoria Espinosa was buried on May 29, 1830 in the Pueblo de los Angeles.

José María Soberanes

BY PATRICIA U'REN

 Founder of the California Soberanes family, José Soberanes came to California with Gaspar de Portola in the expedition of 1769 at the age of sixteen. He was born in Sinaloa, Mexico in 1753 of Spanish parents, Ygnacio Soberanes and Maria Petra Pinta. José was a popular young man, handsome in face, a good musician with a melodious singing voice. With him on that expedition to Alta California were the cross that he wore and a small oil painting. (These were later passed on to one of his descendents, Mrs. Adeline O'Brien.)

These were the first white men to enter the valley of the Salinas, searching for the "Bay Count de Monterey." It was an exhausting trip along the banks of a river whose waters would disappear for miles. They named the river Santa Delfina. They were near starvation and some of the members died. Half dead and able to go no further, they were seen by a few Indians, who gave them pine nuts, acorn meal and fresh, clear water. In December of 1769 Portola and his men left the valley and returned to San Diego.

In the spring of 1770 Portola, accompanied by Padre Junipero Serra, returned to the plains of the Santa Delfina in search of the bay of Monterey. Better equipped and with fewer men so that enough food could be taken, this expedition again included José María Soberanes. Once again, the Indians came out from the canyons of the Santa Lucia mountains and they were happy to see José Maria, one of the young soldiers from the first group that they had nursed back to health.

He then was stationed at the Presidio of Monterey, and later transferred to the Mission San Carlos Borromeo del Carmelo. José was chosen to accompany Fages in 1772 on his exploration as far as Antioch, and later was chosen to accompany de Anza, being then referred to as "a guide of experience." The purpose was for him to establish post roads for the Spanish government. He was used in this capacity on other explorations, and was probably one of California's most capable guides.

Among the colonists of de Anza's expedition was the Castro family, eleven in all: Joaquin de Castro and his wife, Maria Martina Botiller, and nine children. José courted the beautiful, eldest daughter, Ana Maria Josefa Castro — one of California's first love affairs. They were married soon after their arrival in Monterey by Padre Junipero Serra. José confided to the padres that he wanted to live on his own land in the valley of the Salinas and raise a large family.

José was stationed at the Mission San Carlos Borromeo del Carmelo until 1791. When the padres of the San Antonio Mission founded the Mission Nuestra Señora de la Soledad, they were happy to find José Soberanes, now thirty-eight years old, and asked that he be stationed at the new mission. His desire of many children and owning a rancho in the Valley of the Salinas never faded. He and Ana Josefa already had a large family and more were to arrive.

In 1795, at the age of forty-two, José and his father-in-law, Joaquin Castro, were granted 8,446.23 acres by the governor of Alta California. At last his dream was fulfilled! José and Ana Josefa had seven children. (One had died soon after birth.) The beautiful rancho in the Salinas Valley was the Buena Vista Rancho and José was pensioned by the army and became a *ranchero*.

Then Spain decided the Franciscan missions were entirely too prosperous and that they must pay taxes for the privilege of operating the missions. The padres and Indians worked overtime to raise enough hides and tallow to meet the demands of Spain. The missions were drained. When it was remembered that the grant to José Soberanes was only provisional he was ordered to return his land.

José appealed to the governor for justice and the governor ruled against the missions. Though Governor Arrillaga would not evict him, the dream was short lived. José Soberanes died the following year, in 1803. Ana Josefa moved to Monterey with her family. At sixteen years of age, her son, Feliciano, like his father, became a soldier and was stationed at the Monterey Presidio.

The Rancho Buena Vista was situated west of the Salinas River and south of the city of Salinas. There is still a little place called Buena Vista on the Old River Road, which was then the El Camino Real, which ran from Monterey to the Soledad Mission.

Yorba, Grijalva, Avila

BY MARY MERCEDES DE MAZON FRIMAN

 José Antonio Yorba — Born 1746, Catalonia, Spain
On April 29, 1769, the *San Carlos* arrived in San Diego Bay. After its long journey, José Antonio Yorba was one of the few Catalans who was physically fit to make the overland march in search of the bay of Monterey. The sixty-four members of the expedition included men whose family names later became well known in California's history — names such as Sergeant Pedro Amador, Alvarado, José Raimundo Carrillo, José Francisco de Ortega, Soberanes, and Yorba. These troops, known as the *soldados de cuero,* "leather jackets," because they wore protective leather jackets of seven thicknesses of deerskin, carried bull-hide shields on their left arms. Lances and broadswords were among the weapons, as well as short muskets. At their head rode Captain Don Gaspar de Portola, while Captain Fernando de Rivera y Moncada brought up the rear with extra mules and horses.

Juan Pablo Grijalva — Born 1742, La Valle de San Luis, Sonora
On October 23, 1775 the de Anza caravan left Tubac (now Arizona). The expeditionary company consisted of Juan Bautista de Anza, Fr. Pedro Font, Fr. Francisco Garces, Fr. Thomas Eixarch, Purveyor Mariano Vidal, Lieutenant José Joaquin Moraga, and Sergeant Juan Pablo Grijalva, along with eighteen veteran soldiers, twenty recruits, twenty-nine wives of soldiers, one hundred thirty-six persons of both sexes belonging to the families of the soldiers, and four other families, totaling two hundred forty persons and over a thousand animals. Five children were born on their journey

and there was only one death — a woman who died in childbirth. When de Anza arrived at Monterey, his achievement more than doubled the white population in California.

Juan Pablo Grijalva with his wife, María Dolores Valencia, and their daughters, María Josefa and María del Carmen, continued on to San Francisco, arriving in June of 1776.

María Josefa Grijalva and José Antonio Yorba were married November 3, 1782 at Mission San Francisco de Asis, "Mission Dolores," in San Francisco. Her sister, María del Carmen, married Pedro Regalado Peralta in 1785, also at Mission Dolores.

Grijalva served at San Francisco from 1776 to 1786, was *alferez* at the San Diego presidio in 1787, and retired as a lieutenant in 1796. He founded the San Pedro Martin Mission in Baja California in 1784, and died in June 1806 in San Diego.

Governor Don Pedro Fages, representing the King of Spain, granted four land grants — the fourth grant being made in April 1797. In 1814 José Antonio Yorba, along with Pedro R. Peralta, obtained a land grant and, with the Grijalva land, it has been totaled at 141,459 acres. They were called Rancho Santa Margarita y las Flores and Santiago de Santa Ana Rancho.

Josef María Avila — Born 1790, Villa del Fuerte, Mexico

The twelfth child of José Antonio Yorba and Maria Josefa Yorba, María Andrea Ygnacia Yorba, married Josef María Avila in 1823 at Mission San Juan Capistrano.

There were many revolutions in California during the Mexican period, but in nearly every case they were protests against petty tyrannies of Mexican-born governors. In 1831 there was a revolution against Governor Manuel Victoria, who despised the Californianos. Victoria faced his opponents at Cahuenga Pass. Romualdo Pacheco, who elected to remain loyal to his government, was ordered to fire at the enemy. Pacheco, perhaps through a misunderstanding of the order, rode forward alone on his beautiful black horse into the space between the two parties. On the other side was Josef María Avila, a daredevil of herculean size, and said to be the best horseman in Los Angeles.

Avila, who had armed himself with a lance made of a long stake with a bayonet point strapped to it, believed that Pacheco was challenging to single combat, and rode forward to meet him with leveled lance. The two rushed at each other like knights of old. Pacheco swerved to avoid the lance thrust. Avila was carried past by the impetus of the horse, but turning in his saddle, he drew a pistol and shot Pacheco through the heart. The struggle then became general and in the combat that followed, Avila was unhorsed and killed, some say by Victoria himself.

This was the first blood shed between men of Spanish ancestry in California, and it was with the deepest mourning that the citizens, who had taken no part in the contest, carried the bodies of the two young men to the Pueblo of Los Angeles, where they were followed to the grave by all the inhabitants, irrespective of political convictions. Pacheco, a perfect young knight, left a widow to mourn him and a month-old infant son who grew up to serve as Governor of California after the American conquest.

Casa de Avila, built in 1818, was the first adobe residence in Los Angeles. It contained eighteen rooms and a patio. Today, all that remains is the visitors center on Olivera Street, in Old Town, Los Angeles.

Pablo Antonio Cota

BY LUCILLE CORCEL

 This is the story of a *soldado de cuero*, "leather-jacket soldier," who lived in the eighteenth century.

Pablo Antonio Cota, born in 1744 at Loreto, Baja California, was the son of Andres de Cota and Angela de León. He enlisted in the Spanish army on July 4, 1768 at the age of twenty-four. In 1769 he left Velicata, Baja, with an expedition bound for San Diego, the purpose of which was to settle and claim Alta California for the King of Spain. It took fifty-two days to reach San Diego.

About one year later, Pablo was one of seven soldiers leaving from San Diego to accompany the second expedition looking for the Bay of Monterey. This land party was successful and the Mission of San Carlos Borromeo was established. Pablo was stationed at the Presidio of Monterey for about four years, then at Mission San Luis Obispo for another four years. After living a year or two at Mission San Antonio, he was transferred to the Presidio of Santa Barbara, and occasionally had duty at Mission Buenaventura.

While stationed at San Luis Obispo, Pablo was married, on November 30, 1776, to Rosa María Lugo, the daughter of Francisco Salvador Lugo and Juana Villanazul. It is likely that Pablo was there when the Anza Expedition of 1775-6 arrived at Mission San Luis Obispo en route to San Francisco.

By the year 1782, Pablo was *Sargento de Compania Presidial Santa Barbara* (Sergeant of the Presidio Company of Santa Barbara). Some of his duties included leading patrols to search for runaway neophytes and exploring outlying territories. He also was chosen to lead the escort and servants necessary to establish Mission La Purisima Concepción in 1788.

Pablo Cota was commissioned *alferez* of the Presidio of Santa Barbara in 1788. The notification took five months to reach its destination. The escort of La Purisima Concepción was turned over to José María Ortega, and Alferez Cota returned to Santa Barbara. As *alferez*, one of Cota's duties was to periodically inspect the guards and escorts of the nearby missions, San Buenaventura and La Purisima. Once he was sent north to the Monterey area to supervise the construction of a crossing at the Pajaro River near today's Watsonville. These excursions on horseback were from two to four days in length. Alferez Cota was instrumental in choosing the site for Mission Santa Inez, in what we now know as Solvang.

The family of Pablo Antonio Cota and Rosa María Lugo grew to nine children. They were born at various mission sites during Pablo's lifetime of service. Six daughters and three sons carried on the colonization of Alta California, settling at Santa Barbara, San Buenaventura, Monterey, and San Luis Obispo.

In November, 1796 Cota received an offer of an advanced position at Loreto, in Baja California He refused, stating he was not qualified and he was fearful of traveling the distance necessary to reach Loreto, because his wife had gone blind. Rosa María died in January, 1797. She was buried in the cemetery of the Presidio of Santa Barbara. Pablo Cota died on December 30, 1800, and was also buried in the same cemetery.

Today, the sword of Alferez Don Pablo Antonio is on display at the Santa María Valley Historical Museum in Santa Maria, California. The inscription on the 30-inch long sword is:

DO NOT DRAW ME WITHOUT REASON
DO NOT SHEATHE ME WITHOUT HONOR.

It is an honorable tribute to a true pioneer.

A quote from Luann Davis Powell states, "A common man — *soldado de cuero* to *alferez* — in an uncommon era, Pablo served thirty-two years in the wilderness that was California and at the time of his death was approximately fifty-five years old. One thing is certain: all Californians are richer because Pablo Antonio Cota, and others like him, *pasó por aquí!* (passed through here)."

Nearly two hundred years after his death, I am proud to record this story of my third great-grandfather and pass it on to my descendents, and to anyone else interested in California history.

Sebastian Rodriguez

BY CARMELITA BULLOCK

It all started with my grandmother's grandfather, Sebastian Rodriguez. He married María Perfecta Pacheco who was related to the first white child born in San Francisco. Sebastian was a grantee of the Rancho Bolsa del Pajaro, an area north of Monterey Bay, and his children included José Antonio Rodriguez, his first-born. This "Antonio" is described as "founder of one of the two great families of the north shore of Monterey Bay."

The fourth son of Sebastian was Jacinto Rodriguez, who was an important figure in the early history of the state of California. He was *alcalde* of San Francisco and Monterey and the only native-born signer of the California Constitution. The Grand Ball for the signers was held in his home, where the secret meetings to draft the Constitution had also been held. The home has been preserved in Monterey. A copy of Jacinto's portrait is displayed in Colton Hall, Monterey, where the Constitution was signed. The table on which the Constitution was signed is displayed there and came from Jacinto's home.

An interesting family story has been handed down about "a chest from the Orient."

One could tell, it was said, by such chests handed down that the family had been "for the American cause" because so many patriots had had to "get out of town as far away as the Orient. The California Republic had lasted only fifteen days but its patriots had been at it fifty years, and California could be too dangerous at times."

Another story tells about a land transaction that became a well known spot on the Pacific Coast:

> The last point of our land, called Pigeon Point,
> and containing the lighthouse, had been sold to "an
> Austrian countess under, presumably, a 'cloudy title.'
> One had three days in which to contest the sale and so
> my mother embarked on the train and arrived the
> morning of the fourth day, too late to protest."

To return to Sebastian, he described himself as "native of Alta California," in a document dated April 26, 1854. Although he was then living under United States jurisdiction, perhaps his heart remained in the spirit of the old days of the Pajaro Valley, located in the present day area of Watsonville. He had made a leap from a small province of Spain to the great state of California. One wonders how such an enormous change was handled by the new citizens of the United States, those whose spirits perhaps remained in the old province, known for its salutary way of life, and were now challenged by the changes that would sweep the area into the next century.

Juan Francisco Bernal

BY DOROTHY M. WUSS

 Some years ago a friend gave me a cartoon showing an elderly lady looking at a portrait on the wall and remarking, "Why, I didn't know Californians had ancestors." Well, I did, and along with the native Americans waiting for the hordes who came over the Sierra Nevadas were my ancestors — the Californios, my Spanish ancestors on my father's side.

In 1774 Captain Juan Bautista de Anza walked from Tubac (now Arizona) with some soldiers and padres up to the San Francisco peninsula, making a trail for settlers to follow. In 1775, while the eastern coast of the United States was preparing for the Revolutionary War, Captain de Anza was gathering together two hundred forty people — over one hundred of them children — for a walk of about 1,600 miles from Tubac to the San Francisco peninsula to found the presidio and Mission Dolores. Most of the people were from the states of Sonora and Sinaloa, and in order to reach Tubac, they had to walk about another 500 miles. These poor people, and the government of Spain, paid for the entire expedition. No covered wagons for them. Except for the soldiers on horseback, the group walked, unpacking the mules each night before setting up camp and repacking it all again in the morning before starting their walk.

On October 25, 1775 the group left Tubac in the late afternoon. With such a late start, they did not get very far before they made camp for the night. During the night a woman died giving birth to a baby boy. The child was given into the care of another family. The mother was the only casualty, and three more babies were born during the trip. Her name was Señora Feliz, and since I have Feliz in my background. I am searching to see if she might have been a great-grandmother.

The group headed north towards Tucson, then south again, crossing the Gila and Colorado Rivers, and crossing into California about where Yuma, Arizona is today. To cross the southern California desert, they divided into three groups, for if they had taken so many animals at one time there would not have been enough water at the watering holes. One group went to the first water hole, then moved on, and while it was filling up, the second group would be coming up, and so forth. Thus, they crossed the desert safely, reaching Mission San Gabriel on January 4, 1776.

On February 21, 1776 they started north again toward Monterey, then the capitol of California. Some people stayed behind, including the Feliz family, who later became part of the group that founded the city of Los Angeles. Reaching Monterey on March 10, they again set up camp while de Anza, with his second in command, Lt. Joaquin Moraga, the padres, and some soldiers, went up the peninsula to choose the sites for the mission and presidio.

On their return to Monterey, Lt. Moraga took command of the expedition, and de Anza headed back to Mexico. On June 17, they headed for their final destination, coming through the Salinas Valley near Gilroy, through the Santa Clara Valley, reaching San Francisco Bay on June 27, 1776 — seven months after leaving Tubac and having covered nearly 2,000 miles. They immediately set about building the presidio and mission. The group was now down to about one hundred ninety people since some had remained at other missions along the way.

Among this group, were my fifth great-grandparents, Juan Francisco Bernal and María Josefa (Soto) Bernal and their seven children. He is listed as a *mestizo*, born in Sinaloa, so apparently not full

Spanish. He served in the Spanish army and so did his sons as they grew older, and later, some served in the Mexican army when it broke away from Spain in 1822. One of Juan Francisco's sons was my fourth great-grandfather, José Joaquin Bernal. He married María Josefa Sanchez and they had ten or eleven children. They had both come with the de Anza expedition. He was thirteen years old; she was seven at the time. As these one hundred children of the expedition grew and intermarried, I am sure if I searched enough, I would find myself related to a great many of them — Berryessa, Peralta, Pacheco, Higuera, and so on.

When José Joaquin retired from the army the family moved to Branciforte, now Santa Cruz. The government was encouraging retirees to move there to build up the community. Around 1825 the Bernal family moved to the Santa Clara Valley, settling on some land about six miles south of the pueblo of San José de Guadalupe, which had been founded in 1777. It supplied food for the presidios of San Francisco and Monterey. Around 1834 Joaquin applied to the now Mexican government for a grant of the land where the family had been living for many years. He was granted 10,000 acres and it became known as the Santa Teresa Rancho. José Joaquin died in 1837 and is buried at Mission Santa Clara, probably in what is now the rose garden, as that was the cemetery at that time.

In 1846 John William Kottinger arrived in New Orleans from Austria. He sailed up the Mississippi to Louisville, Kentucky, traveled around the eastern part of the United States, and finally ended up in Rio de Janeiro, Brazil. After a while he walked over the Andes to Valparaiso, Chile. At first I could not believe he had walked across the Andes, but research has shown that some forty-niners did actually walk the old Indian trails.

By now the Gold Rush had started in California, so Kottinger laid in a supply of mining equipment and boarded a ship bound for San Francisco, arriving there September 16, 1849. After selling the equipment, he headed for San Jose, where he became friends with the Juan Pablo Bernal family. Kottinger was an educated man, speaking French, German, Spanish, and English, and had certificates to practice law and to teach. He acted as an interpreter for Juan Pablo in his dealings with the United States government. In April, 1850, when John William was thirty years old, he married María Refugia Bernal, fifteen-year-old daughter of Juan Pablo.

My great-grandfather, John David Kottinger, married Marie Souc of French parentage. Her parents had come separately from France. Pierre Souc was a sea captain from Bordeaux, arriving in San Francisco around 1850. Marie Fichet came later, walked across the Isthmus of Panama, and took a ship up to San Francisco, arriving in 1853. They met and were married in 1856, ran a grocery store on Fourth and Clementina Streets in San Francisco, and had four children.

Guadalupe (Welsh) Castro

BY BETTY J. WATTS

 Long after she had died, I found a newspaper clipping about my grandmother, Margaret Castro Schmidt, in her old scrapbook. Dated October 21, 1921 in *The Daily News* of an unknown city, the headlines state, "Aged Woman Lays Claim to $100,000,000 Estate; She is the Oldest Native White Woman." At the time of the article, my great-grandmother, Guadalupe, was evidently living in a "rickety cottage" in East Oakland and was eighty-eight years old.

The story begins, according to the article, back in 1829 when William Welsh, an Irish trader, was working along the coast of California among the Spaniards. He married Galinda Antonio Peralta and was subsequently given a Spanish land grant of 13,000 acres between Martinez and Walnut Creek. Their daughter, Guadalupe, who was born in Santa Clara, married Ramon Castro, grandson of Francisco Castro. Guadalupe is quoted as saying their honeymoon was a trip across the Bay. "In those days we used the Indian's tullie [sic] canoes; it was the only way to get across."

The Castro land grant was in San Pablo, comprising 19,000 acres extending through Richmond to El Cerrito. According to the article, Ramon never secured possession of his portion of the estate but did secure a little strip of land in Fruitvale, where he built the cottage in which she then lived.

Guadalupe had evidently filed claims on three estates: a portion of the Peralta estate (which stretched over land now in the heart of Oakland), as well as the Welsh and Castro estates. She had deeds to land held by the Standard and Shell oil companies in

Richmond. In 1918 the U.S. Department of the Interior stepped into the court actions, and, according to the newspaper article, a decision was promised by 1922.

Guadalupe's cottage was described as having walls covered with old photographs and a shrine of the Savior and Virgin Mary. There was also a piano in one corner, and a phonograph. "That's all we saved from the fire — we lived at 85 San Carlos Ave. [San Francisco?] in 1906. We were renting a place there. We saved the photographs and the piano. We used these chairs and this lounge in wheeling the stuff out . . . but I lost all the jewelry." She earned money by making fancy Spanish lace and was proud she did not wear glasses.

The old Spanish side of my family was never mentioned in my home. Occasionally, when I was a child and visiting my grandmother during the summer, she would tell me that she was the last child born in the Castro-Alvarado Adobe in San Pablo (razed in 1954, but now rebuilt as a museum). She also identified herself as a descendant of Alvarado, a Spanish governor of California, and said that a great-grandfather was the first white child baptized in Mission Dolores in San Francisco. She gave me a small slip of paper with a minimum of information concerning her past which I somehow saved through the years.

However, with that limited information, my first cousin, Vivian Dane, started the research into our heritage. Several items in the *Daily News* article differ from what we have uncovered, either through a faulty memory on Guadalupe's part, or faulty reporting on the part of the interviewer. Guadalupe's mother was, in fact, María Antonia Galindo y Bernal, and not Galinda Antonia Peralta, although she was related to the Peraltas. María Antonia was the daughter of Juan Crisostomo Galindo and Ana María Jacoba Bernal, whose parents and grandparents were among the ten members of the 1775-1776 Anza party, the original soldiers and settlers of San Francisco. (Nicolas Galindo, María Teresa Pinto, her parents Pablo Pinto and Francisca Xavier Ruelas, Juan Joaquin Bernal and his parents, Juan Francisco Bernal and María Josefa de Soto, and María Josefa Sanchez and parents José Antonio Sanchez and María Dolores Morales).

Guadalupe's husband, José Ramon Castro, also had grandparents and great-grandparents who were members of the Anza Party (Castro, Boutiller, Berryessa, Peralta, Soto, Espinosa and Valenzuela).

Ramon's grandfather, Francisco José de Soto was, in fact, the first child baptized in Mission Dolores, entered first in the *Libro de Bautismos* by Father Francisco Palou, on August 10, 1776.

María de los Angeles Cota

BY LUCILLE CORCEL AND MARY ELISE BAUMANN

The Legend of the Burned Trunk

 At the Royal Presidio of Santa Barbara, María de los Angeles Cota was born, and on August 21,1791 she was baptized at Mission Santa Barbara. María was the seventh child of Pablo Antonio Cota and his wife, Rosa María Lugo, both natives of Sinaloa, Mexico. She had three older brothers, three older sisters, and two sisters born after her. She was our great-great-grandmother.

A young, handsome cadet, José Joaquin de la Torre, born in a small village in the mountains of Santander, Spain, became a *soldado* of the *Compania de Monterey.* He had come to Mexico City at the age of ten to attend military academy. After five years of training, he arrived in Alta California to begin his career. José Joaquin spent some time at the Presidio of Santa Barbara, where he met the young girl, María. According to old records, María de los Angeles was married at the tender age of twelve years. The wedding took place at the San Carlos Mission in Monterey in August 1803. As a military family, the young couple moved from one mission to another in the Monterey Presidio area until settling permanently in Monterey. María was probably comfortable with this life because her father was a *soldado*, as was her grandfather, Francisco Salvador Lugo. In moving from place to place there was an important item, Joaquin's trunk, that always commanded special attention. He had brought it with him from Spain.

María de los Angeles de la Torre became the mother of eight sons and three daughters. Her children were born at Mission San

Miguel, Mission San Antonio, and at Monterey. Like most of the women of that era, she was strong-willed and fearless, but a loving person who handled adversity in a matter-of-fact manner. Her husband, known as Joaquin, was given a land grant of 6,915 acres in 1822 by Governor Pablo Sola. It was on that Rancho, called Bolsa de Potrero or Familia Sagrada, that María nurtured her family. It is not known whether she was educated, but she saw to it that her children were. Upon his retirement from the military, Joaquin acquired a taste for gambling and liquor.

Whenever we begged for stories about the "old days," our mother fondly told the following tale:

One day, Joaquin saddled his horse and rode off, saying he had business in the pueblo. Night fell and he didn't return home. Burdened with the responsibility of caring for eleven children, besides overseeing the rancho operations, María's anger grew. In the morning she discovered that Joaquin still had not returned home. María decided to teach him a lesson. Seething with fury, she thought only of revenge. She dragged Joaquin's beloved trunk outside and set it on fire. It burned completely, contents and all. Later, when Joaquin arrived home and saw what she had done, his only comment was, "Woman, you have burned your children's heritage."

No one will ever know what was in that trunk. The legend certainly lends itself to some fantastic daydreams. Royalty . . . a castle in Spain . . . wealth . . . perhaps just papers containing the names of his parents and family members — the incident apparently was never brought up again.

Life continued on the Bolsa de Potrero for the de la Torre family. The children matured and left home to begin their own lives. Several of María's sons became soldiers. The rancho was sold in 1829. John B.R. Cooper bought it for $2000. José Joaquin de la Torre died in 1845, and María spent her last years living with a son and his family in Monterey until her death in 1877.

Four Pioneer Lines:
Arellano, Martinez Tennent, Tennent

BY ANNE T. PROTOPOPOFF

 Four lines of ancestors brought me to the Society of California Pioneers: Manuel Ramirez de Arellano, who came to California in 1776; Ignacio Nicanor Martinez, who came in 1799; Dr. Samuel Johnson Tennent, member of the Society, who came in 1849; and Thomas Tennent, member of the Society (no relation to S.J. Tennent), who came in 1849.

Manuel Ramirez de Arellano (later known as Arellanes) was born in Puebla, Mexico in 1742. His Ramirez de Arellano ancestors had left Spain and been in Mexico since the 1500s. He and his wife, María Agueda Lopez de Haro, came with Juan Bautista de Anza in 1775-76 with the first overland group of settlers from Mexico to California. They first settled in Los Angeles where, in 1784, he became *alcalde* (a position which combined the offices of mayor and justice of the peace). The family later moved to Santa Barbara. His youngest daughter was María Martina de Arellanes, who had been born in Los Angeles in 1787.

Ignacio Nicanor Martinez was born in Mexico City in 1774. His parents both came from the vicinity of Burgos, Spain. It is not known whether they were married in Spain or after arrival in Mexico. Ignacio arrived by ship with the Spanish military in 1799 at the Presidio of San Diego. He served there and at the Presidio of Santa Barbara where he met María Martina de Arellanes. They were married in the Santa Barbara presidio chapel in 1802. Their first children were born in San Diego.

Ignacio Martinez was transferred to San Francisco in 1821 as *commandante general* under Spanish rule, just before Mexico freed herself from Spain. He retired from the military in 1832 and spent some time in the pueblo of San José where he served as alderman. In 1834 he became the fourth *alcalde* of San Francisco, then known as Yerba Buena.

He had applied for a Mexican land grant in Contra Costa County. This grant, called El Rancho de Nuestra Señora de la Merced, more commonly known as El Rancho Pinole was about 17,000 acres of hills and meadows. It extended from the Rancho San Pablo, which was the Castro grant, to El Arroyo del Hambre (now called Alhambra Creek because later inhabitants did not want the name "hunger") from where that creek discharged into Carquinez Straits, and from Carquinez Straits to the source of Pinole Creek. The adobe house in the Pinole Valley to which Ignacio moved his family in 1836 may have been built as early as 1824, although this land, along with several other grants, was not officially granted until 1842. There he and María raised their eleven children. When Ignacio Martinez died in 1848 he was buried under the floor of the Mission San Jose. The city of Martinez was named for him after his death.

The ten sons and daughters who lived to maturity married mostly into families of the area. I mention them because of their connections with local history. María Antonia married William Richardson, who built the first wooden structure in San Francisco; Juana María del Carmen married José Joaquin Estudillo of the Rancho San Leandro; María Encarnación married José Altemirano (their adobe, still standing, later became the home of John Swett); José Jesus, member of the Society of California Pioneers (and known as an outstanding horseman), married first Carmel Peralta, and second Catherine Hannah Tennent; Vicente married first Guadalupe Moraga, and second Nieves Soto (his adobe in Martinez, his second house, is now part of the John Muir National Historic Site); María Luisa married Victor Castro (El Cerrito Plaza is on the site of his adobe); Susana married first William Smith, second William Hinkley, and third Benoit Vassero Merle; Francisca, twin of Susana, married José de los Santos Berellesa; María Rafaela married Dr. S.J. Tennent; María Dolores married Pedro Higuera.

Dr. Samuel Johnson Tennent, my maternal great-grandfather, born in Liverpool in 1817, was a graduate of the University of London. In 1845 he arrived on a whaling ship in Lahaina, Maui, then the capital of the Hawaiian Islands. There he became physician to Kamehameha III.

At the time of the Gold Rush he sailed to San Francisco, and then traveled up to the Pinole Valley with a letter of introduction to Ignacio Martinez, where he found that Martinez had died. The Martinez family invited him to stay for a visit. They were living in three adobe houses, the original one of Ignacio and his wife, and the others built for the two sons. Tennent did not go to the gold fields, but stayed and married María Rafaela Martinez, who had been born at the Presidio of San Francisco in 1826. They were married in 1849 at Mission San Jose. The trip back to the Pinole Valley on horseback and with following ox carts took three days as they visited and partied along the way. He became county physician and managed Rafaela's share of the land grant.

Their eventual home was a house in Pinole, which had been shipped in numbered pieces from New England. He became a member of the Society of California Pioneers. His brother-in-law, José Martinez, also became a member, his date of entry into California being listed as the date of his birth in 1815. I am descended from a daughter of Dr. Tennent and María Rafaela, Ana María Gertrudis Tennent, born in 1865 in Pinole, who married Thomas Burns, a chemist from Ireland.

Thomas Tennent (no relation to S.J.), my paternal grandfather, born in Philadelphia, arrived in San Francisco by ship in 1849 and became a member of the Society of California Pioneers. Thomas Tennent was a builder and repairer of chronometers and other nautical instruments, serving the sailing vessels. He edited a nautical almanac for the port of San Francisco. Thomas Tennent also kept the first weather reports for the Bay Area, beginning in 1849.

His daughter, Jennie Tennent married George E. Plummer, son of a sea captain, who had a ships' supply business in San Francisco as well as lumbering interests. He and Jennie raised their family in Alameda.

Their eldest son, George Tennent Plummer, married Kathryn Josephine Burns, born in Pinole in 1884, who was the granddaughter of Dr. Samuel J. Tennent. I, their daughter, am Anne Tennent Plummer Protopopoff, with the middle name of Tennent, which, I am told, comes from the maternal side.

Louis Pombert
(Luis Pomber)

BY ANITA CLARK

 Louis Pombert was born on December 1, 1798 in Louiseville, Quebec, a small town along the St. Lawrence River. Little is known of his childhood, save that he came from a large family. Several of his female ancestors were known to be *Filles du Roi*, or King's Daughters — those French women who volunteered to emigrate to Quebec and become a settler's wife in exchange for a marriage dowry provided by the King of France.

At the age of twenty, Louis traveled to the Great Lakes region and was hired by the American Fur Company, at Mackinac Island on June 24, 1819. He worked for the American Fur Company for a period of a year as a boatman.

Records of Louis Pombert's movements during the next few years are sketchy at best. There is an unsubstantiated rumor that he was a member of the Etienne Provost fur trapping party, which traveled into the area now occupied by the state of New Mexico. It can be assumed that he attended the July, 1827 rendezvous near the Great Salt Lake in what would become the state of Utah. The rendezvous was a wild gathering held each year during which trappers could catch up on news, sell furs, and buy supplies, not to mention having a "saturnalian" good time. Here, if not earlier, Pombert met Jedediah Smith, who had led the first American fur-trapping expedition into California in 1826, only to be expelled by the Mexican government.

Louis Pombert joined the second Smith expedition into California, which left the rendezvous in mid-July 1827. Just as before, the Smith party was expelled from California and headed north in

December of 1827 towards what would become the state of Washington. In January of 1828, while trapping along the tributaries of the San Joaquin River, Louis and an Australian blacksmith named Reed were given eleven traps and a boat, with orders to meet the rest of the party in a week, further north along the Consumnes River. As the rest of the Smith expedition headed north, Reed and Pombert headed south, never to return.

Louis Pombert next turned up in San Jose, where he worked on the Higuera Rancho. In his April 5, 1829 declaration *"firmado con una cruz"* (signed with an "x"), Louis said, *"Que se llama Luis Pomvera, se frances, soltero y de 28 años de edad."* ("My name is Luis Pomvera, I am French, single, and 28 years of age"). For the rest of his life, Louis Pombert was known as Luis Pomber. The two year discrepancy in age is a mystery.

It was during this period that Luis met the young Filomena Carmen Rudecinda Pico, born on March 2, 1815. On June 18, 1830 a marriage of necessity was celebrated at San Carlos Mission, as Filomena was carrying the first of their thirteen children, ten of whom lived beyond childhood.

By 1832 the family was living in Monterey. Luis supported them by constructing wooden carts, building adobe houses, and raising dairy cattle. It should be noted that the cattle were raised within the town itself, on a lot next to the one owned by Filomena's widowed mother, Isabel Cota Pico.

Though he married into an established Mexican family, Luis Pomber was still considered a foreigner. As one of fifty or so foreigners living in and around Monterey, Luis would have been concerned by the many revolutionary schemes (at least those not directly in favor of his own interests) that were being acted out within California. In order to protect their business interests, nearly all the foreign residents of Monterey organized a *compania extranjera* for the defense of the city. Luis joined the company on January 24, 1832.

In 1836, when the Californianos revolted against Mexico and gained their independence, Pomber joined Isaac Graham's company of riflemen and was appointed as sergeant to act as third-in-command.

Filomena did not limit her activities to being a housewife. As a native Californian, she could ask for more land to raise her growing family. The request, dated April 10, 1839, is a good example of her concerns.

"I, Filomena Pico de Luis Pomber, a native of the Mexican Republic, and at present a resident of this municipality, before Your Honor appear and say: That having a numerous family, and needing a tract of land suitable for the raising of stock, I apply to Your Honor asking you to be pleased in consideration of my family, to grant me the place called Canada de los Osos, together with the neighboring hills. . . ."

Though the family remained in Monterey County, they did not always reside in Monterey itself. Beginning in the late 1830s and culminating in 1846 with the official grant by then Governor Pio Pico (Filomena's first cousin), Luis Pomber looked to settling his family at the place called "El Tucho".

Rancho Tucho, as it came to be known after several more additional land requests by Filomena, was located northeast of Monterey on the side of the rich artichoke fields of later years. It was here, along the banks of the Salinas River, that the Pombers raised the rest of their children, including José Manuel, my great-great-grandfather.

As the family reached its full size, including twins, so came the influx of American settlers, and with them a new set of problems. It must be noted that neither Luis nor Filomena could read or write Spanish, much less English. With the changes that came with the americanization of California, the family would be left at the mercy of the Yankees. Though the children learned to speak, read, and write English, the oldest was only twenty years old in 1850.

In 1847, Luis Pomber applied for a renewal of the title deed for the lot in Monterey, first granted in 1836. Though he had lost the original deed in the interim, local Mexican records proved his claim to the property. This was nothing as compared to the problems of settling land claims after California became a state.

During the winter of 1851-1852 the Salinas River flooded, forcing the Pomber family to flee to higher ground. Upon their return, the Pombers found American settlers squatting on the land. The Act of 1851 set up a complicated system of settling land claims that essentially forced the burden of proof *and* the legal costs upon the original owners. In such an environment, the Pombers were never able to pursue the battle for Rancho Tucho with the Land Commission.

In an effort to raise funds to support the family, the Pombers sold what land they still owned in Monterey and even part of Rancho San Cayetano, once owned by Filomena's father, José Dolores Pico. Luis and Filomena's last years together were spent on San Cayetano where the small town of Pajaro had sprung up.

On January 23, 1864 Luis Pomber died and was buried the following day in the cemetery adjoining the Valley Church which is still standing today. Unfortunately, the family was only able to afford a wooden cross to mark his resting place. With the passage of time, the cross has either so faded as to make reading an epitaph impossible or has disintegrated altogether.

A more permanent memorial lies within the town of Castroville, founded by Juan Bautista Castro in 1863. Castro married Catalina Pomber, one of Luis' daughters. To this day, there remains a Pomber Street in Castroville, in memory of the founder's father-in-law.

Daniel Hill

BY DELPHINA HILL

 My great grandfather, Daniel Hill, arrived in Santa Barbara in 1822 when he was twenty-three. He came from Billerica, Massachusetts as first mate of the ship *Rover*, which was engaged in the Sandwich Islands trade.

He liked what he saw of Santa Barbara, especially Rafaela Luisa Sabrina Ortega, whose family owned the Ortega Hacienda north of Refugio Beach. He quit the sea, joined the Roman Catholic Church so that he could marry Doña Rafaela, and turned to ranching.

He soon became a "man of affairs of Santa Barbara, one of four cities in California to enjoy pueblo status." With construction and masonry skills, he was much in demand. He became a Mexican citizen in order to purchase land, and he learned Spanish, although with a Yankee twang. He owned the Goleta Ranch north of Santa Barbara.

Secularization of the missions in 1831 brought ruin and decay to nearly all of them, with the exception of Santa Barbara. Because of Daniel Hill's diligence and guile, he was able to keep the mission as a parish church. Later his son-in-law, Nicholas Dan, purchased the property, and as landlord of Mission Santa Barbara, he spared it for the ages.

Daniel Hill spanned the eras of greatest contrast in California history. As an American who became a Mexican citizen during the days of the Californios, he became an American again when California became a state. As a devout Catholic, he saved Mission Santa Barbara. As a loyal citizen of America, he was a great influence in bringing stability to California.

Daniel Hill died in January of 1865 and is buried in the graveyard of Santa Barbara Mission.

James Black

BY CHARMAINE A. BURDELL

 James Black Jr. was born in Carnwath, County Lanark, Scotland, on January 1, 1810, the son of James and Janet (Scott) Black. He arrived in California on January 2, 1832. Sick with typhoid fever, he was put off the ship at Monterey, taken to the home of John B.R. Cooper, and nursed back to health by Mrs. Cooper — Encarnación Vallejo, sister of Mariano G. Vallejo. Returning to the sea, he wrote the following letter to his father:

James Black
No. 29 Adlington St.   Callao, Peru
Liverpool, England   17 May 1832

Dear Father and Sisters,

    As *Dawson* is to sail tomorrow, I embrace the opportunity of writing you a few lines to let you know how I am getting on and in the first place I must inform you that I have left the schooner *Dolphin* and am now on board the Brig *Catalina*. We are bound down (up) the coast to California and from there to Hamburg (Germany). I think if I complete this voyage I will have the pleasure of meeting with you all in about sixteen months perhaps a little more. I am sorry that we have been parted so long. I was happy to hear of sister Margaret's union with Mr. Jones. Give them my best respects wishing them much joy with health and happiness in store. I must stop, hoping this will find you in as good health as it leaves me. Your Son & Brother

James Black

A Scottish sailor, James Black met Edward Manuel McIntosh, also a Scotsman, probably in Monterey, who invited Black to accompany him on a sea otter hunting expedition. "Mac," as he was called, became a naturalized Mexican citizen in 1833, and requested permission from the Mexican Republic to engage in sea otter hunting for four months along the coast of the territory, extending from San Luis Obispo Mission to the Port of Bodega, with the specific condition that he equip his craft with at least two other parties, people from the region. The permit was granted at Monterey, November 20, 1834, signed by José Figueroa. Black hunted with Mac for the next two years, forming a friendship between the two men that lasted a lifetime. (They are buried side by side in Mount Olivet Cemetery, San Rafael.)

When not hunting with Mac, Mr. Black lived part of the time at Bodega and part of the time in the redwoods on John Reed's Farm in Marin County. By 1835 he settled on the Cañada de Jonive Rancho, consisting of 10,786 acres, which had been granted him by Pio Pico on February 5, 1845 in what was to become Sonoma County.

Mr. Black married María Augustina Sais/Saez on May 19, 1844 at the Mission San Rafael Arcangel. Born at the Presidio of San Francisco and baptized at Mission San Francisco de Asis on February 17, 1828, Augustina was the daughter of Juan María Saez and Dominga (Valenzuela) Saez. Her grandparents were Justo Nazario Saez and Micaela (Sotelo) Saez, who had come to San Francisco with de Anza's second expedition, consisting of fifty-one persons, soldiers, and their families, arriving in Monterey May

James Black

23, 1775. James and Augustina had two children: James III (October 29, 1848-March 19, 1849) and María Augustina (1845-1900), who married Dr. Galen Burdell D.D.S., son of James and Sila (Lamon) Burdell. After Augustina's death in 1864 James married María Antonia Expectacion Loretto (Duarte) Pacheco, widow of Juan Ignacio Pacheco, daughter of Mariano and Teodora (Peralta) Duarte.

During the Gold Rush, Black drove large herds of cattle to the

Mary Augustus Black Burdell

mines, where he found a ready market for them. Their sale helped to make him a very wealthy man. In August of 1850 he purchased the 8,877.48 acre Olompali Rancho from Camillo Ynitia, an Indian, and in 1865 he deeded to his daughter, Augustina, 6,335 acres of this rancho with a band of cattle as a wedding gift.

By 1851 Black was driving herds of cattle up the Russian River Valley to a tract of land adjoining the Sanel Rancho on the north, for grazing purposes. Walter Skidmore, Deputy Assessor of Marin County, listed Black's property in 1853 as, "Two leagues of land in Nacasio, Nacasio houses, three lots in San Rafael, one and two-thirds leagues of Olompali, tame horses, wild horses, mules and asses, six yoke of oxen, tame cattle, wild cattle, swine, fowl, mortgages, bonds, money due, growing crops, potatoes, and grain, script."

James Black was baptized at the Mission San Rafael Arcangel on March 8, 1840 and became a naturalized Mexican citizen in September, 1843. In 1845 he was the second *alcalde* of San Rafael. On May 1, 1849 he applied in San Rafael to register his brand, the number "3" with vent and ear mark. In 1850 he became Associate Justice of the Court of Sessions and the first coroner of Marin County.

He was a plain, straightforward, honest man, strong in his likes and dislikes, and his word was as good as his bond. He was a man of strong will and decision and not likely to be influenced by others, a man of few words in business matters. His principal business was stock raising, and he seemed to understand that business thoroughly.

Mr. Black's will was contested by his daughter, Mrs. Maria Augustina Burdell. She claimed it was not the will of her father, that her father at the time of signing the paper was not of sound mind, that he was under restraint, undue influence, and fraudulent misrepresentation. This controversy was submitted three times to the juries of Marin County. A fourth trial took place in the Probate Court of San Francisco on March 16, 1874 and was concluded April 2nd. The decision of the jury: the will shall not stand, one half of the estate will go to Mrs. Black, and the other to Mrs. Burdell.

The fees for the three attorneys for Mrs. Burdell — Messrs. Shafter, Sewell and Southard — were established at $100,000, or something over $30,000 each. Mary A. Burdell's will divided the

Maria Augustina Sais/Saez Black

property between her son, James, and her daughter, Mabel (a.k.a. Mary), with Galen receiving a life interest. The home ranch became Olompali State Park in 1977. Some of the property is still retained in the family by great-granddaughter Charmaine Burdell.

José Abrego

BY MARCELLINE (ABREGO) BLAKE

 I am a great-granddaughter of Don José Abrego, the progenitor of the Abrego family in Alta California. José was a young, intelligent, and industrious Spaniard of twenty-one who welcomed the challenge of California as a Hijar-Padres Colonist in 1834. He participated in the purchase of the *Natalia* (a refitted brigantine), which had been purchased by the *Compania Cosmopolitana* to transport the colonization group. The *Morales* (a Mexican sloop of war) and the *Joven Dorotea* (a Mexican schooner) also made the trip. The colonization group consisted of approximately two hundred people, families, and equipment. After their first landing at San Diego, some colonists were escorted north along the El Camino Real from mission to mission, depositing families needed for developing those areas. The Hijar-Padres project was destined to secularize the Spanish missions of Alta and Baja California and grant the mission lands to those Indian, Mexican, and Spanish families who had originally helped in establishing the California mission system lands. José settled near Monterey.

Through the idyllic yet turbulent years of José Abrego's residence in California, he dispensed a prodigious hospitality, aided by his loving family. His winning personality, unfailing source of goodwill, and tolerance combined well with contemporary California and provided him with a life full of exciting events. In 1836 he married Josefa Estrada y Vallejo, the daughter of two prominent founding families of California. Her father was Raimundo Estrada y Ruíz; her mother, Josefa María Vallejo y Lugo. Josefa Abrego was closely related to everyone of note in Monterey and throughout California through various sisters, brothers, aunts, and uncles.

As José Abrego acquired wisdom about his newfound homeland and friends, he labored ceaselessly along with his family to create order in this chaotic country of his adoption. He had many public offices from 1836 to 1846. He held the offices of *Commissario* of the San Carlos Borromeo Mission at Carmel, *Subcommissario* and Administrator of the San Antonio de Padua Mission, Customs Officer, Member of the Assembly, Substitute Member of the Tribunal, *Alcalde* of Monterey, and Treasurer of the Territorial Finances until the occupation of the United States. Abrego's influence has endured in the laws that govern California to this day. No one questioned his ability or integrity and few distinguished foreign visitors failed to pay their respects to the Abregos.

After the occupation of the United States, Don José Abrego continued the operation of his mercantile business and numerous land holdings. During his lifetime he was a devout Catholic and upon his death in April 13, 1878, at the age of sixty-five, he was buried in the Catholic Cemetery of Monterey, an honored pioneer settler of California.

Bernarda de Villar Lyons
and George Lyons

BY TERRIE DI GANGI AND DEBBIE DI GANGI
IN MEMORY OF TERESA LYONS DI GANGI

 George Lyons was a native of Donegal, Ireland. Born in 1823, he was the son of Daniel and Catherine Kirkpatrick Lyons. George Lyons first came to America through New Bedford, Massachusetts, then sailed around the Horn for California, where he arrived in San Diego in 1842, according to the 1860 census.

María Bernarda de Villar, known as Bernarda, was born in 1833, the daughter of Lusana Bauega and General Francisco Roman de Villar, at one time *Commandante* of the San Diego Presidio. Francisco Roman de Villar was an officer in the company of artillery which came to San Diego in the autumn of 1825 with Governor José María de Echeandia. Bernarda and her sister Martina were orphaned at an early age. Both girls were raised by their mother's sister, María Bauega, and her husband Pio Pico, California's Mexican Governor.

Soon after George Lyons' arrival in San Diego, he met and married Bernarda de Villar. They had eleven children. The first, Jayme, died at the age of ten in 1857. His grave is one of five in historic El Campo Santo in Old Town, San Diego. The eldest child was William, who was to become involved in both real estate and mining in lower California. William was married to Sara Ames, daughter of the publisher of the *San Diego Herald* (San Diego's first newspaper), and descendant of Oliver Ames, an early industrialist and Governor of Massachusetts. Another son, Daniel, became a prominent San Diego civic leader, was owner of Lyons Implement

George Lyons

Company, and a former partner of Hamilton and Marston in a general store. He was also Director of the 1915 World's Fair. He married Maude Adams, daughter of William Portney Adams, a direct descendant of President John Adams. Other children of George and Bernarda Lyons were: Alexander, John, Benjamin, Bernecia (Mrs. Fred Thomas), Andrew, Mary Dolores (Mrs. Hinton), George, and Bernarda.

Martina de Villar (left) and Bernarda de Villar Lyons (right) with
Governor Pio Pico and his wife (from *California: An Illustrated History*
by T.H. Watkins).

George Lyons was a successful merchant and so active in politics and public affairs that he must be counted as one of the men
who turned San Diego from a Mexican village into an American
city. The 1850s were busy years for George. He was a prominent
builder in early San Diego and built many of the historic buildings
both in Old Town and New Town. He kept a store in Old Town
from 1851 to 1858. He was owner, founder, and on the Board of
Directors for the San Diego-Gila Railroad, which ran between the
city and Gila, Arizona.

As a citizen and civic leader George distinguished himself, hold-
ing numerous government offices — some of them several times.
He was postmaster from 1853 to 1855. In 1857 he was a member
of the Grand Jury. He served as Sheriff for two terms (1853 and
1862). During those years, he presided over the court-directed
auctions of some of the county's most historic properties — land

George and Bernarda de Villar Lyons with their children (standing, left to right) Bruce, Marjorie and Kenneth, and (seated) Daniel Jr.

grants dating back to the period of Mexican rule, which included Rancho Santa Isabel, Warner's Ranch, Rancho Tecate, San Luis Rey, and Pala Ranchos. George served as judge at the elections of 1873 and served as school trustee as late as 1878. In 1856 George was first named a delegate to the state convention in Sacramento and thereafter served as delegate over the next twenty years.

George and Bernarda Lyons' home was across the San Diego River from Old Town. It attracted attention because of its verdant beauty and the productivity of its orange orchard and other fruit trees. On June 12, 1873 the *San Diego Union* reported, "One of the most beautiful places in this vicinity is that of Mr. George Lyons near the river at Old Town. The pepper trees are the finest we have seen this side of Los Angeles and their graceful foliage is gladdening to the eye of the wayfarer." A family diary in the San Diego Historical Society recorded the fate of this home: "A flood in early 1860 washed their home and orange orchard into the sea. The

Maude Lyons

family escaped with their life. A boat was sent from Allast Point from the whaling camp to save them and everything was lost."

On November 5, 1899, Bernarda de Villar Lyons died. George Lyons lived for another nine years. At eighty-four, he died on March 10, 1908, in Old Town. He enjoyed the reputation of being one of the oldest American citizens and one distinguished from before the time of California's conquest by the United States. His obituary in the *San Diego Union* named nine of their children as survivors.

Both George and Bernarda Lyons were buried in the old Catholic cemetery, now Pioneer Park, near the presidio. Today this historic cemetery has been turned into a public park still surrounded by its original adobe wall. As a poignant reminder of the early pioneers, only a few of the hundred or more headstones remain on the site. One of these, that of Bernarda de Villar Lyons, reads:

Bernarda, beloved wife of George Lyons
Died November 5, 1899

Amiable she won all,
Intelligent she charmed all,
Fervent she loved all,
And dead she saddened all.

The Women Who Settled
La Frontera del Norte

BY MARTHA ANN FRANCISCA MCGETTIGAN

 The strength and character of Sonoma's First Lady was an attribute prominent in the women of her family for generations, and was significant in the settlement of California and the Northern Frontier.

Francisca María Felipa Benicia Carrillo de Vallejo (1815-1891) began a journey of approximately 800 miles to meet her husband of one year, Don Mariano Guadalupe Vallejo. The year was 1833, and she was a young pregnant bride of seventeen, leaving home on her own to start a new life. A true pioneer of Alta California and the *Frontera del Norte*, she traveled for four weeks by burro, escorted by a military guard of twenty troopers under the command of the General's brother, Salvador Vallejo. Although the country was beautiful, covered with flowers and roaming animals, "a volume of description could not give a more complete picture of the loneliness of the peninsula at that time." This amazing and dangerous journey was just one event in the life of Francisca Benicia that showed the courage and bravery that was necessary for the women who struggled beside their husbands for their families in this desolate land.

Francisca Benicia was born the daughter of Joaquin Victor Carrillo and María Ygnatia Lopez in San Diego. She had eleven brothers and sisters who would all figure more or less prominently in the history of California. She solidified her own position in California with her marriage of fifty-eight years to General Mariano Guadalupe Vallejo. She took great pride in having the city of Benicia, on the Carquinez Strait, named in her honor in 1847,

Francisca Maria Felipa Benicia Carillo de Vallejo, from
a painting. (Photo by Warren White, courtesy of California
State Parks, from donation of Frances Vallejo McGettigan).

and thereafter she signed all documents and letters Benicia F. de
Vallejo. The island named by Don Felix Auyala, was renamed Isla
de la Yegua, for Francisca's white mare, and then became Mare
Island — home to the U.S. Navy for 142 years. She provided exceptional homes for her husband and sixteen children along with
music and education. Her first son, Andronico, became the first

Californian to be admitted to West Point. Another son, Platon was the first native-born physician in California, and the first California physician commissioned in the U.S. Navy. She was host to dignitaries because of her husband's position in the country. She was witness through all the stages of California from frontier to statehood, and her thoughts and opinions are recorded in her letters to her husband and children. She is described by the travelers and visitors in California and to her home. Her son, Platon, says, "She was what we would call a level-headed woman." Her life consisted of adjustments that ranged from housekeeping in a dilapidated military post to years of affluence, and finally to curtailing in years of financial reversals. She held her own with the land, elements and foreigners, standing alongside her husband. She drew this strength of will from her mother.

María Ygnatia Lopez de Carrillo (1793-1849) was a woman who truly knew her place in life and that of her children. She was born in San Diego in January 1793 to José Francisco Lopez and María Feliciana Arballo de Gutierrez. María Ygnatia married Joaquin Victor Carrillo in 1809 in the presidio chapel in San Diego. Her husband was a soldier for over twenty-two years and together they had thirteen children. They lived in the first house built outside of the presidio. An orchard adjoined the house. This orchard was a gift from Don Francisco Ruíz to three of the Carrillo children who were his god-children. It was in this orchard in 1830 that *Alferez* Vallejo saw Francisca Benicia for the first time. And it was for this orchard that María Ygnatia took a stand against her husband. When Joaquin tried to sell the property, María Ygnatia appealed to the Governor to protect the rights of her children who owned the property, and she was successful.

After Joaquin's death, María Ygnatia packed all her belongings on horses, pack mules, and *carretas* and with seven Spanish trunks containing her finery, and with the nine children still at home, followed the same route her daughter had taken three years prior to the northern frontier to start a new life. In January 1838 a petition for a grant of land along the banks of Santa Rosa Creek was requested for her. On September 30, 1841 the two leagues (over 8,000 acres — the Cabeza de Santa Rosa Rancho) were granted to María Ygnatia Lopez de Carrillo. It was here that her tenacity and independence was proven. She took charge of her rancho and through it provided for her family. A large adobe home was built and a work force was recruited from the local native Indians. Her own horse had been trained by her sons for her special use in the fields. "She supervised everything that was done on the rancho, but left the managing of the livestock (over 3,000 head of cattle, twelve to fifteen hundred head of horses, and a few sheep) to her sons. She cultivated large fields of wheat, barley, oats, beans, peas, lentils, and vegetables of every variety. She was as good a rider as any man and willing to do any kind of work, on or off a horse." She had a vineyard and was the first woman viticulturist in what would become an important wine growing area. It was known by the Yankees in the late 1840s "not to trespass upon the hospitality of Señora Carrillo who, it is said, affections not our countrymen." She, too, held her own with the land and against foreigners, and she, too, drew this strength from her mother.

María Feliciana Arballo de Gutierrez (1754- ?) made the 1,800 mile journey from the present-day Mexican State of Sinaloa with the Second Anza Expedition of 1775-1776. She was the widow of José Gutierrez, a soldier who was killed in Mexico, and so traveled with her brother-in-law, Ignacio Gutierrez, and his family. María Feliciana was twenty years old when she became a widow and she had two daughters, María Tomasa and María Estaquia. Her daughters were six and four years old. This expedition brought the first families of Spain to Alta California. New research on information and documents of this expedition and its members, the de Anza family and their associates, and the frontier they were entering give additional insight to this tremendous struggle to reach new territory. It has now been established that there were closer to three hundred persons on the trip. María Feliciana signed up after the first recruits in Culiacan. This expedition she joined was an immense undertaking of people, cattle, horses, mules, and supplies. The difficulties they encountered were debilitating sickness, extreme weather — hot and dry to excessive rain — and loss of livestock. Where they were going there were no roads. They had to bring everything for their way of existence with them.

Soon after arriving at San Gabriel Mission, Doña María Feliciana married José Francisco Lopez, March 6, 1776. José and María Feliciana had six children. They were one of the first couples in my heritage to start their family in California. When they arrived, they had to make the unfamiliar their home. María Feliciana was the first of the women to "pack up and leave for a new start," and she was one of the first women of my family line to set foot in California.

It was because of the courage and spirit of María Feliciana Arballo de Gutierrez de Lopez in taking the enormous chance of going into the unknown, and her iron strength to see it through that her daughter, María Ygnatia Lopez de Carrillo and granddaughter, Francisca María Felipa Benicia Carrillo de Vallejo, were able to find their place in California history. It is also women such as these who provide the great tapestry and color of California.

Granddaughter of Monterey

BY CONSUELO ASHE SMITH

 This story begins even before the arrival of the Ortega expedition to California in 1774. The Vallejo family had been in Mexico for generations, but Ignacio Vicente Ferrer Vallejo decided to settle in Alta California and made the trip north and married María Antonia Lugo in Santa Barbara in 1791. There were thirteen children born to the couple, but María Antonia's child rearing was not completed with her own children. She also raised some of her grandchildren. One of these was María Josefa Abrego, who called her "Nana Antonia."

María Josefa married Don José Abrego in 1836 in Monterey. The memoirs of her granddaughter, Julia Bolado Ashe Davis, recall:

> To this home [in Monterey] my grandmother
> came as a bride. She was idolized by her husband who
> showered her with all the loveliest things that could be
> purchased from incoming sailing vessels that arrived in
> Monterey from the Orient, China, Japan, and Manila.
> My grandfather Abrego came on the French sloop of
> war *Natalia*, which was the vessel that took Napoleon to
> Elba and was wrecked in the bay of Monterey. Being a
> great admirer of Napoleon he had planks from this
> vessel used in building the ceiling of his ballroom,
> which was frequently the scene of balls and receptions
> in which American uniforms added no small part to
> the beauty and elegance of the scene — for the early

California *doñas* dressed most sumptuously in their Spanish lace *mantillas, mantons de Manila,* high Spanish combs of shell or gold.

Davis further describes life in Monterey in those early days:

Monterey's main street had lovely symmetrical adobe houses down as far as the old custom house and the water's edge, some with overhanging balconies on which the señoritas mingled with the flowers in the cool of the evening. At noon the chickens roosted down the streets and men sat in their shirt sleeves at the *cantinas* discussing the news of the day, but as late afternoon came on, the street assumed a different aspect as the young gallants on their mounts came out to caracole around the houses of their *inamoratas.* Like all Latin towns, Monterey came to life late in the afternoon. The Californians were happy, trusting, easy going children, basking in the sunshine of life until the Americanos came. Do you wonder that we who cling to the old traditions and romances still weep at the desecration and destruction of all the beauty, poetry, and romance that was our heritage?

Julia's sad memoir concerning her father:

"The Last of the Dons" was the title of the
obituary written on the death of my father, Don
Joaquin Bolado, and I know of none more appropriate;
for with him passed the old regime, the courtly
haciendados, gentlemen land owners, whose homes were
always open to passing guests and whose unfailing
hospitality and courtesy is still remembered with
appreciation and affection by those who knew him.

From the shores of Spain to the shores of Mexico had come
the tradition of gentility that was also the hallmark of living in
early California. As Julia Bolado Ashe Davis wrote in her memoirs,
the generations had changed and the old way of life was gone, but
the oral history of the family was passed down to the descendants
of today who fondly recall the words of their eminent ancestors.

William Money and Isabel Abarta

BY GABRIELLE FLAVIN

 William Money was born in 1807 in Scotland, a good Protestant Scot, to be sure. How did he manage to marry one of the most beautiful girls in Sonora, Mexico, thousands of miles from his birthplace? His is a story of high adventure, unrealized dreams, and pursuit of knowledge that few men experienced in early California.

His education is something of a mystery, since his credentials in natural history, philosophy, law, medicine, and theology are clouded. Edinburgh University shows that he did not attend classes there, so it may be that he was a self-taught observer of the world around him. By 1824 he had left Scotland and by 1825 he had arrived in the United States. The following year he was issued a passport as a British subject by the President of Mexico, Guadalupe Victoria. Money's profession is listed as "naturalist." He apparently collected specimens and sent them back to England, probably receiving enough money to support himself. From Mexico City, he set off for the Sonoran desert in northern Mexico, spending from 1835 to 1840 in the Mazatlan area. It was during this time that he met and married Isabel Rada (or Herrada). She was considered one of the most beautiful women in nineteenth century Mexico, and was much younger than Money. In order to make her his wife, Money had to convert to Catholicism, and in the process, took the name of José María Money (pronounced Mo-nay) This new status entitled him to marry, to own land, and to carry on business in Mexico and its possessions. He was noted for his mastery of the Spanish language, writing the first book in California that was bilingual, Spanish and English.

As a good Protestant Scot, Money made no effort to conceal his disputes with Catholic theology, and during his stay near Mazatlan commenced his long series of commentaries on religion. He was not a popular man among many of the Mexicans; the conflict with the Church made him unwanted in the area, hence the move to California. However, Money was a good draftsman and made many maps of California's land grants, some of which are currently in the Bancroft Library at the University of California in Berkeley. He also produced watercolors and other works of art of the flora and fauna of Mexico, spending twenty-two years in the process. This collection was a masterpiece of the natural history of California and Northern Mexico. The subsequent destruction of his life's work is a sad note in the evolution of the West, and the story, set in the chaos of the Mexican War of 1846 is almost unbelievable.

With the threat of impending war, Money gathered his pregnant wife, seven servants, several friends, all their possessions, and with forty-five horses left Los Angeles on November 18, 1846, heading south towards Mexico. Money obtained a passport from José María Flores, the commander-in-chief of the Mexican-Californian troops in Los Angeles. It reads

> I hereby give a full passport to William Money, a British subject, who leaves this country with his family and servants for the state of Sonora. I hereby charge all authorities let him pass on his journey, giving him all necessaries conveniently, paying a just price for compensation. Given in the general command of the city of Los Angeles, twenty-fourth day of October 1846.

Surely this was authority enough for a journey to relative safety in Mexico, far from the outbreak of the Mexican War in California. Unfortunately, the war caught up with the refugees, with tragic circumstances.

Fear of the reports of the advancing Yankee forces made the trip imperative. Fortunately, by November the Sonoran desert had cooled, and with the usual rains at that time of year there would be enough grass for the horses. One can only imagine the supplies needed for such a hard and long trip: horses, rope, bridles, saddles, guns, clothes, food (beans, dried beef, dried corn), and water, which was always in short supply.

The horse train set out for the south. It is known that they stopped at the Rancho Santa Ana del Chino. There Isaac Williams reported that Money and his family stayed at his house for several days. The Williams family extended the time-honored tradition of putting up travelers who passed on the trail to the south. The next stop was the Warner's Rancho, which formed the midpoint between Yuma (Arizona) and present day Los Angeles. This rancho was the farthest outpost of civilization. The sandy desert lies to the east. Yuma was well over a hundred miles away. They would leave the familiar oaks, sycamores, and palms of California, and the trail would lead steadily down toward the desert.

As Isabel and the others rested at the camp at the confluence of the Colorado and the Gila Rivers, Money, true to his inquisitive nature, left to explore some hot springs in the neighborhood, probably west of Gila Bend, Arizona. While the group awaited his return, tragedy struck. In the middle of the night the forces of General Kearny (the U.S general noted for his prowess in the Mexican War) raided this unarmed band of civilians who had nothing to do with the war. As the travelers slept by the campfires, the American forces silently crept onto the scene. Then violently the Americans attacked. Isabel, now in the eighth month of pregnancy, roused the servants and other party members from their sleep only to see the American invaders rounding up the forty-five horses. Frightened and neighing, the animals were led away.

The dismayed party helplessly watched as the troops rode from the camp with their only means of transport. How to proceed? Where to proceed? Proceed or return? Destitute in the desert with no means of going forward or back, Ygnacio Rodriguez, who had been left in charge of the camp in Money's absence, together with the others, set forth on foot to plead with General Kearny for the return of the horses. Too late! The General had marched on towards California. Meanwhile, during their absence, Indians appeared and confiscated all of their supplies, baggage, and possessions, including Money's manuscripts of natural history, notes, maps, and instruments. The Indians commenced the indiscriminate plunder of property, destroying all in a few minutes. Money's entire life-long work was gone, left to float away on the river, page by page, the inks fading and the watercolors bleaching and rotting under the Sonoran sun.

When Money finally returned, he was greeted with the news of his ruin — the loss of his horses, the destruction of his property. He procured a few horses with the purpose of overtaking Kearny, but this proved to be too difficult as his mounts were not strong enough. He returned to the Indian village in hopes of recovering his lost property, but was bitterly disappointed. Only tattered fragments of his manuscripts were found. The loss of his material now was an accepted fact.

Another fact had to be faced — their future fate. This was not just one man in the Sonoran desert, but his pregnant wife, their servants, and his friends, all at risk. The war had caused the Indians to commence hostilities on the inhabitants of the frontier, destroying their cattle and horses and slaughtering the settlers. Money decided to continue the journey to Sonora with the slender means which he had at his disposal. With no other provision than a little meal that the Indians had given them and beef for jerky, the wretched party departed willingly, compelled to face the dangers of a long and tiring trip into the now unfriendly and hostile desert.

They struggled on riding the few poor horses which Money had obtained from the Indians. For the next forty days they trekked the desert trails, suffering both physically and mentally. There were cold desert nights with little clothing, blankets, tents, or food. All their equipment so carefully gathered in preparation for the trip was now gone, stolen or liberated by the Indians and the American troops. During the space of forty days in the desert, Money and his party subsisted on the flesh of five horses and two dogs, roots, and herbs until they were met by the United States troops under the command of Colonel Cook who treated them kindly, giving them a small supply of provisions.

An eye witness of this encounter between the Money party and the American troops gives us insight into the plight of these outcasts. The following are entries of an American diarist:

December 27, 1846: Struck Gila about sundown. Last night a New Mexican who had been employed in the Dragoon Camp and a Chilean rode into camp. They represent that Mr. Money and . . . women and children are following them (whom they had sent for provisions) living on horse flesh; that Mrs. M. was about being delivered of a child. Terrible situation.

January 1, 1847: We found the party described by the two Mexicans we met. Mrs. M. was happily delivered of a fine child two days ago. She traveled yesterday ten miles on horseback. They tell us it is under twenty miles to the crossing. I asked one of his party we met if there was any news, speaking of Mr. Money. He said, "He is just like a Spaniard and would rather believe a lie than the truth."

January 2, 1847: Mr. Money asked permission to return to California with me alone. I believe it was granted.

January 3, 1847: Early march. Mr. Money has not come, his wife was sick.

Money and his party arrived at the frontier of Sonora in a miserable state. Reduced to nudity, they were compelled to remain outside the town until they could be supplied with some clothing to cover their nakedness by the charity of the inhabitants. Only then, having reached the haven of Sonora and the generosity of family and friends were they treated kindly.

Eventually the beautiful Isabel divorced William Money, married a Frenchman, and was still alive in Los Angeles in 1880. William settled in San Gabriel, his adobe home built in imitation of Holyrood Castle. He was a man of many firsts in California: first naturalist, one of the first physicians, he established the first hospital and the first non-Catholic church; he wrote and published the first book in southern California and the first monthly periodical; he was one of the first surveyors; and the maker of the first document recorded in the Los Angeles County recorder's office. He was a theologian, an astrologer, historian, and poet.

William Money died shortly after 1880 at his home in San Gabriel, a long way from his birthplace in Scotland. Although he had tragedy in his life, he could claim triumphs in his living through the history of early California.

Part Two:
Wagons Westward, 1843-1846

These years reflect the growing interest in the land of California, and the pull of free land was great. Brave and hardy pioneers hitched up their wagons, put the oxen under the span, and headed west. It was somewhat of a small miracle that these men and women ever reached the west coast at all. Maps were practically unheard of, untested if available, and unreliable at best. The stories of the ancestors of the Daughters during this period are another remarkable aspect of the formation of California. It was "Westward Ho!" and the settlers came, in trickles at first, but soon to become a flood.

Isaac Williams

BY DIANE WILLIAMS LANGMACK HOWELL

 The ancestors of Isaac Williams for many generations were pioneers in the westward immigration
movement across the United States. Isaac Williams
Sr. and Susannah Waller arrived in Missouri about the year 1800,
were married around the end of 1803, and settled on a farm near
Jackson, where Isaac Williams Jr. was born on May 23, 1823, one
of a family of seventeen children.

Early in 1843, Joseph B. Chiles formed a company to seek
new homes in Alta California, then a province of Mexico. Isaac
Williams, barely twenty years of age, and his brothers, James, John
S., and Squire, joined it. Thirteen members of the company, including the four Williams brothers, left the covered wagon contin-
gent at Fort Hall and proceeded down the Snake River to old Fort
Boise, thence in a general southwesterly direction through unknown
country, traversing southeastern Oregon, Northern California, and
a portion of Nevada, until they reached the valley of the Sacramento River, and finally Sutter's Fort in November, 1843. In a
letter addressed to the family, James Williams wrote:

New Helvetia, Upper California
March 22, 1844

Dear Brothers,
John, Isaac, Squire and myself arrived here the 10th of
November last, after a long tedious trip. John and
myself are pleased with the Country and expect to

Isaac Williams

remain. John is engaged in tanning for Capt. Sutter. I have for some time been busily at work at my trade, blacksmithing. This is a good country for mechanics, wages being from three to four dollars per day. . . . The climate is much milder than that of Missouri. During the winter the frosts are scarcely severe enough to kill the grass. Pasturage remaining good throughout the year. Snow in the valleys is unknown. The soil is ex-

tremely fertile, frequently producing 60 bushels of
wheat for one sown, red clover and oats growing wild
and very luxuriantly. The climate is one of the most
healthy in the world. There can be no country to
compare with this for game. Elk is most abundant,
frequently going in bands of 4 or 5,000. Black tail deer
are very numerous. . . . The grisly bears are more
numerous than in any part of the Rocky Mountains.
There are also plenty of Antelope frequently found in
bands of two or three hundred. The rivers abound in
fine fish. The salmon came up from the ocean in as
great quantities and up the Columbia River, are equally
as good as Lake Superior. In short, I cannot speak too
highly of the Country.

In 1844 Governor Micheltoreno was in trouble with insur-
gents of the south at Los Angeles, and with an army proceeded to
subdue them. Many recent comers, including the four Williams
brothers, were drafted into the army and participated in the battle
of Cahuenga, February 20 and 21, 1845, which resulted in the
defeat of Micheltoreno, and Pio Pico became governor.

Returning north, the four brothers settled near Santa Cruz
and engaged in farming and stock raising. On July 25, 1846 Isaac
Williams enlisted in the California Battalion, Company D, under
Captain Granville P. Swift, and served until the end of the war
with Mexico, after which he again returned to Santa Cruz and
resumed farming. Isaac wrote:

May the 11, 1847

Dear Brother and Sister,
I again take my pen in hand . . . that I am well and
enjoying health. Hoping that these few lines may find

you enjoying the same good blessings. . . . You wrote that Benjamin was getting well. . . . Wish he was alive to come to this country, the trip across the mountains would make a sound man of him. I suppose you heard of our hot and bloody war which we had with the natives. The war lasted 10 months and the Americans gained the day and our Star Spangled Banner waves over our Country now. Which is a land of the free and a home of the brave. James, Squire, John and myself were volunteers in this war and I could tell you all about it if I could see you. . . . Squire and myself are raising stock we will have not less than 12 hundred bushels of wheat this harvest. . . . Squire and myself, when we left home, we expected to return before now, but I do not know when.

Very soon, however, Isaac's brothers authorized him to go to Missouri and transact certain business for them and close out their interests there, because they all had decided to make California their permanent home. On July 20, 1847 Isaac joined Commodore Stockton's party, which was then returning to the States, arriving at Cape Girardeau, Missouri around the middle of November. He remained in Missouri until May 7, 1849, when he again crossed the plains, in ninety-four days, his destination being Santa Cruz.

On the first day of January, 1850 Isaac married Lydia Patterson, whom he had known since her arrival at Santa Cruz. She was a daughter of Elizabeth Patterson, a widow who was a member of the Stevens-Murphy-Hitchcock party of 1844, which had arrived at Sutter's Fort in March 1845. Lydia Patterson was born October 2, 1832 in Dare County, Missouri.

The Williams brothers operated a saw mill and for a time,

Lydia Williams

during 1850-51, Isaac and his wife lived there. Then they got the gold fever and worked in the placer mines along the Feather and Yuba Rivers and their tributaries until the spring of 1855, then for a short time lived in Stockton. In 1856 they farmed in the Pajaro Valley below Watsonville. The following year they bought a farm on the right bank of the Pajaro River slightly north of Watsonville where they planted an orchard, one of the first in the Valley. They lived there happily until the fall of 1869, when they moved to a ranch in Los Angeles County near what is now the City of Santa Ana. Isaac Williams died there January 26, 1870. He was a member of the Society of California Pioneers, his certificate of membership bearing the date of March 20, 1868. Lydia Williams died December 15, 1884 on the ranch.

Isaac and Lydia Williams had ten children:
William John (married Alabama Tyus)
Martha Lavinia
Julius Albert (married Sarah Ann Jasper)
Margaret Frances (married Grundy McGaugh)
Cynthia Ann (married Frank Holloway)
Isaac Benjamin (married Kate Sonoma Casebeer)
Lydia Alice
My grandfather, Andrew (married Edna Virginia Clugston)

James John Morehead

BY DOROTHY MOREHEAD HILL

 One of the few young men to come west alone in 1844, James John Morehead was only sixteen years old when he left his parents' farm in West Virginia and crossed the plains with an ox team. He was probably lured by tales of the West and its vast open lands, fertile soil, fine climate, wild horses, and cattle. Little is known about his first six years in the West, but the census taken at Mud Springs (now the city of El Dorado) in El Dorado County, California, on October 16, 1850, lists him as a twenty-two-year old miner. By 1852 he had settled along the Sacramento River, where he engaged in the cattle business, and he remained in Butte County for the next thirty-three years, until his death in 1885.

The earliest documentary evidence of Morehead's being in Butte County is the tax assessor's record of August 1857. The 1858 assessment book states that he was living southeast of Jenning's Ranch along the Sacramento River. Morehead built a house on what is now known as Llano Seco (dry plain) Grant, which is near Morehead Lake. He believed that he was homesteading, since Mexican land grants were not legal under American law. It is probable that he had been in this location since 1852 and thought the land was, or would be, unclaimed.

The Homestead Act of 1862 authorized unrestricted settlement on public lands to all settlers who were citizens, or intended to become so. The Act required only residence, cultivation, and some improvements on a certain number of acres. After living on the land and farming it for six months, a person could buy the homestead for $1.25 an acre. Morehead had lived on his site for about ten years, and had been assessed for taxes by Butte County for five. He had probably heard of this Act earlier, and expected the land could be his.

The 1864 assessment book shows a new buggy, and this was probably to escort his bride-to-be, Ardenia Angeline Boydstun, whom he married on February 20, 1865. They moved to Llano Seco Ranch, near Chico, described as a model of California ranch houses. Shortly after, Morehead, together with partners, planted a thousand acres of wheat. By 1867, agriculture produced almost twice as much revenue as mining and Morehead was a rich man.

Close to the Morehead ranch was a large piece of land that had been improved by the Consul of Denmark. The plan was that immigrants from Denmark would come to take over the parcels that had been subdivided. Unfortunately, no immigrants came, and the land was available for the Moreheads to purchase. The family was able to build a large beautiful home. Life was very comfortable for some early settlers.

Morehead had not been feeling well for several months. Though in the care of a local physician, he and his wife boarded the train for San Francisco to consult another doctor. Upon his arrival at the Russ House, he was feeling fairly well, but during the night had an asthma attack and died "in less than forty-five minutes." It was a terrible shock to his wife and children, as well as to his many friends in Chico.

One of the obituary notices stated that Morehead "would be missed from business circles in which he was a prominent figure." Another: "He was an enthusiastic and thorough farmer: frugal, saving, and cautious, he met with few drawbacks to his operations. He was a man of extremely temperate habits, was an excellent citizen, and by his upright and honest course in all his transactions had many friends."

It was Morehead's good fortune to have come west, for in his thirty-three years in California he acquired seventeen hundred acres in Butte, Colusa, and Tehama Counties, thirteen lots in the City of Chico, increased his assets a hundredfold since 1857, and was regarded as a prominent, successful farmer and businessman of the Chico area. He was also fortunate to have had a devoted wife and family. "Morehead, fifty-seven, left his wife, forty-one, daughter Ella, seventeen, son James Franklin, fifteen, and daughter Alma, six."

Ardenia A. Morehead, forty-one at the time of her husband's death, raised their three children and managed his estate for the next thirty-seven years — in later years with the help of her son, James Franklin Morehead — until she died in 1922.

The Great Murphy Migration: California's First Irish Family

BY TERRY TURCO

 The family patriarch, Martin Murphy Sr., was a native of County Wexford near the south coast of Ireland. He farmed with some success, owned his own land, and married Mary Foley. Their first child, Martin Murphy Jr., was born there in 1807, followed by James, Bernard, Margaret, Joanna, and Mary. Bad times after the Rebellion of 1798, a depression (1815-26) and the continued oppression of Catholics caused many Irish families to leave, seeking a better living in the New World. In 1820 Martin set out for Canada with his wife and six children, settling in the small town of Frampton, near Quebec.

Young Martin worked for a time in Quebec, where in 1831 he married Mary Bolger, who had been a neighbor in Wexford. He bought two hundred acres near his father, cleared it for farming, and built a home for his wife and four sons. However, crop failures and a depression caused the family to look south where brighter prospects existed in the United States. The Murphys and many of their neighbors in Canada settled south of the city of St. Louis.

The U.S. Government had bought two million acres of land from the native Indians, and the Murphys acquired some of these through a sale. Though the soil was richly productive, malaria was epidemic and in 1843 two family members died. A visiting priest told them that California would provide opportunities for a good living, and they resolved on another long overland migration.

The story of that remarkable trek stands out in California history. In the spring of 1844 the two Martin Murphys (father and son) disposed of their farms, purchased wagons and supplies,

oxen, and provisions, and made ready to leave Missouri. They joined an Oregon-bound wagon train, departing May 18, 1844 on the Platte River Road toward Fort Laramie. The California party numbered fifty-one men, women, and children, which included twenty-six members of the Murphy family, distributed in thirteen wagons.

The distance from Independence, Missouri, to Sacramento, California was 1,975 miles — nearly a five-month journey with ox teams averaging fifteen miles a day. The Murphys reached the sink of the Humboldt River in western Nevada by October 24, 1844. Determined to strike directly west by the shortest route through the Sierra mountains, they were the first group of American emigrants to arrive at "Lake Tahoe," since known as Donner Lake. Here their camp became the base of operations for getting the wagons up the granite slopes of the Sierras, a superhuman effort.

They continued by way of the Truckee River and Pass, exploring the exact route of modern transportation. When they reached the top of the pass, Martin thought that he had found an earthly paradise at last. The journey brought them to the Yuba River, and soon a new member was added to the group — little Lizzie Yuba Murphy, the first child born to non-Hispanic emigrant parents in California.

The Murphy party had the historic distinction of making the first wheel tracks from the midwestern states across the Sierras and on to the settled portion of California. They were also the first

American settlers to reach the crest of the Sierra divide by way of the Truckee River, thus opening the central immigrant trail and discovering a route used later by the first transcontinental railroad.

In the summer of 1845 Martin Jr. purchased the Rancho Ernesto in the Sacramento Valley. The property, about 9,000 acres on the bank of the Consumnes River, became historic as the site of the Bear Flag Revolt of June, 1846, the first in a series of events which ended with California's becoming part of the United States.

With the coming of the Gold Rush and the subsequent lawlessness and large scale rustling of cattle, Martin Murphy Sr. decided to move on once more — to the fourth and last home for this much traveled pioneer family. With his son, Bernard, he settled in the Santa Clara Valley near San Francisco. Here he purchased land and established ranches and farms centered around present day Coyote, Gilroy, and San Martin. Bernard Murphy married Catherine O'Toole and assisted with the development of the Santa Clara Valley ranches. The family prospered with raising cattle and wheat, and they acquired much land. Unfortunately, the senior Murphy's health declined, and he died on October 20, 1884. The City of San Jose had flags flown at half mast and a day of mourning was observed for his funeral.

A plaque has been installed at the site of the old Murphy home, but probably not many persons passing it in the rush of today's Silicon Valley bother to read it. Nevertheless, Martin Murphy, son of a Wexford farmer, became one of the most influential figures in the history of the state of California.

Riley Septimus Moultrie
and Mary Lucy Lard

BY NANCY DE LARA

 St. Joseph, Missouri was the jumping-off place to the West for most pioneers headed to California. Mary Lucy Lard, a native of Washington County, Missouri, cousin to Jefferson Davis, future President of the Confederacy; and to Jesse James, the renowned outlaw, would leave the South with her parents, Fielding and Nancy Belle Lard. The reason for their journey west was the fear of a civil war. They disposed of all their properties to prepare for their departure.

Mary Lucy was fifteen years old at that time. Her father hired a young man, aged twenty-two, also a native of Washington County, Missouri to be driver of the Lard wagon. His name was Riley Septimus Moultrie. The trip was uneventful to Fort Laramie, Wyoming. It was there while the wagon train took a short rest that the two young people were married on June 14, 1846. It was an eventful day as a birth, a marriage, and a death also took place. It was also the day that in faraway California the bear flag was raised. At this time in Wyoming the group later to be known as the Donner Party separated from the main wagon train and went across to Utah instead of following the California-Oregon trail. The young Moultries stayed with the Fielding Lard group and arrived safely at Sutter's Fort on October 1, 1846.

When word of the Donner Party's plight reached the fort, Commodore Sloat induced Riley S. Moultrie to become a member of the first relief party to aid his former companions. Moultrie along with several others formed the first of four relief parties to rescue the snow-trapped pioneers. In the winter of 1847 they walked from Sacramento to Donner Lake, making their way through un-usually deep snow. Moultrie carried out Virginia Reed, aged twelve, on his back and assisted her sister, Martha, as well.

In the meantime, Mary Lucy grew tired of waiting for her husband to return. She decided to make her way to the town of Sacramento with a few others and a Mexican woman to assist her, and from there to head to San Francisco. This group embarked on a raft trip down the Sacramento River, finally reaching San Francisco Bay. As they reached the bay, a severe storm developed with fog so thick that for a period of about two weeks the raft was unable to touch land. The group narrowly escaped with their lives because all of their supplies were lost except for a small quantity of tea. The raft finally made its way to the south end of the bay, which took about six days. When the raft landed, Mary Lucy stayed at Mission Santa Clara on the Guadalupe River, and was later joined there by her husband. However, she was soon to be in for a further adventure.

When General Fremont battled the Mexicans, Mary Lucy was captured and held prisoner for six days. Of her captors she always spoke warmly, telling of the extreme kindness they exhibited to herself and her family.

Her first child, William Moultrie, was born in September, 1847 at the Mission. Mary Lucy had ten more children for a total of five sons and six daughters. She often would ride horseback over the Santa Cruz mountains to visit her sister Sara Daubenbess, who lived in Soquel, and would occasionally take one of her children with her. Since the trip was overnight, she would spend the night in a roadhouse at the mountains' summit. On one occasion, Joaquin Murieta and his *bandidos* were staying in the same roadhouse. She heard him warning his men in Spanish not to hurt the señora and her "little one."

The Moultrie family stayed in the Santa Clara Valley.

Riley Septimus Moultrie died December 7, 1910 at the age of eighty-six; Mary Lucy Moultrie died in July, 1923 at the age of ninety-two. Her last offspring died in March 1958. Many members of this pioneer family are buried in Madronia Cemetery in Saratoga, California. This cemetery has a rich historical background and is more than 150 years old. As a final footnote, I can remember one of Riley's and Mary's granddaughters saying, "We can survive anything, as we are of strong pioneer stock." When I look back on the Moultries' adventures, some of which I have related here, I can certainly agree.

Part Three:
Arrival of the Mormons, 1846

The Mormons were determined to find a place where they could practice their religion without the persecution they had experienced in Nauvoo, Illinois. Elder Samuel Brannan was commissioned to charter the *Brooklyn*, load two hundred passengers and supplies, and sail around the Horn of South America to land in San Francisco to settle the Mormons in California. When the *Brooklyn* finally landed in San Francisco on July 31, 1846, Brannan found warships in the harbor and the American flag flying over the land. The plan to settle Mormons in California was scrapped, and Salt Lake City became the center of the Mormon church communities.

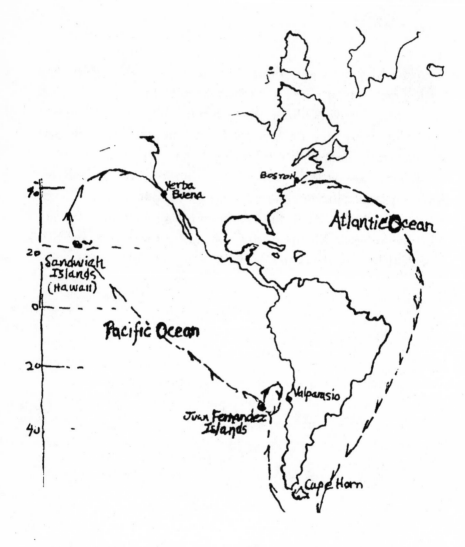

Simeon Stivers

BY LILIAN H. KELLY

 Simeon Stivers was born July 23, 1826 in Camden, New Jersey. His parents, Simeon and Ann Dorsey Stivers, were lost at sea when their son was three years old. Ann's sister, Letitia Dorsey Marshall, and her husband, Earl Marshall, adopted Simeon, but wanted him to keep his family name. The Marshalls lived in Philadelphia and Simeon was educated there, graduating from Philadelphia High School.

The Marshalls were Mormon. After ongoing problems relating to the Church, Mormon leader Brigham Young decided to move his flock out of the United States to seek a new Zion in the West. Those living on the east coast were advised to travel by ship under the leadership of Elder Samuel Brannan. Brannan chartered the 450-ton ship *Brooklyn*, and hired Abel W. Richardson as captain. The *Brooklyn*, a fully-rigged merchant ship built more for work than beauty, was well-worn from eleven years of hard service. She had survived such disasters as a sprung mast and a head-on collision. She was in her declining years, but was well-patched and about to embark on one of the longest voyages in the world — 24,000 miles, from New York, via Cape Horn, to California.

Mormon carpenters refitted the hold of the ship with small cabins for the passengers (who would spend six months in crowded unventilated quarters) while Brannan bought huge supplies of merchandise and farm equipment to start a new life in a new land — flour mills, lumber mills, a printing press, the most modern farming equipment, seeds, fabric for clothing, household goods, furniture, and a stock of food to last a month after landing. On February 4, 1846, 238 Mormons, who had sold their homes and packed their belongings, boarded the *Brooklyn*. With tearful farewells they were leaving families, friends, and their native land, not knowing where they would settle.

Lying ahead were storms so severe that their captain feared losing his passengers and the ship, but with his good seamanship they rounded the Horn and dropped anchor at the Chilean Island of Juan Fernandez (Daniel Defoe's Treasure Island). The Chileans warmly welcomed the Mormons and helped them resupply the ship with water. The Mormons were happy to launder their clothes, enjoy fresh fruits, and explore the island. This was their first landing since leaving New York.

After a week, Captain Richardson struck anchor and sailed for Honolulu, where Commodore Robert Stockton was in command. Advising Brannan that the United States was at war with Mexico, he supplied the Mormons with arms and ammunition, and told Brannan to plant the U.S. flag in Yerba Buena (as San Francisco was still called) to claim the settlement for the United States. But by the time the *Brooklyn* sailed into San Francisco Bay, "Old Glory" was already flying from the mast in Portsmouth Square. The next day, July 31, the *Brooklyn* was moored at Clark's Landing (near the present Broadway) at Yerba Buena. The passengers debarked, finding shelter in abandoned huts and in tents brought on the *Brooklyn*, or in the abandoned Mission Dolores. During the course of the voyage there had been two births and eleven deaths.

The arrival of the Mormons doubled the population of Yerba Buena and brought new energy to the community, as many of them were skilled workmen who contracted to build wells and shelters. Simeon Stivers worked for William Leidesdorff, building the first schoolhouse.

By 1847 Earl Marshall had decided to buy land to farm. He bought a mule, and walked and rode down the Peninsula, around

Alviso and on to Mission San Jose. He bought land a few miles north of the mission at two dollars an acre to develop a wheat and dairy ranch. Letitia and Simeon joined him there, and they lived in an abandoned adobe building until a home was built.

There is a family story that when gold was discovered, Earl and Simeon went to mine gold, leaving Letitia to manage the ranch, and that she did as well selling milk at twenty-five cents a quart, and the services of the bull at fifty dollars per visit, as Simeon and Earl did panning for gold.

Young Simeon, on a visit to San Francisco, met and later married Anna Maria Jones, a Mormon who had been with the group in Nauvoo, Illinois that fled to Utah. They were married September 12, 1858 and raised their seven children on the ranch.

The ranch was sold in 1957 to the Henry Kaiser Company, and is now the center of the city of Fremont.

Quartus Strong Parks
Mormon Teacher and Preacher

BY MAXINE BARRACLOUGH GROPHER

 Quartus Strong Sparks was one of the early converts to the Mormon Church. He had a most unusual and colorful life, a large portion of which was devoted to his religion, and he has become a part of the Church's history.

He was born October 20, 1820 in Hampshire County, Massachusetts. He became a teacher and moved to Long Island, New York. It may have been there that he was converted to the Church of Latter Day Saints, also known as the Mormon Church. Sparks became a leader in the Church and was described as "of gentle manners and a ready flow of language." During this time he met and married Mary Holland Hamilton.

As the early Church was threatened by local mobs, it was decided to move the congregation to Nauvoo, Illinois. There the leader, Joseph Smith, was killed. His death convinced church officials that they must move farther west. Sam Brannan, a Mormon of early California history, was instructed to charter a ship and settle a new country. He proceeded to charter a 450-ton sailing vessel, the *Brooklyn,* for $1,200 and made plans to go to the far west by sailing around Cape Horn and then north to California. The ship was stocked with food and supplies. Other items in the cargo were three flour mills, a printing press, and a one hundred-seventy-nine-volume library. Then, with two hundred thirty-eight men, women, and children aboard, the *Brooklyn* set sail from New York on February 4, 1846. Among the passengers were Quartus and Mary Sparks and their son, Quartus Jr., who was not yet a year old.

The journey lasted nearly six months. Two babies were born

on the trip, a little boy named Atlantica and a little girl, Pacifica. Ten persons died and were buried at sea. The ship make two stops for supplies and water, one at Juan Fernandez Island, the other at Honolulu, the ship having been blown off course. After enduring storms, bad food, and illness, the ship finally reached San Francisco on July 31, 1846.

The Sparks family settled near the Mission Dolores in San Francisco shortly after leaving the *Brooklyn*. Quartus continued to have a keen interest in the Church's activities and was a member of a group of men who established a community near the confluence of the Stanislaus and San Joaquin Rivers. A plaque has been erected on National Highway 99 to memorialize the event. It reads:

NEW HOPE — 1846
FIRST WHEAT

Approximately six miles west twenty Mormon pioneers from the ship *Brooklyn* founded first known agricultural colony in San Joaquin Valley. Planted first wheat; also crops they irrigated by pole and bucket method and erected three houses; operated saw mill and a ferry across Stanislaus. Settlement later known as Stanislaus City.

The Sparks family lived in San Francisco for several years, then in 1853 moved to San Bernardino. Quartus taught school there. He was admitted to the bar and became a prominent political figure in the community. He and Mary were divorced, and Sparks later married three more times.

Quartus Jr. was but a small baby when he went with his parents on the long voyage around Cape Horn. After his parents' divorce he went to the Utah territory with his mother, and later

married Caroline Carlow. They were my great-grandparents.

The patriarch of the family, Quartus Sr., lived a long and productive life. He died on August 5, 1891 at the age of seventy. The death announcement in a newspaper stated,

> He was a pioneer of the state as early as 1852, and took an active part in the formation of the American Party in California. In 1856 he organized the proceedings for the first Fourth of July celebration ever held in San Bernardino County. The press of that county and southern California speak of him in the highest terms of eulogy, as one who helped to create the county and the state.

Part Four:
Breaking Ground, 1847

Meanwhile, as the Mormons were sailing around Cape Horn and settling in San Francisco, there were others headed across the plains to California.

Joel Clayton

BY VIOLET L. MEYER

I am a native Californian, as were both my parents. I was born in San Francisco on February 13, 1913 to Mr. and Mrs. Alvin Lane Calhan. My father was born on May 2, 1887 in Martinez. My mother was born in Santa Maria on August 16, 1887. She was the daughter of Eliza Clayton Clark, whose father, Joel Henry Clayton, founded the community of Clayton in Contra Costa County. My mother was Edna Laurel Calhan, who served as president of the Daughters from 1950 to 1952.

There are many anecdotes about Joel Clayton and his adventures in the new world, but few dates are given. He guided four wagon trains west from St. Joseph, Missouri along the Oregon Trail. On the third trip he brought his seventeen-year-old brother, Charles, with him, and they arrived in San Francisco aboard the brig *Henry*, out of Oregon, on September 3, 1847.

Charles eventually became active in San Francisco politics and was a member of the Board of Supervisors. He served on the Finance Committee to procure land for Golden Gate Park. Later he became the first congressman from San Francisco. Clayton Street is named for him.

Joel Clayton was born in England in 1810, the oldest of twelve children. They lived at Brierly Green Farm at Bugsworth, now Buxworth, in Derbyshire. His family were dairy farmers and miners. In 1837 he and a brother, William, arrived in Boston en route to Pittsburgh, Pennsylvania to stay with their uncle, Peter Bare, their mother's brother. In 1838 the two young men went to Missouri where they acquired land for a farm in the suburbs of St. Louis. They planted fruit trees, vegetables, and flowers and built a large house. When it was finished the rest of their family came from England. Later, some of the family moved to Galena, Illinois, leaving William in charge of the farm. In Galena they worked in the mines.

It was in Galena that Joel met and married Margaret McClay, who was a teacher. One of her pupils was Tad Lincoln.

From Galena they moved to Wisconsin, where they bought a farm at Mineral Point and laid out a town named Mifflin. They worked in the lead mines at New Diggins. During this time Joel would leave his family and conduct the wagon trains. All of them were successful, so I do not believe that he divided his interest by prospecting along the way, but he probably observed and then explored and prospected on the way back to his family. He was likely in California many times before 1847, as he had mines all up and down the state as well as in Idaho, Washington, and Oregon. His pattern seemed to be that he would strike ore, get a partner to help develop and supervise the mine, build a store or trading post and find a partner to manage it, then take off, leaving the managers in charge. If the land was suitable for farming, he would acquire acreage for future use.

With the fourth and last wagon train, Joel brought his youngest brother, James, who eventually settled in San José, where he became an important figure in banking and water rights.

In the meantime, Margaret got tired of being alone so much and decided that if her husband was going to spend most of his time in the West, she would join him. She wrote to him at Bellingham Bay, where he had a coal mine and trading post, to tell him that she and their three children were on their way to meet him at San Diego. She took passage on a ship to the Isthmus of Panama, where she was able to purchase two good mules for the journey across to

Panama City. With her youngest child she rode one of the mules, the two other children riding the other mule. My mother told me that her grandmother never talked much about the hardships she endured. She just said that she devoted herself to keeping her children fed and well.

When Margaret got to Panama City she managed to find lodging and food, and waited in patience until she could find a ship to take them north. She sold the mules and finally left Panama City aboard an overcrowded ship with little privacy or sanitation. Then she began to worry!

For the first time, it occurred to Margaret that Joel might not have received her letter. She was getting low on funds and wondered what she would do if her husband did not meet her! So she was greatly relieved, when the ship entered the harbor at San Diego, to see him standing on the dock searching for her among the people crowded along the railing.

After resting from their ordeal the family traveled by ox team to San Francisco Pass, the site of Fort Tejon, north of Los Angeles. A stage company had been formed to carry passengers between Los Angeles and San Francisco with an overnight stay there. Joel was to be in charge. He had a man to see to the horses, and an Indian girl to assist Margaret.

Margaret had three more children while they lived at San Francisco Pass — two little girls and a boy. All was well until diphtheria swept through the area. All three little ones were stricken and died. They were buried on the shore of Elizabeth Lake, named for my grandmother.

Joel and Margaret gave up the stage business and traveled west through Cuyama Valley to the Santa Maria River, near the coast. Before Margaret had come, Joel had built up a wholesale and retail meat business in Stockton and thought they could settle there. Margaret, however, thought there might be malaria in Stockton and worried about losing more babies, so Joel took her to Oregon, where he had some land in the Willamette Valley. Margaret liked Oregon, but most of Joel's interests were in California, and he wanted to return to his forty acres on the slopes of Mt. Diablo. He had a house built there on Mitchell Creek and they moved in as soon as it was finished.

Joel thought that the railroad would eventually come that way en route to the Bay Area ports so he laid out the town, which he called Garibaldi, after the great Italian patriot. He established a right-of-way for the train, with land set aside for a depot and warehouses. He built a hotel and hired the Ryan family to run it, and a store, hiring Charles Haskell Clark as manager.

Joel discovered coal on Mt. Diablo and established the Black Diamond Mine. He sent to Wales for miners to operate it. When the California Homestead Act became law he took up 1,200 acres adjoining his forty acres and was able to purchase more land.

A town meeting was held at Garibaldi, and it was voted to call the town after its founder, so it became Clayton. Daughter Eliza Clayton and Charles Clark were married in 1864. They had an elaborate wedding with the famous Phoebe Hearst as matron of honor.

Joel owned a grocery store in San Francisco located on Pleasant Place, near where the Fairmont Hotel was later built. He offered son-in-law Charles a job as manager, so the newlyweds moved to the City. They lived at first on South Park, but later they moved to Clay and Taylor to be closer to the store. They had a Jersey cow which had been born to one of the herd of dairy cows that Joel had brought west with his last wagon train.

Sometime around 1850 Joel started a dairy on twenty acres he had "proved up" in San Francisco. I was told that he was the only one who had ever acquired land in San Francisco in this way. He named it the Guadalupe Dairy and hired a man to operate it. Later he sold the dairy to John Bell, who enlarged it and continued to operate it until he moved it to Bellvale, the name he had given his ranch on the San Mateo coast. The original twenty acres in San Francisco is still known as Cow Hollow.

Joel Clayton, immigrant from England, left his mark on California history. His little town of Garibaldi is now the suburb of Clayton, near Mt. Diablo, a bedroom community for Silicon Valley and the San Francisco Bay Area. The Clayton name lives on in the twenty-first century, reflecting the accomplishments of Joel.

Panama, the Gold Rush
and the Railroad

Even before the United States acquired California after the Mexican War (1846-48), many heading for California used the Panama isthmus crossing in preference to the long and dangerous wagon route across the vast plains and rugged mountain ranges. Discovery of gold in 1848 increased traffic greatly. In 1847 a group of New York financiers organized the Panama Railroad Company. This company secured an exclusive concession from Colombia allowing construction of a crossing, which might be by road, rail, river, or a combination. After surveys, a railroad was chosen and a new contract so specifying was obtained in 1850. The railroad track followed generally the line of the present canal. The first through train from the Atlantic to the Pacific side ran on the completed track on January 28, 1855.

Gold rush traffic, even before the completion of the railroad, restored Panama's prosperity. Between 1848 and 1869 about 375,000 persons crossed the isthmus from the Atlantic to the Pacific, and 225,000 crossed in the opposite direction. Prices for food and services were greatly inflated, producing enormous profits from meals and lodging. The railroad also created a new city and port at the Atlantic terminus of the line. The town that immediately sprang up to accommodate the railroad offices, warehouses, docks, and shops, and to lodge railroad workers and passengers, soon became, and remains, the second largest in the country. United States citizens named it Aspinwall after one of the founders of the Panama Railroad Company, but the Panamanians christened it Colon, in honor of Columbus. Both names were used for many years, but because the Panamanians insisted that no such place as

Aspinwall existed and refused to deliver mail so addressed, the name Colon prevailed.

The Gold Rush and the railroad also brought the United States' "Wild West" to the isthmus. The forty-niners tended to be an unruly lot, usually bored as they waited for a ship to California, frequently drunk, and often armed. Many also displayed prejudice verging on contempt for other races and cultures. The so-called "Watermelon War" of 1856, in which at least sixteen persons were killed, was the most serious clash of races and cultures of the period. In 1869 the first transcontinental railroad was completed in the United States. This development reduced passenger and freight traffic across the isthmus and diminished the amount of gold and silver shipped east.

The Family of Eli Moore

BY VALERIE ETCHEBER JONES

 When returning to the Bay Area from Reno, one has to marvel at the pioneers who crossed the majestic, rugged Sierras in covered wagons. Eli Moore and his family were such people. These brave people left Missouri on May 8, 1847 bound for Oregon, and arrived in California on October 2, 1847. The family consisted of Eli Moore, born in 1808 in Guilford, North Carolina, his wife, Elizabeth Palmer Moore, born in 1804 in Tennessee, and their children: Alexander, born in Cock County, Tennessee in 1826; his bride (whom he married in February, 1847), Adeline Spainhower Moore, born in Stock County, North Carolina in 1822; Rachel Elizabeth; Thomas, age fifteen; William, eleven; and four-year-old Martha Emeline.

While crossing the plains, "the party was informed of the close of the Mexican war by Fremont and his party, whom they met soon after reaching Fort Hall, whereupon a portion of the party, including the Moores, took the route for California." Charles Hopper, a trapper in the Bidwell Party of 1841, became the guide of the "twenty wagons and one hundred people" group that was the first party to follow the Donner Party.

According to George Stewart in *California Trail,* "The immigrants this year [1847] seem to be almost exclusively farming people." According to Alexander Moore himself, "There was neither bridge nor ferry across the San Joaquin River." A raft eleven by sixteen feet was constructed and a rope was used to tow the raft across the river. Some had to swim across the river with a rope to tow the raft. The wagon had to be unloaded, rolled on to the raft, and reloaded. This process took an entire day.

The family settled in Santa Cruz on November 15, 1847, probably because Eli could go no further. Adeline and Alexander's son, Eli Moore, born December 12, 1847, has been credited as being the first child born of white parents west of the Rocky Mountains.

Eli Moore was quite impressed with Pescadero because "it produced wild oats that reached his horse's back and he coveted it for his children." Alexander built the first school in Pescadero and paid the teacher himself. Most of the students were his own children. Eli Moore died in 1859. Alexander and his wife celebrated their golden wedding anniversary. Some of the farming tools that Alexander used impressed the natives — especially his steel plow and grain cradle.

Adeline Moore was the mother of eight children, and also practiced as a midwife. One of Eli's granddaughters, Ida Mesquite, became a president of the Daughters of California Pioneers. There are many descendents of Eli Moore today. Alexander Moore's brother, William, remained in Santa Cruz. Rachel, Thomas, and Martha are presumed to have also settled in the area.

John Churchman and
Caroline Jagger Churchman

BY LOIS CHURCHMAN PATTERSON

 Three of my ancestors came to California in 1847: my great-grandparents, John C. and Caroline Jagger Churchman, who had married in Indiana in 1832, and their son, Schuyler, born in 1839. John, the second son of a large family, and Caroline had made two westward moves and were living in a small farming settlement on Spring Creek, in Illinois, at the time of Schuyler's birth.

Though the land was forested with sugar maples and oaks, many of the settlers contracted "ague and bilious fever" and found the winters severe. John Churchman decided to follow the westward migration to California, leaving Spring Creek in 1846.

The family moved temporarily to the Iowa home of a brother to make preparations for the trip west. In the spring of 1847 John and Caroline, with their six children aged fourteen years down to one month, traveled by wagon to the town of Savanna on the Missouri River, where they joined a small company going to California. My grandfather, Schuyler Churchman, was seven years old at that time and remembered the experience of "crossing the plains" all of his long life.

The family's only tragedy on the trail was the death of their three-year-old son, William, in Thousand Springs Valley. Schuyler had his eighth birthday in late summer as they traversed the Sierras. He remembered seeing the cabins the Donner Party had built on top of the previous winter's deep snow, which had since settled crookedly when the snow melted. Treetops had been cut off far above the ground, a reminder of what might befall late emigrants.

Before snow fell, Schuyler and his family had reached the Sacramento Valley, though by that time they were almost out of food supplies. They were able to buy flour and beef at the ranch owned by William Wolfskill. The rains kept them from traveling south to find land, and that proved fortunate when, in January, 1848, gold was discovered. John and his oldest son went prospecting on the Yuba River. At Rose's Bar they staked a promising claim and moved the whole family there to camp for the summer. Following a vein of gold, they mined as much as possible before winter. Then it seemed prudent to find a house, so John sold the claim for a fair price and went southwest to the village of Sonoma. There he found a one-room house with a dirt floor where they lived for over a year. Son William, named after the deceased brother, was born there on January 3, 1850.

There were shortages of food when storms delayed ships bringing wheat from Chile, and John searched diligently for farm land to buy. He rode out on horseback to the Bodega country where the vast El Molino Grant was owned by Captain John Cooper. On May 1, 1850 John Churchman moved his family to the land. Along with several friends, he bought land from Captain Cooper for six dollars an acre. His share was three hundred and forty acres, and he homesteaded seventy adjoining acres of government land. The first United States census in California, taken in October of 1850, shows a community of settlers living in the fertile area west of Sebastopol.

Grandfather Schuyler remembered how beautiful Green Valley looked when he first saw it in the spring of 1850, with abundant grasses high enough to hide the cows when they lay down.

Planting was the first necessity — before shelter. John rode a few miles to the Coleman Valley to buy twenty-five pounds of seed potatoes, for which he paid twenty-five dollars. The first crop sold for a high price.

Until this time, agriculture in this part of California had produced little except wheat and cattle, though the Russians at Fort Ross had planted an orchard about thirty years earlier. In the Green Valley settlement three men, — John Churchman, Mitchell William, and Major Sullivan — were among the first to plant orchards.

> In 1851 they heard that a man named Weeks had
> brought out a lot of trees from the East and had them
> buried in the sand where the old Zinc House stood,
> about three and a half miles north of Petaluma. They
> purchased about one hundred and fifty trees, at one
> dollar and fifty cents to two dollars apiece . . . and they
> were the first orchards planted. For many years after,
> the profit on these trees was enormous, and fruit
> culture soon grew into a trade of the first importance.

The earliest trees planted on the Churchman Ranch were plums. San Francisco was a ready market for produce of all kinds. Twenty-two miles from the farm, Petaluma was the trading center where goods were transferred to boats to go down the river to San Francisco Bay.

John Churchman and his sons would yoke their oxen to the loaded wagon and start for town at two o'clock in the morning. They kept good strong "cattle," as the oxen were called, in order to travel the distance in one day. In Petaluma the animals rested in a feed lot while the farmers did their trading. Laden with whatever tools and supplies they had bought, they drove to the Washoe House, a wayside inn, where they stayed overnight, returning to the Green Valley farm the next day.

Their first home was a log cabin. In the late 1850s John built a two-story house large enough for the family of ten. Having learned cabinetmaking in his youth, he was a meticulous craftsman, and the house was still standing ninety years later.

My grandfather, Schuyler Churchman, grew up on the ranch and in 1852 attended the newly organized Ash Creek School. Farming became his life work. Around 1869 he married Eliza Ann Wilson, daughter of another pioneer family, and they established a home on a farm near Red Bluff.

Schuyler's sister, Mary, and two of his brothers were also married. In 1871, John, still vigorous, conceived a new pioneering project that he hoped would involve his whole family. Accompanied by his twenty-year-old son, William, he traveled by ship to Chile, then across the Andes to Argentina to the province of Entre Rios, north of Buenos Aires. He envisioned great farming opportunities there for immigrants.

The following year he sold the farm in Green Valley and persuaded most of his family to move to Argentina. Only daughter Mary and her husband, and Schuyler and Eliza with one son and another on the way, refused to go. Caroline did not want to leave California, but she was a devoted wife.

In 1873, John, aged sixty-eight, died suddenly from a ruptured appendix. He is buried in Parana, Argentina. Caroline remained there with her family until 1882 when they all returned to the United States. She lived with her children in Ashland, Oregon until her death on January 13, 1898, at the age of eighty-six. While following her pioneer husband she had borne eleven children, of whom seven were still living.

Schuyler and Eliza raised four sons: Schuyler Elmer, John William, Harry, and Charles. The elder Schuyler and Eliza moved back to Green Valley in later years. After Eliza died in 1898, Schuyler lived with my father, John William, who farmed a portion of the large Thomas Ranch in Green Valley that his first wife had inherited from her family. My father and grandfather carried on the tradition of planting and cultivating one of the first Gravenstein apple orchards.

Schuyler was fond of reminiscing about pioneer days, and his son, John, collected many of the stories he had heard as a boy. After moving to Santa Rosa in 1920, Grandfather continued to work daily in his garden until a month before his death on February 5, 1923 at the age of eighty-three. He is buried beside Eliza in the Green Valley Cemetery among the graves of many of the pioneers.

Part Five:
The Mexican War and
Stevenson's Regiment

In the spring of 1846, as the United States entered into war with Mexico, President James Knox Polk appointed Colonel J.D. Stevenson to head a regiment of New York Volunteers. Stevenson's assignment was to recruit a group of "skilled artisans, sturdy young farmers, wheelwrights, blacksmiths, and others" and take them by ship around Cape Horn to California. The men were to be colonists of a new American province. The government chartered three vessels, each with a capacity of seven hundred tons, to transport the volunteers: the *Susan Drew*, the *Loo Choo*, and the *Thomas Perkins*. The regiment numbered fewer than six hundred men.

The three ships sailed into San Francisco Bay in March of 1847, arriving within a few days of each other. Soon the bay would be cluttered with Yankee vessels — sloops of war, transports, storeships, and frigates. General Kearny's dragoons had come in overland, and soldiers and sailors outnumbered all the previous American settlers in California by more than two-to-one. Getting a late start, many of the New York Volunteers could serve no useful purpose except as an army of occupation.

The men of Stevenson's regiment would become the mayors, legislators, congressmen, judges, sheriffs, tax collectors, and county clerks of the new state. Seven of the regimental officers were among the forty-eight delegates who drafted the first California constitution. The first millionaire of San Francisco, the first sheriff, the first port collector, the first published author, and the first editor of the first important newspaper were from the regiment, as well as the gunfighters, knife throwers, ballot-box stuffers, and disturbers of the peace.

Charles Henry Lipp

BY MARIE ELAINE COLLINS

 Charles Henry Lipp, my great-grandfather, was born to Heinrich and Veronica Lippe on July 14, 1824 in Baden-Baden, Germany. Christened Karl Heinrich, Charles was one of several Lippe children and believed to be the only family member to emigrate to the United States. A search of ships' passenger lists has not revealed Charles' name, but it is likely that he left Germany from either Bremen or Hamburg, the main ports of embarkation in the mid-1800s. By the summer of 1846 Charles had arrived in New York City where, according to family lore, he found employment as a clerk. At this time, he was known as Carl Heinrich Lipp, having deleted the final "e" from "Lippe."

In 1846 President James Polk enacted his plan to send a regiment of volunteers around Cape Horn to serve in the ongoing war with Mexico in California. On June 21, at Fort Hamilton, New York, Charles enlisted as a private in Company D of Colonel Jonathan Stevenson's First Regiment, under the command of Captain Henry M. Naglee. On August 19, 1846, at Philadelphia, Charles and ninety-nine other recruits boarded the *Susan Drew*, one of three ships transporting the volunteers to California. The ship arrived in San Francisco in March, 1847, having stopped briefly in Rio de Janeiro the last week of November, 1846. At San Francisco, the Volunteers transferred to the *Lexington*, sailed to Monterey, and boarded the *Isabella*, March 5, 1848, for Mexico. Under the command of Lt. Colonel Burton, Company D battled Mexican forces at Todos Santos. It was "the last command of American troops to leave Mexico after the close of the Mexican War." The

Volunteers returned to Monterey on the *U.S.S. Ohio*, where Charles was honorably discharged October 24, 1848.

It had been President Polk's intention, although unknown to the recruits, that the Volunteers be of sufficient moral character to "serve as a nucleus for the Americanizing of the new province." Upon their discharge, many of the Volunteers did remain in California as miners, possibly because the California land grants alluded to by Mexican War recruiting officers did not materialize. Although Charles is known to have been in San Francisco in 1850 — trying, ironically, to acquire land he believed was owed him — he did mine in California, perhaps for many years. No further information is known about him until 1864 when, as "a miner," Charles volunteered to serve in the Civil War in California.

Described as a "veteran volunteer," Charles was mustered into Company A, Third Regiment of Infantry, August 17, 1864 in San Francisco. On October 28, 1864 he transferred to Company H, Second Regiment Infantry, California Volunteers, for the duration of the Civil War. He served as a hospital attendant at the San Francisco Presidio throughout the war, traveling briefly to Arizona as an Indian scout.

Charles was honorably discharged July 2, 1866, receiving a Grand Army of the Republic Veteran's medal. He remained in San Francisco, marrying Katharina Elizabeth Michel (or Carmichel) at St. Boniface Catholic Church, October 28, 1866. Katharina, fifteen years Charles' junior, was a native of Wiesbaden, Germany. She had emigrated to San Francisco in either 1865 or 1866 in the employ of the Frederick Casselman family. Katharina was the mother of a small daughter, Elizabeth Graffe, left in the care of the child's grandparents in Wiesbaden.

Charles and Katharina's first child, Amelia, my grandmother, was born October 31, 1867 in San Francisco. In 1869 the family relocated to Vallejo, probably to 408 Florida Street, where they were known to reside in 1870. On May 26, 1877 Charles purchased a two-story, wood frame home at 600 Alabama Street, Vallejo from Dr. L.C. Frisbie, Mariano Vallejo's son-in-law. It remained the family residence until 1958. His remaining four children, Ernest Louis ("Lou"), Charles William ("Willie"), Emma, and Laura Veronica, were born in Vallejo between 1869 and 1878. Katharina's daughter, Elizabeth, joined the family in 1884.

By 1874 Charles was employed, at least occasionally, at Mare Island Naval Shipyard's Ordnance Department, where he "was noted for his faithful and industrious ways and habits." He was a member of the International Order of Odd Fellows (I.O.O.F.), San Pablo Chapter No. 43, and of Farragut Post No. 12, Grand Army of the Republic. He also maintained some contact with Francis D. Clark, a former member of Stevenson's Regiment. In New York in 1870, Clark had begun soliciting information about his surviving Mexican-American War comrades. In 1882 he published *Stevenson's Regiment in California.* Charles' copy is among the Lipp family memorabilia.

According to his obituary, Charles lived the remainder of his life as an "esteemed resident" of Vallejo. He died of heart disease April 12, 1896, and was buried in the Lipp family plot at Sunrise Memorial Cemetery, Vallejo, under the auspices of the I.O.O.F. Reverend T.F. Burnham officiated, with N.D. Hoffman, A. McLean, John Brownlie, J.S. Souther, George Rounds, and H.D. Richardson as pallbearers. Charles was buried beside Emma, who had died in infancy, and Willie, who had died of diabetes at age twenty. Katharina died in Vallejo in 1919; Lou, Amelia, and Elizabeth in the 1940s. Charles' youngest child, Laura, lived in the family home until her death in 1958.

Charles married relatively late in life and was unknown to his four grandchildren, all of whom were born to his daughter, Amelia, after his death. His Mexican-American War records describe him as "ruddy complected, with auburn and blue eyes, five feet six inches in height." Three photographs of him exist, showing him to be a slight, regular-featured man. Deceased for almost a century, his character and personality can only be surmised. He was adventurous and hard-working, and perhaps Hubert Howe Bancroft's appraisal of the New York Volunteers is apt:

> Their real achievements, as wisely intended by the government from the first, were not as soldiers, but as settlers and citizens of a new country, under circumstances in some respects more wonderfully favorable than had been dreamed by the youthful adventurers in New York.

The Russ Family

BY JANE V. R. BERNASCONI

 Emanuel Charles Christian Russ (later to be known as I.C.C. Russ) was born in Hildburghausen, Duchy of Saxe-Meinengen, Germany in 1795. The family was of Polish ancestry, the noble name "Rienski" having been changed to "Russ" when his parents fled Poland at a time of continuous turmoil.

I.C.C. Russ was a silversmith by profession, as well as a pyrotechnist — supplying fireworks for the Duke of Saxony. When the Duke moved his court away from Hildburghausen, I.C.C. was no longer able to support his large family as a jeweler. Thus in 1832, at the age of thirty-seven, he decided to leave for America and sailed for New York, leaving his wife, Christiana, and five children behind. He resumed his trade of silversmith and sold watches and jewelry throughout New York, New Jersey, and Pennsylvania. Industrious and successful, within two years he was able to send for his family.

By then he had re-established a pyrotechnic business (there were many occasions for fireworks in New York) as well as a profitable jewelry store. Four more children were born. For the next several years the family led a comfortable though thrifty life in New Jersey on three dollars a day. By careful management, they eventually accumulated a small fortune of some twenty thousand dollars.

However, luck was not to last long. In 1845, scarcely thirteen years since I.C.C.'s arrival in America, the family suffered an economic blow that was to disillusion I.C.C.'s faith in humanity. While

Christiana Russ

the family was attending the memorial procession for Andrew Jackson across the river in New York, the jewelry store was burglarized and everything of value stolen; nothing of it was ever recovered. The family was devastated and for the following year had to resort to living in the poorest of tenements. I.C.C. decided to go away to begin a new life on new soil.

I.C.C. was attracted by stories of California, a new land of opportunity where John August Sutter was building an agricultural empire. The United States was at war with Mexico at the time and Colonel Jonathan Stevenson was recruiting his regiment of New York Volunteers for the outpost in California. I.C.C. had repaired a watch for Colonel Stevenson, and meeting him on the street one morning soon after the disaster was offered passage for his family to San Francisco if he (I.C.C.) and his sons would enlist in the regiment.

Thus in the winter of 1846, when three sailing ships — the *Susan Drew*, the *Thomas Perkins*, and the *Loo Choo* — set sail from New York harbor, the entire Russ Family was aboard the *Loo Choo*: I.C.C. and his eldest son, Adolph Gustave Russ (age twenty-one), enrolled as privates; Charles Christian Edward (nineteen) and Augustus Phillip (fifteen), as fifer and drummer; plus mother Christiana and the rest of the children — Carolina (eighteen), Elizabeth (thirteen), Frederick (ten), Henry (seven), Emeline (three) and Louisa (two). The voyage around Cape Horn was to take six months. Family legend adds that "Mother Russ had some sound ideas when it came to caring for her brood. . . . She insisted that a barrel of sauerkraut be loaded aboard the ship and moreover saw that her husband and children ate plenty of this time-honored scurvy preventative."

The *Loo Choo* sailed into San Francisco Bay on March 26, 1847. The day after their arrival, I.C.C. with his two older sons, Adolph and Charles, bought three 50-vara lots at $16.65 per lot — two on Montgomery Street and one on Bush. They then purchased lumber from the *Loo Choo*, wood from which their bunks on board ship had been built, as well as the partitions between the rows of bunks that housed the military. With this lumber, I.C.C. and his sons built the first family home, on the corner of Bush and Montgomery. A bare shanty at first, he soon improved the house by lining it with adobe. Later, as he was able to gather more used lumber, he built a number of small cottages, some thirty of them, which he rented as soon as completed. The immigrant Russ Family had begun to set down their roots again — joining San Francisco's early population of approximately 200 inhabitants, which occupied

Adolph Russ

twenty-five houses scattered from Pine Street to North Beach.

The Mexican War was virtually over by the time the Russ Family arrived in San Francisco. Adolph had the opportunity to partici- pate in the regiment but a short while, without ever seeing a day of battle. He spent the six months left for him to serve peacefully, in an outpost in Sonoma, while his father was allowed to stay in the city to settle his family.

In January, 1848, a little less than a year after the family's arrival, gold was discovered on the American River. During the following summer and fall crowds began to arrive and the young city started to boom as the first Gold Rush began. Adolph, with three friends, set out with an ox team for Sutter's mill, where they extracted four pounds of gold worth $800. In 1849, after the family was established in San Francisco, I.C.C. and three sons went to work in the Marysville area, returning soon afterwards because of scant returns — about one ounce a day of hard work worth about $16. Adolph made other attempts at gold mining but met with several mishaps along the way. A donkey that he had bought to carry his gear broke down and died. Then he was robbed of his gold and most of his belongings by Indians while he was bathing in the river. He was lucky to snatch his clothes just in time, before the Indians could make off with them also! Finally, he decided that mining was not for him and returned to San Francisco to work with his father.

Meanwhile the family business was thriving. It proved to be the right business at the right place and the right time.

Christian Russ made the first rings of California gold, and miners had such faith in him that the slogan at the digs was, "Take your poke to Chris Russ." He added to his business that of assayer, testing the gold that was brought in to determine its quality. After the discovery of gold, the merchants generally refused to receive it as genuine, but when Mr. Russ made a test of it and pronounced it genuine, the merchants held a meeting at which they resolved to take it for $14 an ounce in trade and $10 an ounce in exchange for coin.

By 1850 San Francisco had become a wild gold frontier town. The neighborhood around Montgomery Street, where the family lived, had become "quite rough, so he [I.C.C.] decided to move the family to a safer and more quiet place." A wise decision in view of the fact that there were four young daughters in the family. He bought seventeen 100-vara lots of "perfect wilderness" for $500. This piece south of Market, a large sector boarded by Bryant and Howard, Sixth (Simmons) and Eighth Streets, was where he built the new family home. From Christiana's obituary we know that, "The frame of the house on Sixth and Harrison came from Boston and the windows and sashes were imported from Germany. He [I.C.C.] imported a quantity of apple trees, paying $600 in freight, and planted them around his home." These apple trees were some of the first to be planted in California.

By 1854 the Russ residence was the destination of many visitors. At the suggestion of friends, I.C.C. opened his large garden to the public, establishing the "Russ Gardens," which became the center for San Francisco's various national groups to celebrate their holidays. Representing all that was entertainment, some of the celebrations included the German colony on May Day, the French on Bastille Day, the Irish for St. Patrick's Day, and the American Fourth of July. The Russ Gardens continued to operate until replaced by other parks.

After returning from the mines, Adolph Russ helped his father with the duties of their real estate business, writing out leases and collecting rents. Although I.C.C. continued with his jewelry store and Adolph began a grocery business (he was also the one official San Francisco Morocco case maker, having learned the skill while living in New York), real estate was the source of the family's growing fortune. Besides their rental property, for several years I.C.C. and Adolph maintained the old American Hotel, which had been built next door to the original house built from the timbers of the *Loo Choo*. In 1862 the hotel was replaced with the prominent 400-bedroom Russ House Hotel, which preceded the Palace as San Francisco's most popular and fashionable hotel.

Lilly Russ Bruckman

Adolph married Frances Simon in 1851. She had arrived in San Francisco from Alsace, Lorraine with her twin sister (age seventeen) and an older brother, having traveled over the Isthmus of Panama. The family story tells of Adolph being at the pier when her ship arrived. Seeing Frances and her sister disembark, he said to his friend, "I'm going to marry the little one," to which the friend replied, "I'll marry the other." The young couple began housekeeping in the original house I.C.C. and his sons had built over the grocery store. It was there, on the original site at Bush & Montgomery streets, that their first child, Lilly Caroline Russ (my great-

Francis Simon Russ, Adolf Russ, Ann Sievers Russ, Henry Russ.

grandmother), was born in June of 1852, the first of the Russ Family to be born in California. Adolph and Frances were to have ten children, of whom five lived to adulthood.

I.C.C. Russ died in 1857 at the age of sixty-two. His widow, Christiana, died in 1880 at the age of seventy-eight, having lived long enough to see her sons and daughters established in the ever-growing city. For the most part the family remained in California, except for Elizabeth, who married the German Consul in San Francisco and returned to Germany with him.

The home at Sixth and Harrison remained until after Christiana's death. Some of the property of the original Russ Gardens was sold. A block between Harrison and Folsom streets known as Columbia Square was designated as a park and given to the City. Several of the Russ Family clan built homes facing Columbia Square: Louisa Russ Wegner, Emeline Russ Gutzkow, Henry B. Russ and Adolph Russ, who also built homes for his daughters, Lilly Russ Bruckman and Laura Russ Westphal. The Russ Family virtually remained centered in the old neighborhood of the former Russ Gardens (and around Columbia Square) until the 1906 fire and earthquake took its toll.

The neighborhood still holds legends of the Russ family history. Columbia Square (erroneously now called "Columbia Park") remains, with a few eucalyptus trees amidst endless bustling traffic, within a few blocks of the new Pioneer Hall. Of the original offspring of I.C.C. and Christiana Russ, Adolph, Frederick, and Henry Russ were early members of the Society of California Pioneers. Adolph's daughters, Lilly and Laura, were among the original members of the Daughters. Present membership of the Daughters includes descendants of both Adolph and Henry Russ, eldest and youngest sons of the original Russ family who arrived in 1847 with Stevenson's Regiment.

My great-grandmother, Lilly Russ Bruckman, died in 1938 at the age of eighty-six. Excerpts from an editorial in the *San Francisco Examiner*, August 1, 1938, reflect on the surroundings of her life:

> . . . This lady who died in San Francisco last week was born in this city in 1852, and it has been given to few persons in the history of the world to see in their lifetime so much that was new, so much change. Her childhood was passed in a tumultuous settlement that was little more than a mining camp without mines. From sand and mudflats she saw magnificent buildings arise. She saw railroads and cable cars replace ox teams

and horse cars; she saw electricity revolutionize living. She saw sailing ships pass and great steamers come. Then the automobile and the airplane.

Had this woman been born anywhere in the civilized world in 1852 her life would have been a constant adventure among what was new, but born as she was at the very outpost of civilization, the changes she saw were more pronounced than they would seem elsewhere.

Whatever changes there may be in politics, government, manners and customs, it is doubtful if the human race will ever again see the revolution in material conditions of life, during a like period, which this "oldest daughter of San Francisco" saw in her four-score years.

William and Philippina Hamel

BY VIRGINIA M. HERNDON

 William Hamel, born in 1816 in Marburg, Germany, embarked on a voyage for America with his future bride in the spring of 1846. He left Germany to escape mandatory military duty. The voyage, which was scheduled to take six weeks, took six months due to an unsound vessel and the captain's lack of navigational skills. They disembarked in Newark, New Jersey and were married there in September, 1847 by the Reverend Stagg, a Methodist minister. The bride was the former Philippina Gegling, born on March 31, 1819 in Bernbach, Wurtenburg, Germany. They took a ship from Newark to San Francisco, arriving in late 1847. William Hamel enlisted for service in the Mexican War on December 28, 1847 in Monterey, California.

William was wounded in the Mexican War and received a medal of valor. He was discharged December 28, 1852 in San Diego. He owned a sizeable ranch in Monterey County and operated the Custom House and the Colton Hall Jail in Monterey. William Hamel died on March 1, 1884. Philippina Hamel died on November 5, 1901.

William and Philippina Gegling Hamel had four children:

Hannah Minerva Hamel, born August 10, 1852. Married John Bostrom, June 2, 1870.

Robert Hamel, Unmarried.

Clotilda Hamel. Married Charles E. Olason, November, 1878.

Mary Hamel, born 1857, Monterey. Married Levi B. Galloway, July 28, 1878.

My great grandmother, Hannah Minerva Bostrom, was christened in the Episcopal Church of Monterey. When her parents' housekeeper learned that the child had been named Minerva, she said, "Why don't you give the child a pretty name like Hannah, instead of Minerva, which is so wretched." Hannah married Johan (John) Bostrom, born in Umea, Sweden on August 9, 1839. He was a cousin of Erik Gustav Bostrom, the Prime Minister of Sweden in 1891. Hannah truly embodied the pioneer spirit. Before her marriage she loved to go to all of the dances. She did the fandango with great ease and grace. Her husband's premature death, on March 10,1888, in Monterey, brought financial hardship to a woman who had only known financial ease. She turned to baking cakes and pastries and making wedding gowns in order to make ends meet.

The ladies of society would whisper to each other, "Why in the world does Mrs. Bostrom work when she has so much land?" Once Hannah heard their whispers. She whirled around on the street and, with a fixed gaze, flatly stated, "You cannot feed land to your children, for the love of God!" Hannah could hitch a team of horses, strike fear in the hearts of her ranch hands, serve an elegant luncheon, and often rule early Monterey society. She could certainly hold her own with whomever. My great-grandmother was a well-educated, well-spoken, bright lady who fought desperately for the right of all women to vote.

She often said, "Just because a man is a man does not make him intellectually superior to a woman. Often it is the opposite." She was one of the earliest members of the California Historical Society. She dearly loved her native state and its beauty. She was a great lover of the native flora of California, and learned their medicinal value. Her daughter, my grandmother, May Bostrom Herndon, was an exceptional botanist who knew the Latin names of most plants. Hannah's brother, Robert Hamel, was a friend of Robert Louis Stevenson and the eminent historian Charles Warren Stoddard. The pair lived in one of Hannah's houses and Uncle

Robert loved to go on long drives with them. When Robert died, Robert Louis Stevenson said, "Your brother was such a good man, Mrs. Bostrom."

Hannah instilled a great love of learning, beauty, and elegance in her daughter, May Bostrom Herndon. My grandmother was a graduate of the Colton Hall School in Monterey. She taught school before her marriage and was called "the most proficient educator in the history of Monterey County" in many newspaper articles about her. My grandmother was a brilliant woman who was interested in everything. She loved to entertain, using exquisite family silver and porcelain. She, like her mother, was dedicated to the history of California. She would fly the state flag on special occasions. To me she exemplified the pioneer spirit in an elegant manner. She lived, as did her mother and grandmother, by a credo of self-reliance, independence, and respect for all people. Her children both graduated *magna cum laude* from Stanford University in the wake of the Great Depression. She was a perfect example of the resilience of the pioneer spirit.

James Kenny

BY CONSTANCE K. HOPPER

California pioneer James Kenny was my great-grandfather. The house he built still stands bravely alone on
the east side of Highway One, one mile north of Elk
in northern California. The cemetery where many of my family
members are buried is still there, well cared for.

I have been in the house even though it is now owned by some-
one else who does not use the entire structure as a home. I have
stood at the foot of the stairway in the silent emptiness and felt the
spirit of the pioneers. Where are they now, James and Katherine
Kenny and their six children — Kate, Mary, Nellie, James, John,
and Annie, my grandmother? What stories they could tell, especially if we, the next generations, have played havoc with the facts?
I knew almost all of them, but for such a short time during my
childhood.

I have no first person account of my great-grandfather. To my
sorrow I did not know this pioneer. This bare bones chronicle of
his life is put together from bits and pieces gleaned from the *Historical and Biographical Record,* letters, news clippings, and published
accounts of the early days in Cuffey's Cove and Mendocino. Where
information conflicts, I have decided to go with the family account
as correct.

James Kenny arrived in New York from his birthplace in West
Meath, Ireland when he was eleven years of age. The year was 1840,
five years before the great potato famine. A young man in 1847,
James joined the U.S. Navy, served throughout the Mexican War,
and was discharged at Benicia, California in 1848.

James Kenny has the dubious distinction of being the first ferry boat "captain" on San Francisco Bay. This enterprising young man started a business rowing a boat. For pay, James Kenny ferried sailors interested in gambling and other pleasures of the night back and forth from their ships to Sausalito.

In 1852 James and two partners, Captain Peck and Dudley Shelling, erected what was known as Peck's Mill in Marin County, near Bolinas. Just as the mill was established it burned to the ground. James was so discouraged he left the county.

In 1853 James turned to farming. He engaged in stock raising between Cloverdale and Anderson Valley. In 1855 he reached the Mendocino coast and purchased five hundred and ten acres at Cuffey's Cove, north of Elk. He sometimes made the long trip to San Francisco by horseback, following Indian trails, to obtain supplies for his ranch, and it was on one of these trips that he met the girl who was to become his wife.

In 1858 James met and married Katherine Shannon, in St. Joseph's Church in San Francisco. Katherine Shannon Kenny had come to Philadelphia from Kilkshandra, Ireland, then to San Francisco with a friend. It was Katherine's brother, Father John Shannon, Vicar General of the Church of Ireland, who had encouraged her to come to America.

Kate, the first of James and Katherine's six children, was born in 1860. Sometime before the birth date James took Katherine up the coast on horseback to the home of the nearest midwife, Mrs. Manuel Lawrence, on Albion Ridge. They travelled over a narrow and treacherously steep trail, down the timbered and brushy south side of the Navarro Ridge, across the river in Captain Walsh's dugout canoe with the horses swimming after, and up the even steeper trail on the other side. There was no doctor to call. When Kate was six weeks old she was transported on horseback in her father's arms back to the ranch. Katherine accompanied them home on her own horse, riding the sidesaddle of the day.

Katherine Shannon Kenny died at Cuffey's Cove in 1904.

In her *Early Reminiscences of the Mendocino Coast,* my great-aunt, Kate Kenny Gorman, writes,

> Father came to the States in early youth, wandered hither and yon, eventually reaching the Mendocino coast in 1855 and buying a ranch of 510 acres at Cuffey's Cove. If I remember right, it had been an old Spanish land grant. Others contend he purchased the ranch from Frank Farnier, who is supposed to have been the first settler at Cuffey's Cove.

Kate also writes that in the area of Cuffey's Cove there were only two or three other farms, the rest of the population — Indians and bears.

To refute the Frank Farnier story and to confuse the date of purchase:

According to the *Historical and Biographical Record,* in 1865 James Kenny purchased from the Spanish the Albion Grant on the coast, supposing it to contain five hundred and ten acres. Sometime later, by government survey, it was said to contain only three hundred and thirty acres. Following the survey James Kenny bought another small tract of forty acres of redwood near Elk and embarked in the lumber business.

According to a miscellaneous record book recorded April 1, 1876, James Kenny purchased more land from Albert Miller in 1865, from Clinton Gurnes in 1869, from Thomas Musgrove in 1873, and from James Coffee in 1877. By 1880 Mr. Kenny owned, on both sides of the main road, land from the gulch north of the Catholic Cemetery to the gulch south bordering the present Greenwood School. James Kenny donated land for the cemetery, a Catholic

Church, and school buildings.

In 1868 Kenny saw the possibility of a shipping point from which local produce and redwood ties could be loaded for San Francisco to supply the demand for food and cross-country rail-road building. It has been said by old timers that by 1870 there were as many as eleven sailing vessels in the harbor and eighty tie teams hauling ties from surrounding camps. The hillsides and fields south of the cemetery were covered with ties. Mr. Kenny was the owner of the landing facilities and chutes. The buyer of railroad ties was John S. Kimball.

Men came as farmers and laborers, buying or "taking up" land where they raised cattle and sheep, grain, and feed, and the famous Cuffey's Cove potato. The coast fields were rich in soil, with sandy loam washed from the bordering hills that were covered with trees and shrubs. The mild climate, level fields, and an abundance of water nurtured crops for local families and left a surplus to ship to the City.

Historical and Biographical Record relates:

> After building his own residence, which overlooks the ocean, he built about thirty cottages for rent, and for several years carried on a prosperous business in this thriving little settlement that he had founded. In 1884, when the post office at Elk, known as Greenwood, was established, a new harbor for shipping was opened, business drifted southward, the houses were vacated, and he subsequently tore some of them down, so that now his residence stands almost alone in its majestic situation by the sea. Its environments are very attractive, and in front is a large pool fed by natural springs, while it is further ornamented by beautiful trees of virgin growth. He then devoted much of his life to cattle, and

from past experience has concluded that oats and barley flourish better than any other grain in this coast region. In addition to his lumber and ranching activities, James purchased a public house in Mendocino, the Occidental Hotel, which he has enlarged, and placed under the management of his daughter, Mrs. Katherine Gorman.

[The Occidental Hotel burned to the ground in 1941.]

Most probably my grandmother, Annie Kenny Kidwell, met John Leonard Kidwell (known as "Big Kid") in August, 1892 while visiting her sister, Kate, at the Occidental Hotel. John Kidwell was registered in Mendocino as "a capitalist, age 26, dark complexion, dark hair, brown eyes." The Kidwells built the house just south of the Kenny place.

Indeed, James Kenny saw the possibilities of shipping timber products from the Cove on his land. Opening a harbor at Cuffey's Cove, he erected chutes and cutting down the giants of the forest began the manufacture of railroad ties, posts, laths, shingles, and lumber of all kinds, which he shipped to various coastal points, making the Cove an important trading port. It remained a busy port until 1890, when L.E. White started a lumber mill in Elk and developed a larger port with better loading facilities than at Cuffey's Cove.

Activity gradually moved down the coast and Cuffey's Cove gradually lost its population and its buildings, until now all that is left are the Kenny and Kidwell houses. During the years when that locality was prosperous, James Kenny had as many as four chutes in operation. It was said that he amassed a comfortable fortune, and then retired.

Part Six:
Before the Rush, 1848

This was the year that changed the history of the world. Gradual settlement of California continued during the early part of the year, but before long the whole scene had changed completely. President Polk announced toward the end of 1848 that gold had been discovered. The announcement set off the greatest migration in the history of the United States. Americans, Europeans, South Americans, and every one else headed for the land where one could pick up gold from the ground.

Madison Hawes

BY NANCY C. THORNBURG

 On February 19, 1856 the following personal advertisement appeared in the San Francisco *Daily Evening Bulletin:*

MATRIMONY — A gentlemen of under thirty years of age, of good appearance and some means, wishes to form the acquaintance of an intelligent and fair young lady, with a view of selecting a good wife. All communications will be addressed to James Xavier, St. Louis P. O., Sierra County, California.

The ad was answered by Nancy Cornelia Hawes, using a pseudonym, who lived in San Francisco with her parents, Madison and Nancy Hawes. James was pleased with his new acquaintance, as indicated in his letter of March 29, 1856. This letter was signed "James Covington," for he, too, was using a pseudonym.

I must confess that I expected to have heard from you more fully than I did. You omitted to state your residence, your Parents, etc. Can't you give me more full details in your next? How am I to find you in case of my visiting San Francisco?

He went on to say:

You mention that you are '. . . demonstrative of your affections, but that age has somewhat tempered it down.' Now for my life, I cannot see how any young lady of 20 years could possibly be tempered down in this short time! Will you explain?

The next letter that has survived was from Nancy's father to James, and is dated June 10, 1856. It was signed "The Father of Cornelia."

I have accidentally ascertained that my daughter Cornelia has been in communication with you for some three months past, in relation to a matrimonial alliance. . . . Permit me to express to you my extreme regret and mortification that my daughter should so far forget herself as to commence and carry on a clandestine correspondence. She is an only and much beloved daughter, and no reasonable indulgence or gratification has ever been denied her, and this fact renders the concealment of this matter from me the less excusable. But I trust you will accord with a father's charity towards her when I inform you that she is <u>not yet fourteen years of age</u>. . . . She is now pursuing her studies, preparatory, I trust, to a life of usefulness, should she be spared, and I am of the opinion her best good requires that the subject of matrimony should not be entertained for some years to come.

Madison politely requested the return of Nancy's letter and a discontinuance of the correspondence. James responded June 24, 1856, explaining the circumstances leading to the correspondence and its nature and stating that, "In her first letter she stated that she was not quite, or rather was under, 20 years of age," and adding that if he had known her true age he would not have answered her letter. He attested that his "motives were purely honorable" and

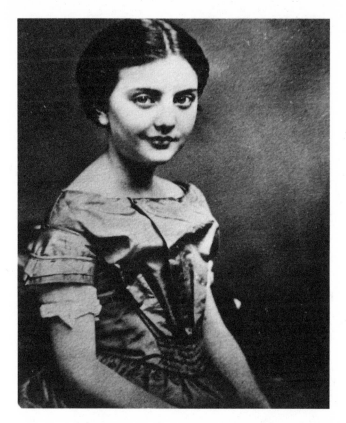

Nancy Cornelia Hawes Critcher

that his "intention was serious." He said that he "should be happy to make the acquaintance of yourself, Lady, and daughter." And he added

It is possible that in the course of this summer I shall spend a portion of my time in your city. I flatter myself that you may find me a different person than those who generally inhabit the mining districts.

On July 8, 1856 Madison responded, giving his full name for the first time and stating as follows:

In answer to the desire expressed in your letter to make our acquaintance, I would say that our house is always open to our friends, and that we should be happy to see you when you visit the city. Our residence is on the N.W. corner of Pine and Taylor Streets, in the suburbs.

In reality, James Xavier, alias James Covington, was Henry Critcher, who was born in 1826 in Westmoreland County, Virginia, and who came to California in 1849. By 1853 he was in Sierra County, and in 1856 he was operating a mercantile store and possibly practicing law in St. Louis, Sierra County.

Madison Hawes was born in 1809 in Massachusetts, and in 1834 married Nancy Nelson Dam. They had four children, three of whom died in early childhood leaving only Nancy Cornelia Hawes, who was born on July 24, 1842. On May 1, 1848 Madison sailed on the ship *New Jersey* bound for California, leaving his wife and daughter in Boston until he could provide for their comfort and safety out west. He arrived in San Francisco on October 11, and established a business as a printer.

In 1852, when Nancy was almost ten, she and her mother sailed around the Horn, arriving in San Francisco on August 13, where they joined Madison. In 1856, when Nancy answered Henry's advertisement, she was thirteen years old.

Apparently Henry did visit the Hawes household in San Francisco, and a warm relationship was obviously established because on July 9, 1857, when Nancy was not quite fifteen years old, she and Henry were married. Henry became a stockbroker, and in 1862 was one of the founders of the San Francisco Stock Exchange. He and Nancy had fourteen children, twelve of whom grew to maturity. One of them, Grace Valentine Critcher, was my maternal grand-

Henry Payson Critcher

mother. Henry died in August, 1904 in San Francisco.

In 1906 Nancy joined a religious organization called the Koreshan Unity (no relationship to the Waco, Texas group) in Estero, Florida. She was on the editorial staff of their newspaper, *The Flaming*

Sword, and was considered to be one of the best posted writers in scientific religion in the United States. Her letters to her daughter, Grace, some of which are in my possession, give insight into the immense reservoir of strength, wisdom, and love which characterized this very special lady. She died in 1917 at the age of 75 and was buried at the Koreshan Cemetery in Estero.

Lester Hulin

BY MARYLYN DEWITZ PICKLER

 Lester Hulin was born in Saratoga County, New York on March 22, 1823. At the age of twenty-one he started westward, traveling by the lakes and the Erie Canal to Chicago, and thence by stage and river travel to Henry County, Iowa. In the spring of 1845 he continued to St. Louis, Missouri. There he met Colonel Fremont and Lieutenant Abert, who were planning an expedition to explore the West; Mr. Hulin joined them.

The company numbered sixty-four men and all were well-equipped with rifles, ammunition, horses, mules, and wagons to carry the baggage. They crossed Kansas to Fort Benton in Colorado, and then turned south to New Mexico, northwest Texas, and Indian Territory, where they surveyed rivers and watercourses, which involved adventures involving hairbreadth escapes.

Mr. Hulin then returned to Iowa, and in the spring of 1847 decided to go to Oregon. With two horses — one to ride and the other to pack — he started for St. Joseph, Missouri. He joined an emigrant party conducted by Captain David Davis. The wagon train was increased to eighty wagons because of Indian hostilities. Mr. Hulin, because of his experience, was appointed camp master and upon him rested the task of providing the camp with feed and water facilities, and with an encampment for defense. They crossed by the south route through Utah and Nevada, through the Rogue River Valley by the Goose and Klamath Lakes, and through Umpqua Canyon. They arrived at the head of the Willamette Valley on November 1, 1847 after five months of weary travel.

Mr. Hulin went on to Benton County, and, because of the recent Whitman Massacre and the beginning of the Cayuse War, volunteered in the company of Captain John Owen. He passed six months in the Walla Walla country experiencing hardship, including cold and exposure. He returned to the Willamette Valley in July 1848 and selected a donation claim.

Hearing of the discovery of gold in California, he crossed the Siskiyou Mountains and began mining on the Feather River. From there he went to Sutter's Fort for supplies, and then to the Middle Fork of the American River, passing the winter at Dry Diggins. Although the weather was stormy and the snow was deep, he averaged twenty-five to thirty dollars each day. In the spring of 1849 he moved to Sacramento and engaged in partnership with Captain Smith freighting supplies to Coloma by ship.

Later on a trip to Oregon, the schooner *Hackstaff* was stranded at the mouth of the Rogue River, and Mr. Hulin, the passengers, and the crew were forced to travel overland through the woods, mountains, and hostile tribes of Indians to reach the Willamette Valley. After twenty-four days of painful travel, days of danger, and starvation, they arrived at their destination.

He located a claim for 320 acres on the site of the current University of Oregon, ten miles north of Eugene. Mr. Hulin, undaunted by previous bad experiences, went back to California to resume mining for gold.

He married Abbie J. Craig of Michigan in 1853. They had four children: Charles, Annie, Samuel, and Lester. Abbie died in 1892, and Lester in 1897, at the age of seventy-four. Samuel Hulin was the father of Goldie Hulin DeWitz, who is the mother of Marylyn DeWitz Pickler. Marylyn Dewitz Pickler is the mother of Cheryl Pickler Davies, who is the mother of Alexandra Lynn Davies and Bryce Anderson Davies.

Hughes Lyons

BY EMELIE WILSON

 When you are hungry and decide to go out to eat at a Lyon's Restaurant, you are reliving an interesting phase of early California history. It all started with the Revolution of 1848 in France when Emperor Louis Napoleon took over the government and caused a general unemployment of thousands of middle-class Frenchmen. During the same year came the call of the discovery of gold in California, and Hughes Lyons, my ancestor, was among the first to heed that call. He was already middle-aged, but applied for a passport to San Francisco, and sometime after June 9 he boarded the *Suffren*, headed for the United States. This ship is famous, or infamous, for its other passengers — the dozen or so unattached women eagerly awaited and received by the almost exclusively male population of San Francisco.

Hughes met another Frenchman and decided to open a general merchandise business in Sonora, in the Mother Lode of the Sierra. The little company expanded and the store became a meeting place for French miners in the area. Hughes started a mail service and was also well known for his syrups and cordials, which he bottled for customers. He decided that California was a good place to live so he sent for his three children who were still in France. He also acquired a new wife and bought out the interest of his partner. The business now was opened up for Hughes' son, Ernest, and soon the firm's name would be E.G. Lyons & Company. Ernest was a good businessman, expanded the operation of the business, and became involved with loaning money.

Hughes died in 1861, "universally and deeply regretted by all who knew him." The business continued for two more years, then local headlines announced that there would be a liquidation of Sonora's "oldest store."

In San Francisco in 1866, Ernest Lyons acquired the Crevolin House, a well-known maker of syrups and cordials. He and his wife, Emelie, obtained an elegant home on Bush Street, and seven children were born to the Lyons. They were both very involved with the local French community, and the death of Ernest from heart failure was, like his father, "deeply regretted by all who knew him."

The Lyons firm was incorporated two years after the death of its founder and continued to bear his name until 1905, when it became known as E.G. Lyons & Raas. By 1913 the company obtained the concession to supply the restaurant located in The Emporium in San Francisco. In 1962 the first independent Lyon's [sic] Coffee Shop was opened, and four years later it was purchased by the Sara Lee Corporation.

After Hughes, six generations of Lyons have lived in California. From its humble beginnings on Washington Street in Sonora, the family-owned business of Hughes and Ernest Gabriel Lyons has lent its name to two major corporations which today service the American West. When you are eating dinner at Lyon's, remember Hughes, the French emigrant who left his imprint on California history.

Rufus Franklin

BY CATHY INNES

 Rufus Franklin was born in Arkansas and made his first trip to California, crossing the plains with an oxen team, arriving in 1848. Apparently liking it here, he stayed in California approximately one year and then returned to the East and married his fiancée, Elvira Lynch, whose birthplace was Missouri. He then returned to California with his new bride via the Isthmus of Panama.

In the early 1850s Rufus Franklin worked on ranches throughout the San Joaquin County and in the early 1860s he took a government claim of 160 acres, six miles west of Lodi. There he raised grain. He acquired more land in the same vicinity where he planted the first large vineyard of wine grapes in the San Joaquin County. These were principally Zinfandels; he got his cuttings from Napa County. Franklin was a member of the Jefferson Lodge of Odd Fellows in Woodbridge.

Rufus and Elvira had eight children. Five surviving children included: Mrs. J. Burrell of Berkeley, Jesse Lewis of Stockton (my grandfather), Amos W. Franklin (who stayed on the homestead and ranched with his father), William Thomas Franklin, and Mrs. Florence Wood of Oakland. The town of Franklin, California was named after this pioneer family.

Part Seven:
To the Land of Gold, 1849

They came by land, they came by sea, by horseback, by wagon, and by foot. Every profession, every trade was represented in the migration — from lawyers to farmers. It was the one great adventure — everyone would get rich. The ancestors of the Daughters are well represented in this group, and their stories cover a multitude of trials and triumphs. Some died on the plains, some at sea, some of disease, but some became the new citizens of the Territory of California, soon to be the newest state in the Union. It was high adventure for these stalwart pioneers, and their descendants are proud to be a part of the great story of El Dorado, the golden place, now named California.

Martin Mulcrevy

BY FLORIAN ELLIOT

 Martin Mulcrevy was born in 1815 in Ennis, County Clare, Ireland. Economic conditions were not good, and with the great potato famine of 1847 Martin took the prudent action of leaving Ireland. He married Catherine O'Connell in 1846 in Limerick and sailed shortly thereafter via steamer to Australia. Catherine gave birth to their first child during this long voyage and eventually had eight children.

The family arrived in San Francisco in 1849, just in time for the Gold Rush. Apparently Martin wanted to stay permanently in California and was naturalized in 1856. Martin became a laborer in the feed and fuel business, a merchant, and a lamplighter, in spite of a limp that had been acquired from his arthritis. The family made their home at 404 Haight Street, and the members always teased that they were now "lace curtain Irish," within walking distance of City Hall on Van Ness Avenue.

Martin's son, Harry Mulcrevy, became a leading San Francisco citizen and was the leader in the family as well. Perhaps his influence provided a job for his father as a lamplighter. San Francisco had gas street lamps very soon after the Gold Rush, and these had to be lighted every evening.

Martin's health only seemed to get worse and in 1900 he died in San Francisco, where he had come a half century before. He was blind and diabetic, and his eighty-four years had been filled with great changes.

Martin's legacy was his children who survived him, who suffered through the great earthquake and fire, and lived to have chil-

dren of their own. The extended family owed much to their ancestor who had the courage and vision to come to California and
become "lace curtain Irish."

The Pedraita Family

BY ROBERTA ARRIGONI SPENCER

 This is the story of my great-great grandfather, Charles Pedraita, and my beloved grandparents, Louis and Anita Pedraita. My mother was the late Lillian Arrigoni, who made her home in San Francisco after her marriage.

Charles Pedraita, who was born in Giubiasco, Canton Ticino, Switzerland, came around Cape Horn to California in 1849. For a time he followed mining, but later took up farming in the vicinity of San Francisco and San Jose. After spending twenty-four years in the Golden State, Charles went back to Giubiasco and married a schoolteacher, Angeline Tomenelli. They were parents of six children. Louis Pedraita was the youngest of the family. Charles Pedraita became the proprietor of a hotel in Giubiasco and also owned a mill run by water power where he manufactured flour.

Louis Pedraita was educated in the public schools. In his youth he learned the miller's trade and also worked as a carpenter. In December, 1882 he left home and started for California. He first visited friends in Eureka, arriving in Cayucos in 1883.

Later that year he married Anita Parachine, who was born and educated in Novaro, Italy, the daughter of Donato and Josephine Parachine. Her family had moved to Giubiasco, at which time she met Louis Pedraita. Years ago I asked my grandfather how he came to marry my grandmother. He said to me, "She followed me to America." First she landed in Yreka instead of Eureka! She went to Eureka, stayed for a time, then left for Cayucos. They had four children: Henry Pedraita, Lillian Pedraita Arrigoni (my mother), Louis "Pete" Pedraita, and the youngest, Alma Pedraita Swain.

For seven years my grandfather was employed on different dairy farms. Then he made a trip back to Giubiasco, his father, Charles, being very ill. During his stay his father passed away. Louis had to remain in Giubiasco for over two years, as he had to serve in the Swiss Army, which he had not done before he left in 1882.

Returning to Cayucos, Grandfather leased a building and opened the American Hotel on Main Street, continuing in the business until 1895 when the hotel was destroyed by fire. Then he bought a lot and built a new hotel, which was named the New Swiss Hotel. Here he met with success until another fire partly destroyed the second building. This building was rebuilt and was called the Cottage Hotel.

Many splendid meals were served at the Cottage Hotel — all you could eat for fifty cents a meal, served with a glass of wine. My grandmother was famous for her fried abalone, and clams baked in the half shells. People came from the Valley, Los Angeles, and as far away as New York. In the town of Cayucos, many dear friends and their children were served meals free. They could drop in for a visit and were served a free cup of coffee.

Senator George Hearst and his wife, Phoebe Hearst, were frequent guests. They came by horse and buggy, sometimes staying overnight. Mrs. Phoebe Hearst loved to have meals at the Cottage Hotel. Often she would bring another well-known person, a Mrs. Cook. William Randolph Hearst often accompanied his parents when he was a young boy, long before he ever thought of building the Hearst Castle. In later years, Hearst would bring guests to the Cottage Hotel; then the dining room would be closed to outsiders.

Ignace Paderewski, the famous pianist-composer, and his wife were frequent guests. Paderewski also brought a famous guest who was an opera singer, Madame Schumann Heink. Paderewski played the piano in the parlor while Madame Schumann Heink sang. Mother told me that people would stop eating just to listen to my

grandparents and Madame Schumann Heink sing together while Paderewski played the piano. As a young girl I remember Paderewski coming there. At the time I was going to St. Rose Academy, a private school in San Francisco, and was always interested in the guests who came to the Cottage Hotel. Among other guests was James Rolph, Mayor of San Francisco and Governor of California.

Living at the hotel were two lovely persons who were very dear to my grandparents, Donna Clara and Saviana, two American Indians. They helped with the care and raising of the children. After my mother married and moved to San Francisco, whenever she returned to her home town they never failed to come from a long distance, by horse and buggy, to bring fresh fruit to my parents. How well I remember those women!

John Parrott

BY FRANCE DE SUGNY BARK

 John Parrott was born in 1811 when his family wagon was on its way from Virginia to Tennessee to settle new country. Little is known of his childhood until he left Tennessee in 1829 to join his elder brother, William Parrott, in Mexico City. "Passport #2711 was issued to John Parrott, on July 5, 1832, describing him: Age 22 years, Stature 6 feet, Eyes Hazel. Nose Pugg, Mouth Large, Chin Broad, Hair Dark, Complexion Fair, Face Round." He joined his brother's mercantile business, Parrott, Talbot, and Co., as clerk, and then eventually applied to the U.S. Government for the position of Consul at Mazatlan. He remained at that post through the Mexican War (1846-1848). During his time in Mexico he was not only active in his consular duties, but was involved in the expanding trade on the west coast, and aided his country throughout the war.

After the war, at age thirty-nine, John Parrott settled his affairs in Mexico and sailed for San Francisco, where he had already commenced some business ventures managed by his agent, Bernard Peyton Jr. Concerned about numerous fires that had already devastated parts of the city, Parrott searched for building material that would withstand the ravages of fire. He purchased a lot on the corner of Montgomery and California Streets (the former site of the old Custom House), on the northwest corner, from William Davis of San Diego, for $19,500, with the intention of building a fireproof granite building. The following are two descriptions of the construction progress:

Of the numerous substantial fireproof buildings now in process of erection in this city, there are none more worthy of notice than the fine granite structure going up on the corner of California and Montgomery streets, and the freestone block at Clark's Point. Mr. John Parrott is the owner of the Granite Block, which will consist of three stories in uniform style. The fronts on California and Montgomery streets will be of granite cut in China, according to plans drawn by Mr. Stephen Heddon Williams, of this city. The contract for this building has been taken by a Chinaman, and judging from the appearance of the stone, we should say that it will be quite an ornament to the city. As a specimen of Chinese workmanship, it will be very creditable. The entire building will be seventy-six by sixty-six feet.

A number of Chinese mechanics and laborers are now engaged on Parrott's splendid granite building. . . . They appear to be a very steady, sober, and industrious set: apparently very slow, but sure. They calculate with great exactness and nicety, and turn out their work handsomely. They are at present building a queer kind of scaffold for the masons. It is made out of small poles and bamboo. It is strong and substantial, and less liable to give way than those generally erected by our mechanics. The building on which they are engaged will, when completed, be the most magnificent structure in California.

In 1853 John Parrott made a trip to New York via the Isthmus of Panama, New Orleans, and Mobile, Alabama. Now, at the age of forty-two and wishing to establish a family and home in San Francisco, he stopped in Mobile to court young Abby Eastman Meaher. She was twenty-two years old and had attended the same school near Baltimore as his daughter, Magdelena Parrott, born out of wedlock in Mexico. Abby Meaher had impressed him by her friendship and correspondence with his daughter and he intended to ask Abby's hand in marriage. He won her heart by engaging musicians and serenading her from a boat in front of her waterfront hotel. The marriage notice that appeared in the *Alta California* stated they were married in the Cathedral of the Immaculate Conception in Mobile, Alabama on February 23, 1853.

The Parrotts arrived in San Francisco on July 19, 1853. They lived in temporary quarters until their home at 620 Folsom Street, between Second and Third, was completed. A son, John Frederick Parrott, was born in December of that year, but died the following October. In one of her letters to her sister-in-law, Helen Meaher, on May 15, 1854, Abby Parrott gives us a flavor of the times:

> Our own home will not be completed until the first of August, and I fear that untiring care and unlimited expense can never produce even the shadow of beauty on these eternal sandhills. There are a considerable number of Alabamians here, the most of them exceedingly pleasant and agreeable. Indeed as far as mere society is concerned, I see no difference between San Francisco and her eldest sisters on the Atlantic Coast, and there is beginning to be no trifling amount of elegance, display, fashion, and dissipation. But how a person whose business does not demand his presence here, can choose it for a residence, is beyond my comprehension.

The Gold Rush and the succeeding years into the 1860s set the stage for a wide range of business opportunities. John Parrott was an active man involved in countless, fascinating challenges. Among the areas that particularly interested him were the mines, such as the New Almaden Quicksilver Mine, the fur trade in Alaska, and the acquisition of land. He purchased land throughout California, mainly in the form of two large properties. The first was south of San Mateo Creek — some two hundred and sixty acres which became the family home in 1868. The site was made up of beautiful rolling hills full of native oak and bay trees, with landscaped gardens and a farm with many animals, especially horses, since he particularly liked horseback riding. For many years it was a great gathering place for family and friends. The second property which he acquired was in Butte County — a large ranch, formerly a Mexican land grant, called Llano Seco Rancho. With the acquisition of Llano Seco Rancho, John Parrott added farming to his many other interests and started dealing in wheat and flour, which were replacing cattle as the major industry.

At this point the outbreak of the Civil War, even though located on the eastern coast, had an adverse effect on many businesses and life in general. Fortunately, however, "the established mercantile trade, the mines, and the spread of agriculture in Northern California assured its progress and prosperity." Because of his extensive and diversified business interests, which included banking, John Parrott and his family were able to survive these troubled times:

Throughout the 1870s he continued to develop his land, farm, and garden at Baywood, the name given his home in San Mateo. Little by little he enlarged it to four hundred fifty-eight acres. He added cattle from England and ponies from Mexico for his growing family, and grew several varieties of grape in a glass house on the property. By now the family of John and Abby Parrott had expanded to seven children: Mary Katherine, Abby Josephine, John II, Grace Almaden, Edith Isabelle, Regina May, and Noelie Christine.

As the years progressed, "John Parrott's years of 'sound judgment and careful avoidance of speculative ventures' had brought him success, and 'no matter what financial convulsion troubled the community he never closed his bank's doors for a day.'" In January 1871 Parrott & Company merged with the London and San Francisco Bank. In addition to his continually growing banking business and his numerous other interests, he reserved time for his own community of San Francisco, serving on the boards of the Spring Valley Water Company, the San Francisco Gas Company, the Union Insurance Company of San Francisco, California Lloyds, California Home Insurance Company, and California Lloyds Marine Insurance. During this period he again showed confidence in San Francisco by purchasing lots in the commercial district of the city.

After being in the forefront of most of the areas of development in early California, in the year of 1878, at the age of 67, John Parrott was taken ill. He was no longer able to attend to his affairs. The following year his son, John Parrott II, returned to San Francisco, married, settled, and took on the management of many of his father's affairs. Even though John Parrott could no longer direct his vast business interests, he remained active in the background and enjoyed several more years close to his family and friends, dividing his time between San Francisco and San Mateo.

His good humor and quick wit were shown in the following story. Mr. Parrott's residence on Folsom Street was called Parrott's Palace. One day he was standing on the porch of his residence when two strangers approached him and asked, "To whom does this house belong?" He quickly responded, "To a damned old fool. They call him John Parrott."

From the earliest years at Baywood, John Parrott
had ordered that no one should be turned away from
his home hungry, and feeding the hobos long remained
a rule of the house. The wayfarers were many during
the ensuing years.

His beloved property in San Mateo was a haven for him in his
seventies, where he lived a quiet domestic life surrounded by his
family. All seven of his children lived to marry and have families of
their own, which accounts for the very large number of descendents of John and Abby Parrott who still live in California. They
include the de Dampierre, de Guigne, de Sugny, de Tristan,
Donohoe, Parrott, and Thieriot families.

John Parrott died March 29, 1884 at the age of seventy-three.
His had been a active life, spanning the years of early trade on the
west coast of Mexico and California, the war with Mexico, and the
Gold Rush. His was the age of sail, the pony express, the Overland
Mail, the telegraph, the first steamships, and the building of the
transcontinental railroad.

He experienced the devastating fires of the early years in San
Francisco, the violent days that brought into being the Vigilantes,
and survived the panics in the banking world. Undaunted by loss
of cargoes, mules, and tobacco, a fortune in themselves, nothing
deterred him from surmounting the vicissitudes of his time with
drive and purpose. Friend of many, exacting of himself and others,
John Parrott contributed to the advance of his country, California,
and to the city of his choice.

Grace Canitrot Borel

BY GRACE FICK GHISELLI

My great-great grandmother, Grace Canitrot, was born in New Almaden (now known as San Jose), California on November 10, 1849. Her father was French and her mother Mexican. She was a cousin of the Walkinshaw family, who were involved in the New Almaden Mine. She attended the Old Benicia Seminary (later to become Mills College) with her cousins, Chonita and Josephine Walkinshaw. At school she studied drawing and painting, as well as Spanish.

Not much is known about her life until her marriage to Antoine Borel on May 3, 1871. The story of their meeting has been told in my family as the following: Grace lived with her uncle's family on California Street in San Francisco. Antoine would pass Grace sitting on her porch on his way home from working at Alfred Borel and Company, a shipping and banking firm that his older brother, Alfred, had started after their arrival from Switzerland in the early 1860s. Alfred Borel & Company, located at 440 Montgomery Street, eventually became Antoine Borel and Company, after Alfred returned to Switzerland and turned control over to his brother, who was by then twenty-seven years old.

Antoine was known for his great business sense. He served on the boards of California Street Cable Railroad (which he controlled for thirty years), the California-Oregon Power Company, the Los Angeles Railroad Company, and the Bank of California.

Antoine and Grace Borel lived in a beautiful home at the corner of Franklin and Washington in San Francisco, which included a beautiful glass conservatory. Antoine served as the Swiss Consul

Grace Canitrot Borel

for forty years.

The Borels had seven children: Chonita, Sophie, Grace, Alice, Antoine, Alfred (who died at the age of four), and Lupita. My great-grandmother was Grace Eleanor Borel, the third daughter, born in February of 1876.

In 1874 Antoine and Grace Borel purchased land in San Mateo, where they moved their family. The land extended from El Camino west into the foothills and comprised one hundred acres. The estate's

At Borel Estate, San Mateo: Grace Canitrot Borel (in black), Grace Borel Bouet (far left), Grace Bouet Fick (in carriage).

grounds were beautiful, with gardens, fountains, and a pond with a grotto for row boats to pass through. Members of the family loved to go fishing in the pond, as well as bike and ride horseback around the property. The family was very active in the local community. Every year at Christmas the Borel daughters gave a party for the local children. The children wrote letters to Santa in care of the Borels, stating their wishes. The girls then worked the weeks before so that each child would receive a special present.

In the late 1890s Antoine and Grace purchased the Chateau de Gorgier, near the Lake of Neuchatel in Switzerland. The family would travel between Switzerland and San Mateo. Therefore, Grace and Antoine had two households to manage. It must have been quite an adventure moving the entire family back and forth between continents.

Eventually homes were built on the estate in San Mateo for the children and their families to be near to the matriarch and patriarch, Grace and Antoine. One of these homes belonged to my great-grandmother, Grace Eleanor, and her husband, Louis Bovet, whom she had met in Switzerland. They had seven children, one of whom was my grandmother, Grace Eliza Bovet. The Borels were in Switzerland at the time of the 1906 earthquake. Both the San Francisco and San Mateo houses survived, although there was damage from the chimneys that fell. Antoine and Grace went again to the chateau in 1914, but Antoine developed cancer and died in 1915. Grace returned to San Mateo and lived surrounded by her family until her death at the age of seventy-three, in January 1923.

Today the houses of the Borel Estate are gone, but in the exact spot of my grandmother's home stands a new Borel Bank and Trust Co., started by my father and uncle in 1980. I am very proud to be of the fifth generation of Borels living in California, and to be the namesake of three generous and caring Graces before me.

Edward McLean

BY LUCILLE SWASEY VINSANT

Edward McLean was born in 1807 in Hudson, New York, historic locale of a port of entry, shipbuilding, and whaling. The lure of New York City downriver was too great for him, however, and when he was in his early twenties, he headed for the big city. He became partners with Samuel Throckmorton, a famous merchant, and through the connection married Elizabeth Lewis in 1830. She was a milliner and bonnet maker (not a "hat" maker, as hats were considered "fast" and my great-great-grandmother certainly would have had nothing to do with fast hats!). In any event, both Elizabeth and Edward worked in the vicinity of Broadway, New York City, had children, were living happily, and then . . .

Toward the end of 1848 the news of gold was announced by President Polk. Edward, promptly as ever, rushed off to book passage on the *Falcon*, the mail ship for the west coast. He wanted to be first to reach El Dorado with ore crushing machinery to process gold, and inside the *Falcon* was the machinery that would make him rich. Unfortunately, when the ship reached Panama there was no way to transport the heavy machinery across the isthmus. To this day, the family history is unable to say what happened to Edward's grandiose scheme, and the machinery, which never reached California.

Now that Edward was in Panama, a big riot ensued due to the fact that the connecting mail ship from the west coast, the *California*, had been overbooked. Edward had a through ticket from New York and he was accommodated, and after many an eventful incident at sea the steamer, *California*, sailed into San Francisco Bay on February 28, 1849. There were cannons booming from the warships anchored there, bunting hung from the yardarms, and a band played popular music to welcome the newcomers. The steamer was the first to enter San Francisco Bay, and the event was headlined in the newspaper, the *Alta*, that was published for the celebration. No gold hunting for Edward. He had decided to start a boarding house in the city, and he is listed in the 1850 directory as having such an establishment.

A short time later his wife, Elizabeth, and children arrived in separate ships, one coming around the Horn, and one carrying Elizabeth via Panama. Elizabeth thereafter had attacks of fever from a disease she contracted in Panama. The family was united once more, including the five beautiful, educated, talented daughters of Edward McLean.

Fate was kind to all the daughters. Caroline married first William Chipman, land title attorney for important clients such as General Vallejo. After becoming a widow she married John W. Dwinelle, a famous name connected to the charter of the University of California and author of many books and newspaper articles. Daughter Virginia married Joseph Lord of Benicia and San Francisco, considered "a wealthy man." After about seven years of marriage, Virginia was left a wealthy widow. Daughter Josephine married Timothy Guy Phelps, representative to Congress, Regent of the University of California and Lick Observatory, and owner of the Las Pulgas Rancho. Daughter Emily married and left for the east coast. Daughter Amanda, my great-grandmother, married Charles S. Swasey, longtime employee of the new U.S. Mint on Fifth Street built in 1874. He may not have been rich, but he was a fine artist.

As for Edward, he lived a long and upright life. Wife Elizabeth had preceded him in death so he lived with his daughters, and toward the end of his life resided in the Alameda home of Caroline Dwinelle, where he died. He was kind enough to leave behind a family tree for future generations to treasure.

His descendants can be truly grateful that he had vision and courage to look westwards and set his sights on the high adventure of the California Gold Rush. That spirit endures today, and displays itself in the enterprising attitude of his descendents who approach the twenty-first century with Edward's old cry, "It's Ho for California!"

Jules Francois Bekeart

BY LAURA JACOBS

 Jules Francois Bekeart was born in London in 1822 and emigrated to New York as a boy with his father and four siblings. His mother died in England.

As with many children of that era, young Jules went to work at the tender age of ten. He started as an errand boy for a drugstore, then worked as a tailor's helper before finding employment as an apprentice gunsmith. On the New York street where Bekeart lived, there were numerous firearm businesses, including the shop of A.W. Spies, his employer in the year 1843. Later he was hired as a journeyman gunsmith at the Colt firearms factory in New Jersey.

In 1845 "Frank," as he was known, decided to leave New York and travel to the southern states to find work and adventure. By stage he journeyed to the Mississippi River where he boarded a boat bound for New Orleans. He eventually arrived in Columbus, Mississippi, found a gunsmithing job, and worked until November, 1846.

The Mexican War had begun due to the United States' desire to annex Texas and California, and in 1847 the young man joined the First Mississippi Regiment of the U.S. Army, led by Colonel Jefferson Davis. Later, he transferred to the Second Regiment where he remained throughout the war. It was near Monterey, on the east coast of Mexico, where Frank fought fierce battles that resulted in a leg wound. The enemy took advantage of the ill-equipped infantrymen from Mississippi who carried only short rifles and bowie knives. At one point Frank was pinned down with a long lance aimed at his stomach. Since he hadn't time to reload his rifle, he drew his bowie knife, deflecting the lance that pierced his leg below the knee. On the following morning, reinforcements arrived from General Zachary Taylor's armed forces at Monterey. The long battle was won, and in July, 1848 Frank was discharged from the army in Vicksburg, Mississippi.

By this time, the young veteran had heard the story of gold in California and decided to make the journey west. Wanting to see his parents and his "best girl" before leaving, he went up the Mississippi River to St. Louis, then Chicago, again by water to Niagara Falls, Buffalo, and on to Albany and New York City.

After saying his farewells he, with four other men, booked passage on the steamship *Panama*, only the second ship to sail for the gold fields. But after a few days a broken steering shaft brought the ship back to port. Frank and his friends changed their tickets to a ship called the *Oregon*, bound for South America, but it had just sailed. Passage was then secured on the *Harriet F. Harlett*. Included in his baggage were two hundred Paterson Colt revolvers and two hundred Allen Pepperbox revolvers that were consigned to him by his former New York employer, A.W. Spies.

Leaving the snow-clad city of New York behind, the passengers enjoyed the warmth of the Caribbean, passing near the islands of Cuba, Santo Domingo, and Jamaica. The *Harriet F. Harlett* left California-bound passengers at the settlement of Chagres on the eastern side of the Isthmus of Panama, from where people were to find their way through the jungle to the Pacific Ocean, where they would reconnect with their original ships.

Strange trees, climbing vines, and mud and cane huts typified the little town of Chagres, but Frank and his party feared contracting malaria if they lingered, so they hired two covered boats to take them up the Chagres River. Monkeys, dense forest, and red, yellow, and orange birds were a strange sight, and at night screaming animals kept the travelers awake.

The next day the group progressed up the narrow river by using poles to move the boat along. Gorgona, a town of adobe and thatched huts, was the village at the end of the waterway. The friendly native women were clothed in white chemise-like dresses, and the barefoot men wore white shirts, pants, and straw hats. The children were naked. The travelers were served stewed and roast monkey and iguana steaks. Alligator meat was a staple of the natives, but was declined by the visitors.

After two days in Gorgona Frank wanted to move on, but the rest of the party stayed, remembering the promise of mules and horses that would eventually arrive from Chagres. Frank, being impatient and anxious to see the city of Panama, decided to press on and hired a fourteen-year-old boy, offering him twenty-five cents to chop a path through the jungle.

When they set out Frank was surprised by a torrential rainfall. His clothes were soaked, but the sun emerged and dried them in a matter of minutes. The naked boy was unfazed by the downpour as the rain just rolled off his body. As night fell they reached a two-story cane and thatched hut, and were invited to stay the night by its occupants. After a meal of chocolate and a little stewed monkey, the visitors climbed a pole to a loft where they spent the night sleeping on banana and other leaves.

Early the next morning the two set out for the city on the Pacific Ocean. The church bells pealed out the noon hour as they entered the gates of Panama City. Frank hired a large, sparsely furnished room in a coral and adobe house where he anxiously awaited the arrival of his companions.

In three days they arrived from Chagres. The party included a man who had letters of introduction to a Mr. Nelson at the American consulate. Soon, the five were invited to dine with his family. On Washington's birthday several hundred people, waving American flags, paraded the streets of Panama. They were given three cheers when saluting the consulate.

Soon the Pacific mail ships began arriving from their long voyages around Cape Horn. In March Frank and the party of five sailed on the *Oregon,* on which their original passage was booked. Hundreds of people were left behind without passage tickets and very little money.

The *Oregon's* points of entry for mail and repairs were Tobago, where they also took on coal and water, and San Blas. A full day was spent in Mazatlan, an important town of the time. They crossed the tip of Baja, then dropped mail at San Diego and Monterey, and on the first of April, steamed into the bay at Yerba Buena (San Francisco). At the time the American fleet was moored at Little Willow (Sausalito). Marines came aboard the *Oregon* and took off nearly all the crew. It seemed that crews from earlier ships had fled to the gold fields, prompting the Marines to seize them from every vessel to prevent desertion.

The *Oregon* finally docked with the help of passengers near Sacramento Street, where they were floated on rafts to shore. The newcomers spent a cold night on the sand on what is now Montgomery Street. In view were stores with hides and tallow, officers' shanties, and tents on surrounding hills.

The next morning Frank set out on foot to see the town. He enjoyed wild strawberries on his way to the Spanish fort on the hill (Fort Point), and then walked all the way to Mission Dolores. He then continued on to El Potrero.

Frank purchased gun powder, shot, and other supplies, and in several days the five friends hired a sailboat and a pilot and left Yerba Buena for the Embarcadero (the city of Sacramento). They spent the first night where the Sacramento and San Joaquin rivers meet. The only signs of life were the startled deer and elk. Strong winds and tides roared though the tules where the men tried to sleep. It was so cold they returned to the boat, then quarreled as each man wanted to row in order to keep warm. The trip to Sutter's Fort took three days.

Captain John Sutter met the group and invited them to stay. The captain slaughtered extra sheep for the occasion and offered wine from his Feather River vineyard. In view were the captain's company of mounted Indians, dressed and in uniform.

Frank hired a man with a team of horses to take him to Coloma, on the south fork of the American River. The other four men remained at the fort. It was a muddy trail and took two days. The first thing he did in Coloma was to dig for gold near Sutter's Mill.

Frank bought an old log cabin in Coloma that he used as his store. He unpacked the crates full of revolvers he had brought from New York, set up shop, and immediately began selling guns, powder, shot, cartridges, and miscellaneous items to the miners and townspeople. When business was slow Frank joined the gold seekers and mined for the magic dust. On one occasion he had been away from home for nearly a month, searching for new sources of the precious flecks. The bag over his shoulder had become laden with gold dust and nuggets, some weighing over a half ounce. By the time he arrived back home, he was weak and hungry and "would have given away my largest nugget for a warm biscuit."

James Marshall, the discoverer of gold, and Frank became good friends. Marshall told him of that January morning, and of the difficulties in verifying that the yellow metal was, in fact, gold. Marshall had pounded it, and tried staining it with lye and vinegar, but nothing he attempted could change the shape or color of the strange rock. Marshall finally took the nugget to Captain Sutter, who poured acid on the piece and joyfully exclaimed it to be gold. When controversy about the find followed Marshall, Frank always defended him. The two remained friends until Marshall's death in 1885.

Frank returned to New York in 1851. While there he married

his childhood sweetheart and brought her back to Coloma. Frank and Mary raised four children and watched two of them grow and prosper during the Gold Rush. But when the miners left, the gunsmith's business waned and the family moved to Hangtown (Placerville). They later moved to San Francisco, taking the business with them.

Frank died in 1903 at the age of seventy-two in San Francisco. His son Philip Baldwin Bekeart, and grandson Philip Kendall Bekeart, continued in the gun business, for Frank had left a legacy that lasted over a hundred years. The store in Coloma stands today as a state historical monument.

Robert B. Woodward

BY CATHERINE MARY MELONE

 My ancestor, R.B. Woodward, reached San Francisco just as the first miners arrived. Being the son of a shopkeeper in Providence, Rhode Island, he naturally chose to supply the miners with the goods and equipment they would need to seek their fortunes in Gold Rush country. He had been born in January of 1824, and so was still a young man when he set out for California on a sailing ship that would take him through the Straits of Magellan and on to the growing city of San Francisco.

He soon set up shop, but noticed that the miners needed more than goods, so he started a coffeehouse in Chinatown. The success of the coffee house inspired him to start a hotel on the corner of Sacramento and Leidesdorff Streets. This hotel was unique in all of San Francisco and it was a safe and moral place to stay — no liquor, no women, and reasonably priced, home-cooked meals. This hotel, the What Cheer House, charged fifty cents a night, twenty-five cents for board, and twenty-five cents for a bath. The hotel included a library, newspapers from around the world, and a museum. The museum continued to grow from the interesting items R.B. Woodward's friends and customers, sea captains, brought him from their world travels. They knew that R.B. Woodward was a business man, a gentleman, and a scholar.

R.B. soon brought his wife, Mary Church Bucklin (also of Rhode Island), and growing family to live in San Francisco. Four of their eight children had died in the great typhoid epidemic. The energetic R.B. built a new home in the Mission District, in what was then the outskirts of San Francisco, in 1866. The land had once belonged to General Fremont. While the house was being built, gardens, fountains, a lake, and vast lawns were laid out. The treasures from the museum at the What Cheer House were added to the home. R.B. also sponsored young artists. The now famous Virgil Williams, from the Hudson Valley School of American art, was commissioned by R.B. not only to paint, but to go to Europe and purchase originals and copies of European masters to be hung in the new house on the corner of Mission and Fourteenth Streets.

The house was eventually finished and the family moved in. This house soon became a favorite spot for groups and organizations to hold reunions, parties, and meetings. Eventually the family moved elsewhere and this house, Woodward's Gardens, became an amusement park and more, with a theater, a dance hall, a skating rink, a race track, a museum, and finally an amusement park with rides. R.B. built one of the first street car lines in San Francisco to bring visitors to Woodward's Gardens. If R.B. had been wealthy before, he was now a millionaire with a net worth of nearly seven million dollars.

However, R.B. suffered from both asthma and Addison's disease and felt that he and his family would be healthier living out in the country. He bought an unfinished mansion, Oak Knoll, in Napa County, finished it to his satisfaction and lived out the rest of his life in this estate. My ancestress, Sarah B. Woodward, was married there on March 23, 1878 to Drury Melone, lately the Republican Secretary of State to Governor Pacheco. They immediately left for a year's tour of Europe. Their trip was cut short by the untimely death of Robert Woodward, on August 22, 1879. My great-grandfather, Henry Clinton Melone, was born shortly afterwards, on September 17, 1879.

Woodward's Gardens amusement park and street car system continued to function for a few more years, but was eventually closed and its treasures auctioned off, in April 1893. Many of its treasures were purchased by Adolph Sutro. The four children of Robert Woodward split his wealth and properties among themselves, with my ancestors, the Melones, keeping the Oak Knoll house in Napa. Drury and Sarah raised their three children in Oak Knoll, although they always spent their winters in San Francisco on their own floor of the Palace Hotel. Their oldest son, H.C. Melone, married Wanda F. Hadenfeldt of Alameda in 1906. My grandfather, Woodward Melone, was their third son, born in 1912.

Although Robert Woodward's lovely country home, Oak Knoll, was lost during the stock market crash of 1929, my grandfather graduated from Stanford University, was an officer in World War II, and had a distinguished career at Fireman's Fund Insurance Company. Like Robert Woodward, he is a moral and caring person. My father, Jonathan Melone, is the oldest son of Woodward Melone. He is a retired teacher in Stockton and has taught English to Asian immigrants to California, something I am sure Robert Woodward would be proud of. Robert Woodward should certainly be remembered as a great enterprising pioneer of San Francisco, the builder of the first decent hotel in San Francisco, and the creator of Woodward's Gardens family amusement park. But I think he would like best to be remembered as a loving, caring man who valued and loved all of God's creation and did his best his entire life to provide safe and educational recreation for his fellow San Franciscans.

Nathaniel Holland

BY KATHERINE FRENCH WILLI

 Nathaniel Holland arrived in San Francisco on June 8, 1849. He was the twenty-seventh president of the Society of California Pioneers (1884-85). Holland was a Philadelphia lawyer whose ancestors came to America in colonial times.

The first Holland ancestor to emigrate was also Nathaniel, born in Chatham, England in 1740. He came to America some-time prior to the Revolutionary War and kept the British stores at Schomokin, Pennsylvania. His mother was descended from John and Jane Sharples, who came to Pennsylvania from Wybunbury, Cheshire, England in 1682. Both families were long associated with the Society of Friends. Pioneer Holland was born on the family farm in Marple, Pennsylvania in 1812, but was educated in the common schools of Philadelphia. He read for the law in the office of a Judge Campbell of that city and later was the law partner of Robert Tyler, son of President John Tyler.

The thirty-seven-year-old Nathaniel Holland sailed from New York on March 1, 1849 on the steamer *Northerner*, "making his way up the Charges River to Gorgone, thence he walked to Panama, a distance of some twenty-five miles. . . . The required ten dollars for a ride on a very poor beast for the journey seemed quite out of proportion to his pecuniary ability." He is believed to have among his companions a Mr. D.O. Mills, a Mr. Pope, and his friend and later law partner, S.W. Holliday.

Upon arriving in Panama City and learning that the expected steamers had not arrived, Holland and some companions took a steamer south to Callao (Peru) and then sailed up to San Francisco on the *Massachusetts*. He immediately began his practice of law, his profession until his death in 1894.

In addition to being a successful attorney, Nathaniel Holland was a concerned citizen of San Francisco. He served as President of the Board of Assistant Aldermen from 1851 to 1853. In 1852 his was the persuasive voice that caused common council to pass Joint Resolution #236 of September 15, requesting that unsold city lands not be sold at auction as planned but rather be set aside for "hospitals, schools, and engine houses." Nathaniel Holland was a Democrat and a member of the seventh session of the California State Legislature in 1856.

While in the Legislature, he contributed to the shaping of the Consolidation Act, that wise piece of legislation enabling the merging of two groups of personnel, buildings, equipment, and land into one governing body, the City and County of San Francisco. It is also known that he was responsible for other legislation.

In 1857 Nathaniel Holland requested a leave of absence from the Legislature and returned to Philadelphia. The reason for his departure is unknown, but as he merely requested a leave, it would appear that he did not plan to be away for four years. We do know that he practiced law in Philadelphia for three years, and then on September 1, 1860 married a widow, Martha Chace Smith. Mrs. Smith had lived with Nathaniel's uncle's family for many years, and she and Nathaniel certainly had known each other well before his going west in 1849.

Mr. and Mrs. Holland arrived in San Francisco on June 24, 1861. Their only child, Martha, was born August 31st of that year. The trip from Philadelphia by boat to the isthmus, the train trip to the Pacific, and the voyage up the coast must have been arduous for the "expecting" Mrs. Holland, who was forty-three years old! Her courage and strength must have been great because at the end of the Civil War the Hollands retraced their steps to Philadelphia. They undertook the journey so as to introduce little Martha to her namesake, Martha Holland, who was the wife of Nathaniel's uncle, and Martha Chace Smith Holland's aunt as well.

Upon returning to San Francisco the Hollands built a house at 1414 Taylor Street. Nathaniel returned to the practice of law at his office in the Wells Building at 605 Clay Street. He also resumed his role as a concerned citizen. He was chosen a member of the State Committee of the Union Party, made up of Democrats and Republicans who supported Lincoln, serving as chairman in 1863 and 1864. He was School Director, 1872-73; United States Chief Supervisor of Elections, 1880-82; and President of the Pioneer Society in 1884. He was also a vestryman at Grace Church.

Nathaniel Holland was known for his cheerfulness and good health, however, he must have relished thoughtful silence as evidenced by the following:

> Mr. Holland and the beloved Judge Edward
> Norton had the habit for years of taking extended
> walks every Sunday afternoon. They would set forth
> from Mr. Holland's office and return after a three
> hour's stroll, having walked side by side the entire way
> without the exchange of a single word.

Nathaniel Holland died in San Francisco on July 31, 1894. He is buried in the family plot in Cypress Lawn Cemetery, Colma, California.

Whitford Pascoe Harrington

BY LORRAINNE ALBACH MCLAUGHLIN

 "Honest Harry" was the nickname his fellow customs agents gave my great-grandfather, because he never took a bribe during the sixteen years he served in that capacity!

Whitford Pascoe Harrington was born on February 27, 1821 in Winfield Township (now known as Ilion), in Herkimer County, New York. The names of his parents and any siblings are still unknown, despite research in this area. According to the information in the Society of California Pioneers' memorial book, given to my great-grandmother upon his death, Whitford finished high school at the age of sixteen, taught school for two terms, then migrated to Ohio. He worked in Cincinnati as a shoe cutter until gold was discovered in California. He then joined the migration across the plains in The Cincinnati and California Joint Stock Company, a wagon train in which he served as First Lieutenant. This train left St. Joseph, Missouri on April 14, 1849 and arrived in California on July 27, 1849. Whitford first mined in the Hangtown (Placerville) area before going north to Nevada City, where he lived many years.

In 1855 he was elected Police Judge in Nevada City and served until 1856, and was a member of the Board of Trustees in 1857. He was also a member of the Nevada Rifles, which fought in the Indian War in the state of Nevada in 1860 and disbanded in 1861. When Edwin Booth, the famous actor, played in Nevada City, Whitford played supporting roles in the Shakespearian plays *Hamlet* and *Richard the Third*. During these years he operated a saloon on

Whitford Pascoe Harrington

Broad Street, and also had part ownership in at least one mine.

Mary Ann Connelly emigrated with her parents, Ardy and Ann Connelly, and brothers and sister from Ireland to Baltimore, and then through the Isthmus of Panama to California. She married Dr. William G. von Poelnitz and had a three-month old son, William J. The doctor was accidentally killed by his gun going off as he crossed a fence stile in 1857. Her family was living in the Nevada City area when she married Whitford on May 27, 1859. They later had a son, Benjamin Pascoe, and three daughters, Mary Ann, Alice Jane, and Ada Isabelle. In 1864 the family moved to Austin, Nevada where Whitford was elected Police Judge for one year in 1865 while working in the Young America mine. The following year the family returned to Nevada City for a year before moving to Virginia City in Nevada. They were living there when their youngest daughter, Ada Isabelle, died in 1870.

In 1871 Whitford was appointed to the post of Customs Inspector in San Francisco, where the family would then reside permanently. "Honest Harry" was true to his nickname during his sixteen years as an inspector.

My grandmother, his daughter Mary Ann, said she never met a finer man in her entire life. With his patriarchal beard and venerable figure, he epitomized the California pioneer to the thousands who visited the Mining Bureau and State Museum located in the Pioneer Building on Fourth Street in San Francisco. After his service as an inspector was finished he operated the elevator at the Pioneer Building nearly until his untimely death on August 3, 1899, at the age of seventy-eight years.

While walking home one evening he tripped and fell while crossing the railroad tracks, suffering a concussion. The police who found him thought he was drunk, but a friend informed them that Whitford was a teetotaler. His death was a shock to his family and friends because of his good health, and he was sorely missed by all.

Simeon Mattingly and
Eliza Thompson Mattingly

BY MARY JANE ERHART PORTER

 The California gold fever of 1849 lured my great-great-grandfather Simeon Mattingly to leave his family in Hinds County, Mississippi to seek his fortune. He sailed to Central America, traveled overland across the Isthmus of Panama and sailed northward on the ship *Alex Von Humboldt*, arriving in San Francisco in August, 1849.

Family records do not detail his journey from Mississippi across the isthmus, but do record that the voyage aboard the *Alex Von Humboldt* required several months. Many passengers sickened and died and were buried at sea. Numerous emergencies arose requiring passengers to volunteer their services for the duration of the trip. Simeon volunteered to take charge of food services. After their safe arrival a number of the passengers founded a club called "The Humboldteers." An annual banquet was held to commemorate their arduous voyage until no survivors remained.

Simeon's degree of success in the gold arena is unknown. However, he did return to Mississippi for his family. Shortly after the birth of his son, John, in Mississippi in 1852, Simeon, Eliza, and their five young children, made the overland trip to California. They also brought two slaves with them, Uncle Charles and Aunt Mariah. In his book *Descendants of Joseph and Hessina Mattingly*, Joseph F. Mattingly Jr. said that "Uncle Charles took Simeon's sons hunting and camping on the grounds of what is now the campus of the University of California in Berkeley."

The 1860 San Francisco *City Directory* lists Simeon Mattingly as a merchant, living at "N. Howard, between First and Second." In

1862-63 he is listed again as a merchant, living at 538 Howard Street. In the 1863-64 *City Directory*, he is a miner and residing at 520 Howard Street. The Oakland *City Directory* of 1872-3 lists Simeon as a miner-developer, living at the southwest corner of Fourth and Jefferson. The 1875 *Directory* lists his occupation as miner, living at 715 Jefferson Street. This appears to have been his address until his death in 1891.

Family records show that he also operated a silver mine in Atlanta, Idaho Territory. One of his sons, Phillip, was killed in a black powder explosion in that mine. Simeon owned and operated an assaying mill for the mines in Idaho. He made several trips to England, seeking financial backers for his mining interests. While on such a trip to London, England in 1891, he died and is buried in London. The children of Simeon and Eliza Mattingly were: Mary, Phillip Daniel, Caroline Theresa (my grandmother), Virginia, John Andrew, William Thompson, and Richard Clarence. Eliza Ann Thompson Mattingly died in Mariposa, California while visiting her granddaughter, Carrie Ledden Wall. She is buried in St. Mary's Cemetery, Oakland, California.

David Saul Levy

BY VERA FREEMAN FELCHLIN

"A California pioneer of great integrity and courage" best describes David Saul Levy, my great-grandfather. He was born in New York City on July 4, 1838 to Saul and Ellen Levy. Ellen Levy was the daughter of Rev. Myer Levy, Rabbi of the Leadenhall Street Synagogue, in London.

Large families were commonplace in the nineteenth century and the Levy family followed that tradition. David Saul's father, Saul Levy, and his wife, Ellen Levy, produced five children: David Saul, Harry Lee, Isadore, Aaron, and Flora. David Saul married around the age of twenty-five a beautiful, artistic woman by the name of Mary Myers. She had eight brothers and sisters and flourished in a comfortable environment where discipline, love of family, education, and religious practice were emphasized.

One of Mary's sisters, Alma Myers, became the first woman Federal Attorney in California, appointed by Woodrow Wilson. Another sister, Emma, married a Norton and produced one child, Marian. Marian Norton Montague became an accomplished artist in San Francisco under the name of Madame Yoreska. She created miniature portraits on ivory and was commissioned here and abroad by many prominent people. Some of her work became part of the Palace of the Legion of Honor collections.

At the age of eleven years, young Saul Levy and his father started for California aboard the steamship *Falcon*, via Charleston, New Orleans, and Havana to Chagres. The voyage to Chagres took fourteen days. The next leg of the journey was by canoe up the

David Saul Levy

Chagres river to Gorgona. Naked natives poled the vessel and were described by Saul in his journal as "kind and honest." He writes further, "From Gorgona to Panama it took one long day by mule or on foot, as mules were scarce."

After crossing the isthmus on foot, they left Panama harbor on August 1, 1849 on the ship *Eugenia*, along with 112 other passengers, children not enumerated. The cost of passage was $300 per adult. Elean Hydenfeldt with his wife and two children were among the number, as well as Almarin B. Paul, who became a noted mining engineer. From the time of leaving the island of Tobaga near Panama, no land nor vessel was seen until land was reached on November 4,1849, just above Point Reyes, ninety-three days out from Panama.

During the voyage from Panama one of Mrs. Hydenfeldt's children died and, in compliance with the heartbreaking wishes of the mother and the demands of other passengers, the body was preserved in brandy from the cargo, paid for by the passengers, and a tin coffin was made from food cans. The body was wrapped in cloth, covered with the spirits, placed into one of the life boats, and brought to San Francisco for burial.

Of his arrival in San Francisco Saul wrote, "Rising over the point, San Francisco lay before us scattered around a horseshoe bend that reached inland to Montgomery Street." After anchoring in the bay on Sunday, all passengers were brought ashore in small boats for five dollars per head to Clark's Point, which was at the foot of what is now Broadway Street.

The first work undertaken by David Levy was to assist his father in upholstery, he having opened a workshop on Clay Street just above Powell on what is now the corner of Prospect Place. They later moved down Clay Street between Pike Street (now Waverly Place) and Stockton Street. At the southwest corner was the post office. During this period David received more formal education, as evidenced by his superb command of the English language, which was reflected in his autobiography.

In the fall of 1850 David Saul wandered off into the interior for adventure. Taking a train at Marysville to Cottonwood Creek in Shasta County, he was taken sick and left at Cottonwood Crossing with Jeff and George Clanton. They had a stock ranch there and made their living taking care of broken down animals left there to recuperate. When well, he struck out for the headwaters of Cottonwood, since rich mines were being reported at Horsetown and Jacksap Flat. There he tried his hand at mining and then headed for Major P.B. Redding's ranch at the junction of Cottonwood Creek and the Sacramento River. He stayed there until Redding was defeated in his election for Governor of the state.

In pioneer spirit, David went on to Oroville to river mine until flooded out by fall rains. Not being successful at mining, he took a trip to Portland, Oregon and opened a bookstore next to the Arizona Hotel on First Street. Portland was "too slow for a Californian" so he returned to try store keeping in Hangtown (Placerville). The next endeavor was working in the post office department until after 1856. During this period, David Saul furthered his education in higher learning institutions.

The excitement of mining surfaced again and David Saul Levy went to Nevada City and worked on Bear Creek until the discovery of the Comstock Lode. Thence on to Virginia City, where he was one of the thirteen men to work the Esmeralda mines. He worked three years tunnelling into barren rock and finally quit mining once and for all. In his own words, David Saul comments, "Though not very successful in a pecuniary sense, mining is the only pursuit that ever keeps a man fully supplied with hope."

Of the incidents occurring during the Vigilance days of 1851-1856, it was David Saul's pleasure to belong to Company Six under the guidance of Captain Ebbetts. He went on to say, "I feel that the efforts of myself and co-members made San Francisco, in particular, and California, generally, a safe place for decent people to camp in. The moral force of an undoubted punishment for crime, had a far greater effect during '51 and '56 than has ever been attained since."

On to a new profession at the young age of twenty-seven, David Saul worked in the Custom House in San Francisco as a collector under Tom Shannon for two terms, and for part of Eugene L. Sullivan's term. For the last thirty years of his life, he served as an adjuster with the Board of Trade in San Francisco. He was a life member of the Society of California Pioneers and served as Marshall of the Society as late as 1919.

My great-grandfather, David Saul Levy, died in 1922 at the age of eighty-four. His courage, great sense of morality, and honesty, coupled with his high regard for God and his fellow man is a legacy to be not only recognized, but to serve as a model of what made our country great then, and what our country needs now to sustain that greatness.

> In this new country north, now in the twentieth century, just arising, it is to be hoped our successors in pioneership will profit by our examples, and be just to one another outside of the technical points now often used to defeat equity.

Dennis Mahoney

BY EILEEN C. CALLAGHAN

Dennis Mahoney was born July 30, 1816 in Michelstown, County Cork, Ireland, where he attended local schools. He was the second of at least five children. His parents were John Mahoney and Margaret Moriarity. Dennis came to the United States in 1838 and settled in Albany, New York. It is reported that he brought his father and possibly some of his brothers and sisters with him, and that his father died in Albany, New York. (If his mother's name was Margaret, then she came with him to San Francisco in the late 1850s and resided close by his residence on Pacific Street, on the south side of Filbert Street between Stockton and Powell.)

Dennis married in 1845 in Jersey City, New Jersey. Margaret Casey, born in 1828, was also from Michelstown, County Cork, one of seven children of Edward Warren Casey and Mira Hennegan who had also immigrated to Albany about 1829. Denis and Margaret had eleven children, three born in Albany; eight survived to adulthood.

Dennis was involved in the butcher trade in that city, but upon the news of the Gold Rush to California he decided to improve the family fortunes. He joined John Woodhouse Audubon (the son of the famous naturalist) who, with a certain Captain Webb, formed a company of some ninety-eight men to attempt an overland route to California by going to New Orleans, then to the Rio Grande, then following that river through Mexico and Texas to reach the California coast. The New York newspapers described this company of men as "highly educated, good appearance, men of good moral habits and unblemished reputations, from the best families of New York."

With much fanfare and outfitted in woolen uniforms with brass buttons (highly unsuitable for the terrain which they were to cross!) they left Baltimore in February of 1849 and went to New Orleans. With a great deal of time lost in loading their supplies and horses they took ship to the Mexican border area. Here disaster struck in the form of cholera and a number of the men died. Dennis apparently became discouraged with the company and returned to the East and took passage around the 22nd of June on the Chilean brig *Copiapo*. The voyage was of some fifty-five days duration, stopping in San Diego and then landing in San Francisco August 16, 1849. This was well ahead of Audubon's ill-fated surviving group that finally reached the coast in November with but a skeleton number of its original members!

Dennis went to the mining district near the middle forks of the Yuba River called Foster's Bar but did not find prosperity and returned to Yerba Buena (San Francisco) where he established himself in the butchering business and in real estate. He established a large ranch consisting mainly of sheep, which encompassed the area from Bush Street on the south to Green Street on the north, Larkin Street on the east, Fillmore Street on the west. It commanded an unobstructed view of the bay, and here he built a large ranch house known as the Mahoney Rancho.

Dennis returned to Albany, New York in 1852-1854 and made preparations to bring his family and his wife's sisters to California. They arrived in 1854 and stayed in the San Jose area from 1854 until 1857 with the famous Burnett family, from which the first Governor of the state had come. Margaret's sister, Ellen Casey, married John Burnett. When the new home, which was being erected near the ranch home, was finished, the family moved to San Francisco in 1857. It faced what is now Pacific Avenue. Dennis' brother,

David (later Senator), and his sister, Margaret, established a residence next to his. It had a rich setting among the rolling fields surrounded by oak trees, lupine, Christmas berry, and yerba buena vines. Indians and Spanish, as well as immigrants from Germany and other countries, were generously employed about the ranch.

Mr. Mahoney was of medium height, broad shouldered and erect, with blue serious eyes only half veiling their twinkling humor. He had a bright complexion, with black hair and black side whiskers worn in the style of that period. Margaret Mahoney was described as a tall woman with brown hair and grey eyes, deeply set under straight dark eyebrows. Their home was a center for early society of San Francisco, graced by the names of John Mitchell, the Irish scholar, George O'Dougherty, lawyer and court reporter, Bartholomew Dowling, poet, Congressman John Coness, U.S. Senator David Broderick, Governor John Downey, General Shields, Col. Baker, as well as the prominent early Spanish families of Ainsas, Estudillos, Pritchards and Vallejos.

Mahoney seems to have avoided most of the political problems of the early years of the city but did take a decided stand in 1856 against the Vigilance Committee. There was a Frank S. Mahoney on that Committee, but it is not known if this was a distant relative or not. Dennis became a member of the Association of the Law and Order Men of the city and was a member of the Society of California Pioneers, joining on December 7, 1853. He was intolerant of anything and anyone who would seek to take away an individual's rights, and was active in the destruction of the Vigilance Committee.

Dennis Mahoney died September 9, 1890 at his residence at 1503 Pacific Avenue. He was buried in the Mahoney plot at Calvary Cemetery, later transferred to Holy Cross Cemetery, Colma. He was seventy-four years old. Margaret died February 2, 1894 and is buried beside her husband in Holy Cross Cemetery.

Dr. Galen Burdell D.D.S.

BY CHARMAINE A. BURDELL

 Dr. Burdell was born near Adams Centre, Watertown, Jefferson County, New York on June 26, 1828, the son of James and Sila (Lamon) Burdell of Ellisburg, New York. Sila was the daughter of Noah and Nancy (Gault) Lamon, also of Ellisburg. Noah's father, Francis, born in 1727 in Palmer, Hampden County, Massachusetts, served in the Colonial War on the Lake George Expedition of 1755 and the Crown Point Expedition of 1756. He died in 1829 at Hounsfield, New York at the age of 101. His wife, Margaret Ray, born 1737, Greenwich, Hampshire County, Massachusetts, died in 1836 at the age of ninety-nine. Nancy's father, James Gault, lived in Halifax, Windham County, Vermont at the time of his enlistment in the Revolutionary War and served in the Massachusetts line.

The Burdells were living in Simsbury, Hartford County, Connecticut in 1790. Galen's grandparents, William and Polly (Cunningham) Burdell, lived in German Flats, Herkimer County, New York in 1810. Polly's parents, John and Rebecca (Taylor) Snyder Cunningham, lived in Salem, New Jersey, where he served with the Jerseymen during the Revolutionary War.

At the age of fifteen, Galen became a student of dentistry under an apprenticeship to his uncles, Doctors John and Harvey Burdell, prominent dentists of New York City. (Harvey was murdered there January 30, 1857 and the case has remained unsolved.) The New York City *Directory* for 1831-1847 lists "Dr. Galen Burdell, dentist, office corner of Franklin and Broadway." He was nineteen years old.

Dr. Galen Burdell D.D.S.

In 1849 Galen decided to visit another uncle, Dr. Lewis Burdell of Rio de Janiero, Brazil, who was physician to Emperor Dom Pedro II. In the archives of the Society of California Pioneers Galen states that he arrived in California aboard the *Duxbury* as her surgeon. He may have been on board the ship when she sailed from Boston, February 10, 1849 bound for Rio. The *Duxbury* rounded

Cape Horn May 22, arriving off the Golden Gate August 21 in a dense fog. Seeking the entrance to the harbor on a calm sea, she ran onto a reef, today known as Duxbury Reef, off Bolinas. At the following high tide she was pulled off by her crew and came into San Francisco harbor August 22, 1849.

Dr. Burdell wasted little time in pioneering a dental practice. In the *Alta California*, September 27, 1849, appears the following ad:

> Copartnership — The undersigned have this day
> entered into copartnership under the firm of Tompson
> & Burdell for the practice of Dentistry. J. Whitlock
> Tompson and Galen Burdell M.D. Office on Clay
> Street, next door to Woodruff & Addison Jewelry.

Volunteer fire and militia companies were considered "places of the highest resort." On January 8, 1850 Galen joined the St. Francis Hook and Ladder Company No. 1. A sense of sympathy and brotherly love bound the members with the closest ties of friendship. When a member was sick, one or more of the members were required to visit him daily and tend to his needs.

Dr. Burdell, with Dr. Horace J. Paine and their friend, Eldridge G. Hall, became partners in a scheme to get rich in Oregon, which they called "the Umpqua Expedition." Unfortunately, Simmons, Hutchinson & Co. went bankrupt and the company lost their entire capital of $1000. The Act of Congress offering a square mile of land in Oregon to settlers expired December 1, 1850. By this date they had not taken possession of any claims. During the autumn of 1850 Congress passed a law forbidding the issue of U.S. patents for lands in Oregon to companies or non-residents whose object was speculation.

Dr. Burdell became acquainted with Maria Augustina, the

daughter of James and Maria Augustina Black, in 1861. They corresponded for six months before their engagement, sending their letters through her father. They were married October 6, 1863 at the Blacks' home in Nicasio, Marin County. In 1865 as a wedding present for his daughter, Mr. Black conveyed 6,335 acres of Rancho Olompali, stocked with cattle. Dr. and Mrs. Burdell moved onto the property December 24, 1866.

A son, James Black Burdell, was born in San Francisco on November 18, 1869. James married in 1892 Marie Josephine Sweetser, daughter of John Robert Sweetser of Novato, Marin County. On March 21, 1876 a daughter, Mabel Isabel, was born to Dr. and Mrs. Burdell, also in San Francisco. She married first John M. Comman in Dublin, Ireland. She married second Edwin V. Smith in Reno, Nevada. Her third marriage was to Rudy Lichenberg of San Rafael, Marin County. In her later years she was known as "Mary." She died in 1956 in Sonoma County.

In 1864 Mrs. Burdell's mother came to Dr. Burdell with a severe toothache, and during the operation she died in his dental chair. This was the first fatal case of using chloroform in dentistry.

On April 21, 1869 Dr. Burdell and Henry Wakelee made a contractual agreement to market "Dr. G. Burdell's Oriental Toothwash." On May 19, 1870 he sold all controlling rights to Oriental Toothwash to B.B. Thayer, a well known chemist in San Francisco. Wakelee continued as sole agent and added Burdell's Toothpowder to the line.

When Mrs. Burdell's father died in 1870 she acquired half of his estate. One of her ranches, on Black Mountain in Marin County, contained many springs from which the Burdells were able to supply their neighbors and the village which later became Point Reyes Station. This was the first water system in this area, before the first train arrived in 1875. By 1876 Galen established a bar and a hotel to serve the needs of passengers and crew. In 1879 Mrs. Burdell deeded her husband 950 acres surrounding the Point Reyes train depot, which he had surveyed off into town lots. At the end of 1883 the town had one hotel, one saloon, a railroad depot, blacksmith shop, livery stable, butcher shop, store, dentist office, and post office.

Galen Burdell was a member of the 1851 and 1856 San Francisco Committees of Vigilantes, badge number 259. He was a charter member of the Society of California Pioneers and served as vice-president in 1894 and 1895 in Marin County.

Dr. Burdell died April 8, 1906 at his home on Rancho Olompali, now known as Olompali State Park, just ten days before the great San Francisco earthquake and fire which destroyed most of the city he loved so much. He and Mrs. Burdell are interred in Mountain View Cemetery Columbarium, Oakland, California.

Milo Jewett Ayer, Wheelwright

BY NANCY POWERS

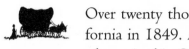Over twenty thousand persons left Boston for California in 1849. Among them was Milo Jewett Ayer, who arrived in California via the overland route. Born July 25, 1820 in St. Johnsbury, Caladonia County, Vermont, Ayer was twenty-nine when he left for California. Not only was he a strict temperance man, but he refrained from smoking, gambling, and swearing. He was known as a kindly and industrious soul with his more memorable characteristic being his correct manner of speech. Milo Ayer was skilled in two trades — he was a carpenter and a millwright. His wife, née Phoebe N. George, was a member of the Bradford family of Mayflower fame. When Milo Ayer joined the Boston-Newton Company in 1849, he and Phoebe had been married since August 10, 1845 and had two children, a son and a daughter.

Unlike the tales of disaster and extraordinary difficulty popularly associated with accounts of migration to California in the mid-nineteenth century, the experiences of the Boston-Newton Company were probably typical of the great majority of forty-niners who undertook to traverse the North American continent.

The men of the Boston-Newton Company were a homogenous group — all New Englanders, mostly from the Boston-Newton area, several of them related. They were average citizens — if any pioneer may so be described — sober and God-fearing family men, not looking for excitement, seeking solely to better them-

selves. . . . The Boston-Newton Company is credited
with being the only organized group of forty-niners to
reach California without a change of officers en route.

Fellow traveler David Staples commented in one of his first
diary entries, "We are strangers with few acceptions, but a remarkable trait in Americans is to have confidence and respect for each
other and only on being disappointed or deceived do they distrust
their ability or zeal to operate together."

They were perceptive men who were among the first to see the
wonders of that great stretch of land from the Missouri River to
the Pacific Ocean before civilization put its mark on it. Witness
Staples' May 22, 1849 diary entry:

> Today we crossed the Wakarusa River. The banks
> were steep. We had to let our wagons down by ropes
> and hired some Santa Fee oxen to get our teems up.
> There is heavy timber for a half mile on each side of
> the river. For three miles we had to pass over a wet
> bottom prara. Had to double teems and much of the
> way the wheels went down to the hub. However, we
> have got through it at dark and camped on fine rise on
> the high prara. Tonight for the first time our ears have
> been saluted by the howling of wolves about our camp.

The long and short of it is that these men left for California
on April 17, 1849, traveling through Massachusetts, New York,
Ohio, Indiana, Illinois, Missouri, Nebraska, Wyoming, and Utah,
southwest through Carson Pass, arriving at Hangtown (Placerville),
California in just over five months. At about noon on September
26, 1849 a site of tall, wide spreading oaks and green grass came
into view, and as they drew near the spot they found a spring and

encamped. That very spot, located in Shingle Springs, California, is now marked by a California historical monument erected on June 4, 1950 and paid for by descendants of the Boston-Newton Company. The Company officially reached Sacramento, California on September 27, 1849 and formally disbanded on October 25, 1849.

At about that same time Ayer's cousin, Dr. Washington Ayer, arrived in California via Cape Horn. Soon the two Ayers began mining together in the Mokelumne Hill area, and Milo Ayer's mining venture paid off at Rich Gulch. In 1850 Ayer and his companions provided financial help to David Staples to purchase a tract of rich farming land on the south bank of the Mokelumne River. Ayer and fellow travelers Easterbrook, Coffey, Thomason, and Fred Staples used the Staples ranch as their headquarters for several years. Also during 1850 Milo Ayer supervised the building of the first two-story frame house in the region.

In late 1850 Ayer bought mining property in Downieville,

where he developed several mines and built a house. His wife and daughter arrived via Cape Horn in March, 1851, having left their young son with relatives in Newton, Massachusetts. They stayed at the Staples ranch for about two months before joining Milo Ayer at their Downieville home. In 1852 friends brought Ayer's son to California and within a few days of his arrival he fell down a mine shaft and was killed. Another son, Clarence Milo Ayer, was born in Downieville in 1856. In 1866 the Ayers moved to Vallejo where they built a home in the hills east of downtown. Although no longer in the family, this home was recently featured in a Vallejo newspaper as having been refurbished by its new owner.

Ayer was an accomplished millwright and is credited with building the first stamp mill in the California gold fields. After his adventures in the gold country Ayer came to San Francisco and established a lucrative business as a millwright. Some of the mills of the early days still stand as a monument to his skill and clever workmanship.

After a brief illness and just before his 80th birthday, Ayer died on June 15, 1900, leaving Daniel E. Easterbrook as the last survivor of their adventurous trip across the plains fifty-one years earlier. Ayer was a member of the Society of California Pioneers, under whose auspices his body was interred after the funeral, which took place at Pioneer Hall on Fourth Street, San Francisco.

James Thomas Lillard Jr.

BY CONSTANCE CECIL LAVENTURIER

 In the 1840s Independence, Missouri was a bustling area and a growing community. Located at the head of the Old Santa Fe Trail, it was the hub of commerce with Mexico for the increasing number of Americans traveling west; it was the place for freighters to secure supplies and equipment. This was the primary occupation of the population. Many of the local boys aspired to become teamsters and wagon masters because the wages were good and there was a constant demand for their services. This was the environment in which James Lillard spent his youth and impressionable years.

Born in Harrodsburg, Kentucky in 1830, J.T. Lillard was the second child of James Thomas and Elizabeth Coovert Lillard. The family lived in a community settled by Captain John Lillard in 1788, but in 1840 James Thomas Lillard Sr. purchased land in Jackson County, Missouri and moved his family to an area just outside of Independence. He died shortly after his arrival so the children were placed in the care of relatives. James' guardian, James Chiles, was a member of a merchant family and related to the pathfinder, Colonel Joseph Ballinger Chiles. Thus James was familiar with tales of challenge, of blazing the wilderness, and life on the plains.

When the United States formally declared war against Mexico, Missouri was called upon to furnish a mounted regiment. The Jackson County Volunteers, A Company, under the command of Colonel Alexander Doniphan, signed men for service from June, 1846 to June 22, 1847. Lillard volunteered and was hired as a civilian teamster to care for the supplies and horses. Colonel Doniphan, sensing the need for a massive attack against Santa Ana, mustered the teamsters into the army, swearing them into active service on the battlefield. Lillard participated in the Battle of Sacramento near the city of Chihuahua. During the battle the teamsters did service on the front lines. Santa Ana's forces were routed and the Americans marched on victorious. In twelve months the Missourians covered 3,500 miles by land and 2,500 by water. The federal government never recognized the legality of Doniphan's actions and denied veterans' benefits to the civilians who fought on the battlefields.

Lillard returned to Independence, completed his schooling, and made plans to move west. Gold was discovered in California and the stories told by friends and neighbors who had been west excited the imagination of many local young men. James Thomas and his brother were no exceptions. With the possibility of great wealth, land, and opportunity, the Lillards made plans to follow Missourians who had moved earlier.

On May 5, 1849 James Lillard and his brother, John, emigrated from Missouri with a small herd of horses. They set out across the plains with the Hudsly Party, arriving at Bear River in July, where they followed a cutoff between Salt Lake and Fort Hall. They traveled the California Trail and the Truckee route, arriving in Sacramento in the fall of 1849. Evidently it was an uneventful trip except for the loss of some horses. The brothers spent many months on the Yuba River at Missouri Bar panning for gold, but they were only moderately successful, so John returned to Independence while James settled in Yolo County. There he managed a hotel in Washington, now Broderick, and operated the ferry across the Sacramento river near the current I Street Bridge. Later he purchased 600 acres of farm land in the Davisville area and engaged in agriculture until 1885.

He married Mary Ann Mears, originally from Ireland, on October 7, 1852 in Plainfield, near Davis, California. They had two children, Eliza Ann and Henry Riggs, whose descendants continue to live in Yolo County. Following Mary Ann's death in 1856, James married a widow, Susan Shelby Hoy, who was a friend and neighbor from Independence, Missouri. The two children born to James and Susan died in childhood. Members of the Lillard family were buried in the New Helvetia Cemetery in Sacramento, however, the cemetery was moved in the 1950s and a school was built on the site.

With the opening of the California Pacific Railroad in 1868, Lillard established a hotel to accommodate the travelers transferring at Davis to stages for Sacramento, Woodland, and points north. In 1882 he built a larger, two-story hotel, Lillard House, across from the new train station. After his death in 1889 his widow managed the business until it burned in 1898.

Lillard participated in many civic activities. He was the coroner for a number of years and was elected supervisor for Yolo County for two terms. He also served as a Justice of the Peace and held membership on innumerable civic committees. In addition, he was a member of the Order of Red Men, Siskiyou Tribe Number Nineteen, as well as the Sacramento Society of California Pioneers. His funeral service was held at the family residence in Davisville under the auspices of the Sacramento Society of California Pioneers. The funeral sermon was pronounced by Rev. Philip Burton of Winters.

James Lillard's life was typical of many of the early Missouri pioneers who settled and developed Yolo County in the 1850s. They cultivated the land, raised their families, and actively participated in the growth and progress of California.

Frank J. Tillman

BY JANICE TILLMAN CLINE

 There is a small street off Grant Avenue in the heart of downtown San Francisco called Tillman Place. It was the site of the original home of my grandparents after their marriage, when this was a residential area. When they moved away it was replaced with a commercial building that may be remembered as the site of the popular Temple Bar for many years.

Although grandfather died before I was born, he left a large family that included my mother, Josephine, and seven uncles and aunts that were very much a part of my life. Here is the story of the Tillman family as I know it.

Frank Tillman was born in Arnesburg, Germany on March 14, 1819, one of nine children of Henry Tillman, a large-scale farmer and the principal land owner in the region. At the age of twenty, fortified with a sense of adventure and a well-rounded education in the Catholic schools of the nearby city of Cologne, Frank left for America in 1839. He was in Philadelphia at first and then followed a brother who had settled in Vicksburg, Mississippi. He was there in 1849 when word came that gold had been discovered in California. Joining the Gold Rush, he set sail from New Orleans on the clipper ship *Alexander McCame.* It was a nine-month voyage around the Horn to San Francisco. When he arrived in San Francisco on October 3, 1849 he made his way to the gold fields of Mokelumne Hill, where he reportedly made a small fortune of $5,000. However, he came down with scurvy from the long voyage and spent it all recuperating back in San Francisco.

Now permanently settled in San Francisco he first turned to locksmithing and then became the sole west coast agent for Tilton and McFarland Company, an east coast manufacturer of safes and scales. He established his business at 318 Battery Street where he operated out of his own building until he retired in 1879.

On August 22, 1867 he married Anna McKenna, a handsome young woman twenty-five years his junior. With the dark red hair and fair complexion of her Scottish-Irish ancestry, she caught Frank's eye shortly after her arrival from Boston to visit a sister who had preceded her to San Francisco.

Anna McKenna was born in Prince Edward Island, Canada on December 11, 1845, but raised in Boston where the family moved after her father's death. Frank was very proud of her and later had her portrait painted by Toby Rosenthal, a European-trained painter of renown in San Francisco at the time. By the time of the marriage, Frank had prospered in his business and had acquired a sizeable amount of real estate. Children were born quickly into the Tillman household and as the family expanded, they moved to a more commodious Victorian home Frank had built on a lot he owned at Larkin and Broadway. There were ten children, eight of whom lived to adulthood. Minna became Mrs. Penner Briggs of Victoria, Canada; Frank Jr. and Tilton became physicians in San Francisco; Frances became a nun in the Holy Family Convent; Harry was a driver for Goldberg-Bowen Grocers; Josephine married Maitland Cline, a real estate developer; Louise remained unmarried; and the youngest, Eugene, died of a ruptured appendix shortly before he was to enter Stanford University, a devastating loss to the family.

Frank retired from the safe business at age sixty and was then listed in the city directories as "capitalist." He died on February 7, 1904 just a month before his eighty-fifth birthday. Later that same year his widow, who long outlived him, had the house moved to a new location at 2826 Van Ness Avenue where it survived the 1906 earthquake and fire. She continued living there until her death in 1941 at the age of ninety-six.

Living there at the time were her daughters, Josephine and Louise Cline, and granddaughters, Josephine and Janice Cline. As one of the last living granddaughters of Frank Tillman, Janice Cline continues to live in the family home, which is the gathering place of successive generations of Tillmans. The latest gathering was on January 1, 2000, when about forty of this pioneer's descendants, down to the sixth generation, connected with one another and with their past.

John Mathews

BY ROBIN POPPERS

John Mathews arrived at Lassen's Ranch on October 3, 1849, having spent five months on the journey from Missouri. John had been born in Kentucky in 1828, and had lived with his family in Indiana and Missouri. In September, 1847 at Fort Leavenworth, he enlisted in Colonel Gilpin's battalion of Missouri Volunteers with a thirty-five dollar horse, and served in the Mexican War for thirteen months. He was mustered out at Independence and six months later, at the age of nineteen, joined the forty-niners bound for California.

John Mathews' future wife, Virginia Elizabeth Goodrich, is listed in the 1850 census in El Dorado County, California. As a girl of thirteen, she experienced the giddy life of the roaring mining camps in the vicinity of Ringgold. Her father, James, was born in North Carolina, and Virginia was born in Tennessee, as was her mother, Nancy. James Goodrich was in his forties when he and his wife packed up their three children and set out on the great adventure of the Gold Rush. The whole family had arrived in California by 1850, most likely from Missouri, where Virginia's youngest brother was born four years earlier.

In 1853, John and Virginia were married in Marysville. Virginia was sixteen and John was twenty-five. For ten years they farmed in Sutter County. Five children were born to them between 1855 and 1863: Alonzo (who died as an infant), James Robert, Laura, California, and Stonewall Jackson, born in 1863 (a revealing clue to the family's political sympathies in those tumultuous times). Two weeks after giving birth to little Stonewall, Virginia died. She was, as her tombstone documents, twenty-five years, eleven months and eight days old. She is buried, along with Alonzo, in Yuba City.

John Mathews was left with four children under the age of eight, one a newborn. In 1866 he moved with his children to Sonoma County and lived on a farm near Santa Rosa for two years. His eldest son, James, eventually joined him in the cattle business, for which they traveled to Nevada. John sent his son, James, to school in Windsor in 1869, and to Pacific Methodist College for two years. James became a pharmacist; he kept books and ran Sutler's Store on the Indian Reservation in Round Valley, Covelo for several years. In 1879 James married Josephine Reid, whose father was the physician and surgeon on the Round Valley Reservation.

John Mathews married a second time, in 1872, to Mary Henry Seawell, the sister of Emmet Seawell, who was to become a California Supreme Court Judge. John had three children with Mary: Oscar, Hamilton, and Milly. John's son, James, with his wife, Josephine, moved to Ukiah, where they built a grand Victorian house and owned J.R. Mathews Drug Store. John died in Ukiah in April, 1878 at the age of forty-nine. He must have been well loved, for his tombstone bears the tender inscription

A Kind Father and Affectionate Husband,
Though Are Gone, but Not Forgotten.

William Craig

BY LINDA LEE KERR

 William Craig arrived in San Francisco on November 3, 1849, according to the records of the Society of California Pioneers. It is assumed that he came by ship, although this is only a guess, and that his homeland was Scotland. William Craig married Mary Bright and they had (at least) one son, William Bright Craig Sr., who was born March 10, 1859.

William Bright Craig Sr. married Johanna Burns and they had four children: Alma (Chisholm), Lillian May (Kerr), William Bright Jr., and Robert George. According to a newspaper clipping (concerning Lillian May Craig's wedding), William Bright Craig Sr. was a "well-known capitalist in the early days of San Francisco." Both William and Johanna Bright Craig Sr. died in their early forties from influenza and are buried in San Francisco's Columbarium.

(An interesting side note here: On both my grandmother's and grandfather's side there was a tradition of passing along the mother's maiden name to children as their middle name, seemingly a way of giving the mother's family name to her children.)

Of William and Johanna Craig Sr.'s children, Alma Craig Chisholm is known to the Daughters of California Pioneers, having served as president twice (1924-25 and 1939-40). In addition, "Auntie" Alma was a San Francisco businesswoman and partner in the W.M. Dickerson Company. Alma was married two times, but had no children. "Auntie" was also my godmother.

Alma's younger sister, Lillian May Craig (my father's mother), married Lansing Bosworth Kerr on September 15, 1909 and they had four sons: James Lansing ("Pete"), William Craig, Donald Robert (my father), and Douglas Craig ("Brim"). Alma's husband, Lansing, was the son of James Watt Kerr, said to be one of San Francisco's pioneer iron founders and cofounder of The Steiger and Kerr Stove and Foundry Company, which for several decades manufactured "Occidental" ranges in San Francisco.

Lansing worked in his father's business as sales manager until the business was sold (which is an amazing story for its time and something right out of today's tabloid rags.) Lansing's brother, Andrew L. Kerr, also worked for Steiger and Kerr as vice-president and general manager.

I shouldn't forget to mention that my great-grandfather, James Watt Kerr, immigrated to San Francisco with his brother, Dr. William Watt Kerr. They came from their family home in the village of Svanston-Midlothian, Scotland (near Edinburgh). Dr. William Kerr was one of the founding members of San Francisco's University Hospital (his picture, last I heard, hangs in the hospital's lobby). According to stories handed down by my grandmother, Lillian, to my father, Dr. Kerr "scared his patients to death" with his stern bedside manner.

Sadly, this is all I have regarding my pioneer ancestors, though I have been told how fortunate I am to know "so much" about my family history. How unfortunate that most people today don't know even this little. I have been carrying around pictures of my grandmother, Lillian May Craig, for many years, and have only recently begun to understand why much of my art work concerns depictions of talking about "family stories." It seems a shame to me to let them all just fade away with time. In talking about my family history, I understand why I am here. And, isn't that one of life's great mysteries that concerns us all?

William John Clarke

BY MARILYN ORNBAUN

 William John Clarke, son of Scottish-Irish parents, Dougal and Jane Tease Clarke, was born January 7, 1820 at Carricknamart, Parish Ray, Ireland. He emigrated to America in 1839 at the age of nineteen. Locating first in Louisiana, then moving up the Mississippi River, he made his home in Mercer and, later, Rock Island Counties, Illinois, as did many Irish from the Donegal area. He was naturalized in March of 1848 at the District Court of Rock Island County.

The lure of the West called him in early 1849. He came with a wagon trail group, which endured a few hardships along the way. We have a copy of his diary in which he tells of shooting a young buffalo along the way, and having a nice buffalo supper. He mentions it being so cold in April that they had to cover the horses with their blankets and do for themselves as best they could. In June, prior to the emigrants cutoff road, or the junction of the Fort Hall Road, he mentions traveling west over some beautiful bottom land all covered with flowers of almost every description. "Well might be said of this that a man can pull flowers with one hand and make snow balls with the other." The next day he states, "The musketoes are most devilish bad here. . . . We came to Bear Springs about twenty in number, where the water tasted like beer of the sharpest kind. Some wood this evening for the first camp of wood for seven hundred miles."

"We had a visit from twenty-five or thirty Snake and half-breed Indians, also some flat heads, which look hard cases. Our camp is at the base of the small Euta Mts." Upon coming into

Carson Valley, his diary states, "It is a beautiful place, the clover here is some three feet long and thick. If I had such land in Illinois I would have stayed there." William's strong character and generous nature show in his notes of the trip.

William had been schooled in the Ray Charter School, built in 1740. This was the only charter school in Donegal, Ireland in the Manor Cunningham area near Letterkenny. He was very well educated; his handwriting is quite formal, and very neat. It is now called the Ray National School and is still very active. Many of the children attending today have the same family names as those attending in the 1800s, including Clarke. Some Clarke family members still live at Carricknamart.

Upon arriving in California, William first tried his luck at mining and was rather successful. He was then employed as a carpenter on the Anchor House, the first brick building in Sacramento, located at Front and M Streets, for which he received twenty dollars a day. Mr. George Zins (Sinze) from Germany was the builder. The bricks were manufactured by Zins near Sutterville. The building was first known as Anchor House, then as The Green Tree, and finally as The Pioneer.

By 1850 William and his partner, John Stewart, were engaged in "packing" — with a train of mules each able to pack about 300 pounds of supplies, of which freight charges could run from six cents to seventy-five cents per pound, depending upon the distance to be packed. Soon after, they purchased 320 acres of property in Yolo County, four miles west of Knight's Landing, where they engaged in farming and the making of Spanish saddle trees. By 1862 William and his partner had purchased 1320 acres of land, and planted wheat. Three years later they had a crop of forty-five bushels to the acre on the dry-plowed five hundred acres sowed in the fall. This acreage was called the Buckeye Ranch.

William's younger brother, Noble Clarke, emigrated from

Donegal to California prior to 1856, where he too purchased land in the same area and farmed. During this time the Clarke brothers showed their Irish tempers in two trials held at Knights Landing. Justice of the Peace Samuel Patrick opened court under the sycamore tree fronting the Sacramento River, where the Snowball Mansion was later built. The case: Noble Clarke vs. I.W. Jacobs on some minor matter. Jacobs, acting as his own attorney, commenced his argument of the defense before a sleepy jury of six. The defendant made a derogatory slur on the character of Clarke. Suddenly the hammer of a pistol directed against his ear snapped harmlessly on a cap. Instantly knives and guns leaped into the hands of the spectators as each took sides. Judge Patrick leaped to safety in the trees along the riverbank with an admonition to the jury to "Run, boys, run, or every devil of you will be shot." Friends interceded and hostilities were averted without much further ado, whereupon the Justice resumed his seat. He opined, as though he had just arrived for the trial, "Here's the court, now where the hell's the jury?"

Three months later, William J. Clarke was called before His Honor to defend himself for a crime of "putting an extension on the head of a legal limb of the law." Clarke had assaulted a lawyer whose name is lost from history. For a day and a half the boring case had continued when Clarke suddenly moved the court to adjourn outdoors where plaintiff and defendant might settle their differences with a round or two of fisticuffs. The party being thrashed was to pay all costs of the suit. Squire Patrick leaped from his seat, adjusted his coat, removed his glasses, and stepped away from the bench. "That's a fair proposition," he ruled. "If anyone wants a squarer proposition than that, he's a damned coward."

William married Catherine Foster Tinney of County Fermamagh, Ireland, later of Illinois. They had seven children: Elizabeth, William Dougal, Margaret Jane, Catherine May, Foster Noble,

Celia, and George W.D.

By the year 1879 they owned a farm two miles southeast of College City, Colusa County, which was in vineyards from which raisins were produced. They had a stately, two-story home in the town of College City for their large family, which included — besides their own seven children — two nieces: Jenny (his sister Margaret Clarke Bourgoie's daughter); and Cora, (the daughter of James Washington Foster, his wife's brother). When the College City Christian College was opened, the Clarke family boarded a few students who were attending school there. This is where my grandfather, Foster Noble Clarke, met my grandmother to be, Martha "Mattie" Belle Gates of Red Bluff, Tehama County.

William was Justice of the Peace in Antelope (now Dunnigan, Yolo County). He served as roadmaster, and was a member of I.O.O.F., Masons, Sons of Temperance, and was a trustee of the College City Christian Church.

On June 2, 1870 William John Clarke applied to become a member of the Sacramento Society of California Pioneers, being recommended by C.F. Reed, his Yolo County neighbor. His large framed certificate of membership, dated January, 1873, now hangs in the Taylorsville Museum, Plumas County. His photo appears in the group of all the Sacramento members. Copies of this photo hang in the Sacramento Valley Museum in Williams, Colusa County, and in Sutter's Fort in Sacramento, as well as some private homes.

William purchased land in Plumas County in the Big Meadows area (now Chester and Lake Almanor) and took his cattle there each summer. The cattle drive to Big Meadows took three weeks from Yolo County. One night was always spent under Hooker Oak in Chico, prior to starting up the Humbug-Humboldt Road. The Clarke family spent all their summers at Big Meadows. Two of their children married members of the Stover family of that area. His daughter, Catherine May "Katie," married George R. Stover. She became the first librarian in the newly constructed Log Cabin Library along the Feather River in Chester, in the 1920s. His son, William Dougal, married Annie Stover.

William Clarke died on October 28, 1894. He had carved a successful and admired life for himself and his family in America. He was civic minded and extremely family oriented.

Elias Beard and James Hawley

BY JEANETTE BEARD KORSTAD

I am a descendent of two early southern Alameda County families — Elias Lyman Beard and James Hawley — both of whom came to California in 1849 to seek their fortunes in gold. Beard settled in Mission San Jose and made his home in the abandoned mission buildings until Bishop Alemany reclaimed the mission property. He then moved across the road and built a home in the estate that is known as Palmdale. Beard had a general store in the Mission and sold supplies to the gold prospectors going to the southern mines.

Meanwhile James Hawley followed his trade as carpenter and built a number of buildings in that area. In 1879 Hawley went to Alaska to manage a silver mine. However, disaster struck and the enterprise was abandoned. Hawley returned to California and followed his trade as a carpenter and farmer.

Meanwhile Beard, not content with a small farming operation, acquired thirty thousand acres and farmed on a grand scale. He planted potatoes when everyone else did, and that year there was an oversupply and barges full of potatoes were dumped into the bay. He was a friend of John C. Fremont and managed his Mariposa grant. Later he tried to develop an oil well in Mattole, Humboldt County, and dealt in various speculations — all of which were unsuccessful. He was the second president of the California State Agricultural Society, the forerunner of the California State Fair. Beard died May 8, 1880.

Reverend Samuel Gray

BY DOROTHY JOHNSON WATERBURY

 The 1830s and '40s were times of bitter religious controversy, prejudice, and persecution. The Mormons, because they were practicing plural marriages, were persecuted, shunned, and stripped of their possessions. They fled from Nauvoo, Hancock County, Illinois in 1841, eleven thousand of them making their way to the desert of Utah, to what is now Salt Lake City.

In the summer of 1849 a Mormon by the name of Jefferson Hunt made up a train of 107 wagons and headed west. The Derr-Gruwell train of twenty-three — among whom were Reverend Gray, a minister of the Southern Methodist Church born in 1814, and the Reverend Jacob Gruwell, and their families — followed them out from Missouri in late summer, planning to winter at Fort Utah sixty miles south of Salt Lake. Learning that Mormons were about to attack the Gruwells, their train gave them horses and mules to go ahead of them to Los Angeles. They broke camp and followed, staying ahead of the Hunt train with a Mexican guide.

About three hundred miles from Los Angeles provisions and supplies ran low. They began to see evidence that others before them had been forced to sacrifice their property by abandoning it near what is now Barstow. Two weeks later the Gruwells met the train again, suffering from lack of the necessities of life. Jacob Gruwell had had fifteen head of cattle when he started west. He walked into Los Angeles with one ox and one cow. The train arrived in Rancho Cucamonga in November, 1849. Margaret Cox Gray, the mother of Samuel Gray's children, died in childbirth.

Reverend Samuel Gray

She and the baby were buried January 24, 1850 in Rubidios Rancho
(now called Downey), twenty miles from Los Angeles. Both mother

and infant were wrapped in the last oxen hide for burial.

Samuel Gray had a blacksmith shop in Sacramento and preached on Sundays. There was a fire and flood in Sacramento and he moved his motherless family to San Jose.

The oldest daughter, Rebecca, was married to Jeremiah Johnson on December 2, 1852 at Squirrel Creek Ranch. Jeremiah and his father, known only as "Mr. Johnson," had traveled in the same wagon train. Samuel Gray married a widow, Rachel Mann; both died of typhoid fever and were buried at Los Noretos, California. Rebecca and Jeremiah Johnson are buried in San Luis Obispo, where he had been a rancher. Melchi Cox Gray, my great-grandfather, was drowned in 1864 at the juncture of the Sacramento and American Rivers. He is in a marked grave in Sacramento.

Jefferson James, Cattle King

BY MAUDEE GRAVES

 "Cattle King" was a popular name for very large cattle-men in the early days of California, and Mr. James exemplified the characteristics "which forcibly illus-trate the effect of America's frontier culture and institutions in developing strong men."

James' father, John Robinson James, a Virginian, and his mother, Elizabeth Thompson, a Kentuckian, were descendents of English people and early settlers in America. They emigrated to the terri-tory of Missouri in 1820. John was a physician by profession and a farmer at heart. He gave his son a keepsake in the form of a note that in turn was given to his grandson, my father, Jeff Graves. The note is signed by Thomas Jefferson, President of the United States of America and promises to pay his dear cousin the money he had so kindly loaned him.

James was born on December 12, 1829. The panic and de-pression in Missouri in 1837-1842 and the discovery of gold in California aroused his curiosity to see California. At about age eighteen or twenty, with his brother, Thomas B. James, a brother-in-law, James L. Alford, and a friend, George Ogle, he joined a train of wagons captained by Jeff Alman, who was passing through South Pass and Green Raft Rivers, Idaho on the way to California. The going was so slow the young men decided to leave the wagon train behind and, cutting up the wagon wheels, they converted them into pack saddles to put on the mules. Since the mules were unused to anything but pulling wagons, they had quite a roundup before the mules behaved.

Jefferson Gilbert James

The group reached Hangtown in August of 1850 and Jeff and Thompson mined at Rocky Creek Bar until 1853, making $3,000 a piece in gold dust. They supposedly went as far as the middle fork of the American River and then returned to Missouri by way of Nicaragua (the Isthmus of Panama), traveling to New York by boat, and then by rail to Missouri.

Thompson stayed in Missouri, but Jeff purchased a small herd of dairy cattle and herded them to California. The heifers were barren and he sold them as beef. This was the beginning of his cattle business. He amassed huge land holdings on the west side of Fresno and built the James Canal. He dug artesian wells, the largest being bored to a depth of 800 feet, yielding 50,000 gallons of water per minute to irrigate the arid land to graze his cattle. He built several towns, one of which, Tranquility, is still in existence.

James was sued by Henry Miller, who said James had no right to take water out of the San Joaquin River to irrigate his land. James won that suit and still retained a friendly relationship with Miller. I must refute one story about James, where gossip has him rowing a boat on top of a wagon to claim marsh lands that the government was releasing. In my family, that story was always attributed to Henry Miller.

By the year 1890 James branded about 4,000 calves a year and shipped more than 2,000 head of beef to his wholesale butcher company in San Francisco. The company slaughtered twenty to thirty bulls and ten to fifteen calves daily, in addition to hogs and sheep. By then he had moved his residence to San Francisco, was elected to the Board of Supervisors and, among other things, ran for Mayor of San Francisco, but was defeated by Adolph Sutro.

James married Lucinda Jane "Jennie" Rector of Missouri. She was the daughter of Jesse Holt Rector and Cynthia Strother. Her brother came with James to California and built and lived in the historic National Hotel in Nevada City, where they also established a bank and developed the town. The name "Rector," originally "Richter," is from an old German family which developed Rictorville, Virginia in about 1714, and who were a part of Germantown, whose people were skilled in mining and steel and came from Nassau-Sieger.

James' only child, Maude Strother James, lived a lavish life in San Francisco, developing the famous Pink Palace on Scott Street near Green. She married Walker Coleman Graves, a graduate of the University of Kentucky Law School. He moved to San Francisco to become Assistant District Attorney of San Francisco. He befriended and defended a Chinese prince by the name of Sue Lock, became the first attorney for the Chinese Six Companies, and was retained by them for the rest of his life. He was a high ranking Mason and was buried with honors. His widow, Maude Graves, traveled to Europe, lived in Paris for a while, and eventually married William Loller, a real estate broker. She was a colorful, flamboyant, witty, talented, eccentric woman in San Francisco, where she became a benefactress of the arts. She still loved to ride the range on her father's vast ranch where she could shoot and hunt as well as any man.

Walker and Maude James Graves had three sons: Jefferson James (my father), Walker Coleman, and Rector Gilbert (deceased at about age twelve to fourteen years.) Jefferson Graves' first love was ranching in the foothills of the Sierras east of Fresno. He and his brother eventually established a small town known as Gravbros, now wiped out by floods. Mr. Graves developed Oak Shadows Ranch where he raised race horses, planted vineyards, and marketed Sample and Graves wine in the late 1930s.

Edmund Valentine Hathaway

BY KATHARINE ANNE BUFFUM HATHAWAY AND FRAN HELMKE

The following account of his life was sent to Brown University at the time of his death. It was hand written by his wife (my grandmother), Katharine Anne Buffum Hathaway. This was probably written in early January, 1900.

Edmund Valentine Hathaway of the Class of 1870 was born in Freetown, Massachusetts on the eighteenth day of January, 1818. His parents were Edmund Hathaway and Betsy Hathaway, both New Englanders by birth.

His early years were spent in the peace and quiet of his native village. At the age of fourteen he was sent to the Friends School in Providence, R.I. and from there he entered the Academy of the Rev. Orville Briggs, one of the early educators of New England, at Middleborough, Massachusetts, where he completed his preparation for college. After graduating from Brown University in the year 1840, he commenced the study of medicine in the office of Dr. Laprelate Miller, one of the first of New England's surgeons, completing his studies at the medical department of the University of Pennsylvania and at the Massachusetts General Hospital.

He commenced the practice of his profession in Providence, R.I., but very soon, upon hearing of the discovery of gold in California in 1849, he joined the army of fortune hunters who were so eagerly rushing to the field of promise. At the expiration of two years, finding pioneer life distasteful, he started on his homeward voyage, making the circuit of the globe on the way, and resumed the practice of his profession in Providence. Three years later he again started for the golden land, this time to enter into mercantile life in which he remained until a few years of his death.

In 1861, feeling the need of a respite from the cares of business, he again returned to New England, after which he made a hurried trip to Europe.

In September, 1862 he married Katharine A. Buffum of Providence, and in November of the same year left for California, never again to revisit the home of his early years.

Carrying with him to his adopted home his New England inheritance of integrity and persistence, he was one of the makers of California, working with zeal and determination for all that concerned her welfare. In the early years of the state, when in that new country crime seemed to be overpowering justice, he was among those sterling men of San Francisco who, determined that wrong should no longer run riot in their midst, banded themselves together in the famous Vigilance Committee of 1856.

During his forty-eight years of life in California he had the satisfaction of witnessing the unparalleled transformation of the little struggling Mission planted upon the sand dunes of the Pacific Ocean in the name of Saint Francis into a great and prosperous city, standing guard upon our western shore and opening wide its gates wherein might pour the wealth of the Orient.

He was from early manhood a Unitarian in religious belief, and was an ardent supporter of that faith by work and deed during the pastorate of Thomas Starr King, and of all others who succeeded him at the First Unitarian Church of San Francisco.

The last few years of his life after retirement from business were passed in the tranquil enjoyment which a well-spent life ensured, in a lovely home amid the beautiful hills of Berkeley, which are the setting of the great University of California. There he passed away after a brief illness on the tenth day of December, 1899 at the age of eighty-two years. His wife, two daughters, and one son survive him.

Hiram Throop Graves

BY HARRIET HENDERSON BROWNE

 Herewith is the history of Hiram Throop Graves as told me by my grandmother, father, and aunt, and elaborated by gleanings from Hiram's papers, various publications, and public records:

Born in Batavia, New York on December 12, 1824, son of Samuel and Polly Bostwick Graves (daughter of William Bostwick, prominent civic leader of Auburn, New York and his wife Hannah Warner), Hiram was named for his godfather, Hon. Enos T. Throop, Governor of New York, 1831-33. In every branch of his lineage the infant's ancestors had been early colonial Americans.

The family (eventually thirteen children) moved back to Auburn, New York in 1826 where his father continued as a silver and goldsmith, horologer, and inventor. He was also an active Mason.

Hiram was a graduate of Auburn Academy, the highest secular school in Cayuga County at the time. Then he became a successful horticulturist/nurseryman, seemingly set for life. However, at the news of the Gold Rush, he and seventy-nine young men incorporated the Cayuga Joint Stock Company, which purchased and provisioned the barque *Belvedere*, and, "with cargo most judiciously chosen," sailed from New York on February 25, 1849, for San Francisco via Cape Horn, stopping in Callao for water and other provisions. They dropped anchor in San Francisco Bay on October 12, 1849, the voyage having taken 228 days. He was twenty-five years old. (His father followed him June-October, 1850 on one of the first steamships, the *Northerner*, but by way of the Straits of Magellan.) The Van Ness House on Stockton between

Broadway and Vallejo Street was built by the Cayuga Joint Stock Co. with lumber brought on the *Belvedere*. It was moved in the early 1860s to the north side of Chestnut Street, between Mason and Taylor Streets. It was the first three-story house in San Francisco.

Hiram stayed in the city until 1850 when he and a fellow "Belvederan," W.S. Lyon, went to Auburn, California where they mined successfully until June, when they moved to the South Fork of the Yuba River. Later they moved to Illinoistown on the Bear River, Hiram leaving for San Francisco in October to meet his father. Hiram never returned to mining, but made a career of business as did so many other successful forty-niners.

In 1853 the young man went back to Auburn, New York, and while there married Melissa Chadwick, on October 24,1854. Their children were Charles Henry Graves (who married Josephine Browell, literally "the girl next door") and Hiram Augustus Graves.

Shortly after returning to San Francisco the ex-miner joined the venerable "pioneer assay office in San Francisco, Moffat & Co.," which later became Curtis, Perry, and Ward, then the U.S. Assay Office, and in 1854 the San Francisco Branch of the U.S. Mint. Mr. Graves continued as an employee through all those changes and became Assistant Coiner at the Mint, a most important and prestigious post. Mr. M. Eckfeldt, whose grandfather had been appointed the first Coiner at the Philadelphia Mint by President Washington, was named Coiner. I well remember my father pointing with great pride at the Old Mint as we drove by, telling his children that his grandfather had had a very responsible position there.

In 1859 both Hiram and John Eckfeldt resigned from the Mint to incorporate the firm Eckfeldt and Graves, when they bought the California Wire Works at 412 Clay Street. The firm made wire as well as wire cable and other products. It was the first wire works on the Pacific Coast, started in 1852 by a Mr. Dennis. Although

Hiram sold his interest in 1874 to Eckfeldt's estate, he was one of the incorporators of the successor company and a director.

Another partner was Andrew S. Hallidie, said to be the inventor of San Francisco's cable cars. Others believe the inventor was Hiram's father, Samuel Graves, who with his inventor's mind, a patent for making rope much the same as wire cable, and his knowledge of manufacturing wire cable was a more likely candidate. Herb Caen once addressed this subject in his column.

"A Life Member of the Society of California Pioneers, Mr. Graves served as a director, 1868-69, was appointed Secretary in 1884, and served until 1890." My grandmother and Roy Graves told me Hiram had a Society of Pioneers' gold pin which was for the original members only. It was lost or misplaced long before my birth. However, there is a silver member's pin in my possession which belonged to Hiram or John Taylor, Hiram's brother-in-law and Grandma's uncle.

After Melissa Graves died Augusta Taylor became the second Mrs. Hiram T. Graves, at Grace Cathedral in 1864. She had come to California from Westport, Connecticut to visit her two brothers. The children of that marriage were Bessie Bostwick (Mrs. George L. Henderson Sr.) and Augusta Taylor Graves.

Hiram was one of the founders of the Masonic Savings Bank, and in 1873 was elected its Secretary, a position he held for the life of the institution. With others he also founded the Mt. Olivet Cemetery in Colma and was its secretary in the first years.

The Hiram T. Graves family lived at 204 Lombard Street, at the corner of Kearny Street, in San Francisco. Bessie, my grandmother and the elder daughter of the family, told me that while she was a student at the University of California in the late 1880s, she would stand in the house high up on Telegraph Hill with its wonderful view of the Bay, watching for the ferry boat to peek out from Goat Island (a.k.a. Yerba Buena) on its way to the City. At that point she would run out of the house, pick up her long skirt, and run down the steep streets to the Embarcadero and along to the Ferry Building in time to catch the ferry boat to the East Bay to attend her classes at the new university in Berkeley.

Bessie's father was far ahead of his time, although well in tune with many men in the newer western part of the United States. Because their women were their equals in their endeavors, from their difficulties in travels to being far fewer in number once they arrived in California, to the influence of Spanish laws favoring women far more than those of England ever thought of doing, California men often encouraged their daughters to attend college or in other ways to prepare themselves to be self-sufficient. Hiram was no exception. Bessie graduated from the University of California in 1889 (as did her future husband's sister and his cousin, Nellie Johnson, who became a much-beloved teacher at Oakland High School). Hiram's other daughter, Augusta, a fine artist, attended the famous Cooper Union in New York City to study painting in various media and won a silver medal for "drawing from the antique."

The Graves family often spent spare time or vacations at Willow Camp, a popular country spot, which I think was near Stinson Beach. At other times the entire Graves Clan, Hiram's brother, Augustus, and all his children would go to Tomales where they and their friends would play games, involve themselves in plays, musicals, or other entertainments of that period.

Physically, Hiram was not large, probably about 5' 6", but his full white beard and white hair made him stand out among the citizens of the area. He had a "wicked" sense of humor (inherited by many of his descendants), was gregarious and genial, albeit autocratic. Happy, he loved children and their tricks and the feeling was reciprocated — and he ruled his empire with a firm hand.

Hiram and his father gave of their time and energy in support of two schools associated with the old St. Paul's Episcopal Church in Benicia, once the state's capitol city. The girls' academy was St. Mary's of the Pacific, the boys' was St. Augustine's College. Hiram's two sons were, of course, enrolled in the college. Unfortunately their attendance was short. One day the boys led a cow up the stairs to the front entrance as a joke, but the cow proved intractably resistant to descending the steep slope of the steps. Both boys were quickly expelled — evidently neither those in the educational establishment nor their parents had retained a sense of humor, but the youngsters had had an attention-getting lesson in responsibility and consequences.

As part of his civic involvement Hiram served on the Board of Directors for the San Francisco City Schools for many years. Feeling it necessary to stop violence in the city, he served on the Committee of Vigilance of 1856.

An Episcopalian, Hiram joined the Grace Cathedral parish in the early years, and served as a Vestryman and Superintendent of the Sunday School. Later the family joined St. Peter's, which he and his father, Samuel, helped found, where he performed the same duties. He was an organizer and Trustee of the Old Ladies' Protestant Episcopal Church Home, and Treasurer of the California Diocese for ten years. He was also instrumental in founding and supporting the Masonic Home in Alameda County.

Toward the end of his life, Hiram and his wife moved to Alameda where they lived happily near their daughter and her family, his other daughter, Augusta T., and his sister, Hannah Sophia Graves, who for many years "kept house" for him and Augusta.

At his death, September 24, 1902, there were two funeral services — at St. Peter's Episcopal Church, and an hour later the ritual at the San Francisco Masonic Temple. A procession was organized by the Masons and their leaders, who, in all their regalia, proceeded to Mt. Olivet Cemetery in Colma, *en masse*, accompanied by the family and other mourners. My aunt, Muriel H. Rich, who was seven years old at the time, told me there were so many partici-pants in the procession that they blocked the streets as they went along.

Ithiel Corbett

BY ELLYNDA MIELER DUNCAN

 My great-great-grandfather, Ithiel Corbett, was born December 4, 1810 in Melford, Massachusetts. His parents were Robert and Lucretia (Madden) Corbett. Ithiel moved from Milford with his father to Mina, New York in 1824. In 1831 he married Catherine Cross, and in 1836, with his wife and two sons, John and William, moved to Andrew, Jackson County, Iowa.

In May, 1849 Ithiel, with his sixteen-year-old son, John, left Iowa for California. Arriving in Salt Lake City they joined Captain Jefferson Hunt, of the Death Valley Party. Upon arrival at the old Cucamonga Winery in San Bernadino County on December 24, 1849 they were among the few persons still remaining with Hunt's party. Ithiel and John walked from Southern California, following the coast, then traveled inland to Stockton, Calaveras, Angels Camp, and Feather River, as far north as Nevada City, California. They mined in these regions for two years, making an average of fifty dollars to one hundred dollars per day.

In 1852 Ithiel returned to Mina, New York (by way of Panama), where his family had been living while he was in California. Later that year he returned with his family to Iowa. In 1857 he made the second trip to California, this time bringing his family by covered wagon. They came by way of Humboldt Sink, arriving in Nevada City that same year.

The family moved to Stockton in 1860. After the flood of 1862 the family moved to Mission San Jose, Alameda County, where Ithiel and his sons took up government lands, which was grain and cattle range. Ithiel was a prosperous farmer.

Ithiel Corbett

At some time before 1860, Ithiel returned a second time to New York by way of Panama. On the return trip, he sailed from New York on the steamer *Grenada* to Panama, from there to San Francisco on the ship *John Stephen*. Ithiel Corbett passed away January 23, 1895 and is buried in San Bernardino, California.

Ithiel and Catherine had eight children:

John, b. 1833, New York. — d. 1876, California.
William, b. 1835, Mina, NY — d. 1882, San Jose, California

257

Walter, b. 1838, Andrew, Iowa — d.1867, San Jose

Jasper, b. 1838, Andrew, Iowa — d. California

George, b. 1845 Andrew, Iowa — d Ferndale, California

Robert, b. 1846, Andrew, Iowa — d. Grass Valley

Henry, b. Andrew Iowa — d. California

Amos, b. Andrew, Iowa — d. California

Dr. Gustave Herman Malech

BY ETHYL C. PAULLY

 Dr. Gustave Herman Malech, my great-grandfather, was a native of Weda-Saxe, Weimar, Germany. His family migrated to Pennsylvania while he was a youth. He graduated from the Philadelphia College of Medicine and Surgery (now University of Pennsylvania), and went on to San Francisco at the time of the Gold Rush. We believe he arrived by sea. My grandmother, many years ago, gave me a jewel box which she said "came around the Horn."

Dr. Malech was a founding member of the San Francisco Medical Society. He is recorded in the official register of Physicians and Surgeons of January 1893, covering the period 1850-1900. He was also one of the early day Odd Fellows in San Francisco, Harmony Lodge 13. He was a musician and composer. At one time he was surgeon for the old sixth Regiment, commissioned by Governor Lowe.

Early day directories of the city of San Francisco show that he had an office at Montgomery and Pine Streets and resided at 105 Post Street. Nearing his retirement years, he moved his offices to 601 Golden Gate Avenue, the location of my great-grandmother's home. Later he moved his practice to 520 Van Ness Avenue.

The Malech family had a medical tradition of long standing. Our family tree shows Johann Malech, 1730 and August Malech, 1801 as "Barber-doctors."

In the January 15, 1900 issue of *The Pioneer,* a local San Jose periodical, Dr. Malech's obituary appears, stating "Dr. Gustave H. Malech, a physician and surgeon, engaged in practice in San Francisco since 1849, died at his residence, January 10, 1900."

Part Eight:
Manuscripts of 1917

   While going through old records from basement storage boxes of Pioneer Hall, an unexpected treasure was uncovered: a collection of manuscripts written in 1917 — brief biographies of the pioneer fathers of some of the early members of the *Daughters of California Pioneers*. As if in anticipation of our centennial project to assemble the stories of our ancestors, seeds planted by our grandmothers were waiting to be discovered.

   In reproducing them here, we have retained the spelling and punctuation of the originals.

Joseph McGregor.

A native of Perth, Scotland, born Feb 28. 1814.
He arrived in San Francisco in Oct. 1848 – coming
from Valparaiso, Chili, where he had gone intending to
become a resident. Within a few months of his arrival
there, the news came of the discovery of gold in California
He then joined the exodus to the land of gold –
He did not go to the mines, but at once established
his business in a tent on the Long Wharf (Commercial St.
wharf) later removed to a one story frame building on Commer
-cial St. west of Sansome. On the completion of the St.
Nicholas Hotel building (S. W. cor Commercial & Sansome Sts.)
he removed to that building where he remained perma-
nantly. As an adjunct to his business, he establish
-ed the San Francisco Observatory. a Transit astronom-
-ical observatory, the first on the Pacific Coast, other
than that maintained by the United States government.
The Observatory was located on a bluff on the south -
-eastern slope of Telegraph Hill. (this location was the eastern
end of Green St. after streets were laid out) From the cu-
-pola of the Observatory a time ball dropped at one o'clk
P. M. daily – Joseph McGregor resided in San Francisco
continuously until his death on October 28. 1867.
He was survived by his wife, four daughters, and
four sons –

Fannie McGregor Weber.
Flora McGregor Egert

262

William H. Hargrave

BY AURA HARGRAVE KYSER

 William H. Hargrave was born in March, 1818. In March, 1843 he joined a party of emigrants at Independence, Missouri and started on a long journey overland to Oregon. In the spring of 1844 he started down the coast on horseback for California by the old Oregon and Sacramento River trail.

Mr. Hargrave was Fremont's guide and escort north of the bay and received from his hands a first lieutenant's commission. He was an active member of the noted Bear Flag party that captured Sonoma on June 14, 1846. He settled in Napa Valley in what is now Calistoga and on April 22nd, 1857 married Anna Collino. He moved to Napa in 1869, living there until his death Sept. 21st, 1890.

Captain Edward Augustus King

BY LIZZIE KING GUINAN

Captain King was born in Salem Mass Sept 2nd 1817 and came to California July 1846 on his own vessel, the Brig *Elizabeth*, which sailed from Boston through the Straits of Magellan. Brigadier General Riley of California, when it was a territory, appointed Capt. King first harbor master of San Francisco.

Captain King was married in Monterey by Walter Calem, Alcalde, May 23rd, 1848 to Miss Sophia P. Clark of Springfield, Mass, who also came to California, July 1846 in the ship *Brooklyn*.

Captain King was interested in the shipping business in San Francisco, the name of the firm was King and Piper. Mr. King was one of the members of the Vigilante Committee.

Mr. King died December 19th 1860 and is buried beside his wife in Salt Lake City, Utah.

Gustavas Wetzlar

BY PAULINA W. DOHRMANN

 My father, Gustavus Wetzlar, a native of Germany, came to America in 1836, and in September 1839 married Louise Dumbach, born in Dixon, Ill.

He came to California in a sailing vessel and settled in California. He engaged in merchandising, then in mining. He resided at various times in Sacramento, Virginia City, Nevada City, and San Francisco. He returned to Germany early in 1851 and spent some time with his family at Leipsic, where I was born, and returned to California early 1853. He died in San Jose, California in 1878, being 74 years old. He was a Charter member of California Society of Pioneers and created and arranged their mineralogical collection.

He had eight children.

My father was identified with Mr. A. Sutro in the "Sutro Canal Cos." and various enterprises. Was one of the founders of the "German Savings and Loan Bank." Among his associates were A. Sutro, Sam Brannan, Gov. Bigler, D.A.B. Stout, John Tallant, W. Chamberlain, Dr. Franklin, Leland Stanford, Mr. Pioche, Dr. Baehr, John Koster, H. Mensdorfer. He spoke seven languages and was graduated from Heidelberg University.

J.H.P. Gedge

BY LUO GEDGE KNOPF

J.H.P. Gedge was born at Tasmania July 18, 1843.
Arrived in San Francisco May 17, 1849.
Married Jarella Marguerite Vallejo, daughter of Salvador Vallejo and niece of Gen. Vallejo.
Is present President of Society of California Pioneers.

Isaiah W. Lees

BY ELLA LEES LEIGH

 My father was born in Yorkshire, England on Christmas Day, 1830. He was the youngest child of John and Elizabeth Lees. His mother brought him to Paterson, New Jersey when he was nine months old, his father having preceded his family. He died when my father was four years old. At the early age of eight years, he was bound out to learn machinery and locomotion building, also learning how to make guns, etc. at the Colt Arms Co. I have a pistol he made. Becoming so proficient in his work as a machinist, he was sent to Cuba to set up machinery. He was between 17 and 18 years old. On the 20th of December 1848, just five days before he was 18, he left New York for California. He was in company with Messrs. John Nightingale, C.C. Updike, F.B. Cadden, R. Lewis, G. Grosvenor, Dr. Barlow and others. He crossed Mexico and sailed from San Blas on the Hawaiian barque *Mary Frances,* arriving in San Francisco May third, 1849. He was the owner and engineer of the first tug out of San Francisco Bay, the *Firefly.* My mother had such strange dreams about the boat that she persuaded him to sell it. A week after he sold it, the *Firefly* was blown up, and her crew drowned.

At the age of 19 he returned to Paterson, New Jersey, and married my mother, Jane A. Fisher, who was born in Lancashire, England, having come to America when she was three years old. Two months after they were married, which occurred February 22, 1850, he sailed again for San Francisco. My mother followed him in October 1852. Mr. Nightingale, who was then Alderman, appointed my father as patrolman on the police force October 26th, 1853. My father lacked two months of being 23. The police force consisted of eight men and he served three months as patrol man. He was then ordered to detective duty and rose rapidly, becoming Captain of Detectives in 1856 and later Chief Detective. He was appointed Chief of the San Francisco Police in 1897, ten weeks after my mother died. He resigned his position January 2, 1900 having served forty-six years, three months continually. He was as well known in Scotland Yard, England as he was in his beloved America. He founded the Rogues' Gallery in the United States, paying for the photos of criminals out of his own pocket. All other states borrowed his invention.

He was a many-sided man and had great mental abilities with a phenomenal memory. Like all public men he led a dual life — the turbulent existence of the official, and the home life where no care but those of his household and family intruded. His home life was ideal and as a husband and father he was adored by his wife, son, and daughter. He was married nearly forty-seven years when my mother died and they had five children. Fred and myself were the only two who lived beyond babyhood. My brother Frederic, who was a Jr. Pioneer, died in his sleep February 21, 1903, just two months after my father died.

My father died on Sunday morning at five minutes past seven December 21, 1902, aged 71 years, 11 months, and 26 days. He was buried from Masonic Temple Fidelity Lodge, December 23, 1902. A sad Christmas for Fred and myself.

William Downie

BY ADELINA BELL DOWNIE

 William Downie was born in Irvin Airshire, Scotland, in 1819. Came to America arriving in Quebec in 1940. Sailed on Lake Ontario and Lake Erie in freight and lumber business for eight years. Heard of gold discovery in fall of 1848, went to Boston, shipped on Brig *Monterey* for New Orleans. Upon arrival there found the clipper ship *Architect* of Baltimore in command of Captain Grey, waiting one man to complete the crew, signed the papers and sailed for San Francisco around the Horn, dropping anchor in San Francisco Bay on the 27th of June, 1849.

Left for the mines on the 5th of July, landed in Sacramento on July 16th, resuming his journey to the Yuba by way of Nyes, got to Foster Bar on October 5th, saw the forks of the Yuba and the site of the place which is now Downeyville, Sierra Co. Picked up 400 lbs of nuggets in six weeks that fall. Called that home till he heard of the Fraser River Strike. Left Downeyville and went north, arriving in Victoria in July 1858. The gold strike not proving to be as rich as expected, returned to Victoria and went on an exploring expedition for Governor James Douglas to find a pass for a railroad. Finding the pass, posted a notice on September 22, 1859, claiming it for the Great Canadian RR.

Later years brought the Cassiar and Caribus strikes. Was interested and arrived in both districts; the best was on Williams Creek in Caribus. In 1874 went to Panama to dig gold from Indian graves, spent six months down there; obtained very little gold, but found ancient pottery in large quantities. Brought back several boxes. I gave the Pioneer Society of San Francisco some, also the Nevada Pioneers at Carson City. Visited Alaska during the summer of 1876

Was married in Victoria in 1862 to Miss Adeline Davidson of Charlottowne, Prince Edward Island. Of this union three children were born: Flora Ellen, William John, and Adelina Bell.

Robert Joyce Tiffany

BY EMMA TIFFANY MCGREGOR

Robert Joyce Tiffany (my father) in company with nineteen associates, purchased the bark *Josephine* at New York, and embarked from that port January 10, 1849, via Cape Horn, for San Francisco, and arrived July 9, 1849 after an uneventful voyage.

After resting in San Francisco for a few days, they left for the various mines. Shortly after locating at the mine, my father was stricken with Panama fever and returned to his former home in New York.

Before finally settling here in 1856, he had returned to New York at least three times. In 1857 he opened the hat store on Washington Street between Kearny and Montgomery Streets, opposite Maguire's Opera House. At the organization of the old Clay Street Bank, my father was made director of that well known institution, and retained that position for many years.

In 1866 he was elected president of the Society of California Pioneers, and while in the chair he founded and liberally contributed to the benevolent fund of that body. This fund has since become most helpful to many of the old Pioneers who through sickness or misfortune have needed this aid.

Albert Kuner

BY BERTHA KUNER

 Albert Kuner was born in Lindau, Bavaria, October 9th, 1819. He emigrated to America and arrived at New York early in the year in company with three fellow townsmen. Being an expert goldsmith and engraver, he found lucrative employment at t . . . in the metropolis, but when the news of the gold discoveries in California reached New York, he decided in company with friends, to strike out for the New El Dorado and on January 1, 1849 they embarked on the ship *Sutton* for San Francisco via Cape Horn. Everything went well until they reached the Caribbean Sea, when they were overtaken by a severe tropical storm and the ship began leaking so badly that the captain decided to make for the port of Rio de Janeiro. On arriving there, it was found that it would take three weeks time to make the ship sea worthy. During the enforced delay, Mr. Kuner made trips into the interior, visiting the Palace of Dom Pedro, who was king of Brazil at that time and other places of interest. After repairs had been accomplished, they again set sail, all went smoothly until they reached the lower latitude of the continent, where they again encountered frightful storms; for weeks the ship was tossed about, endeavoring to get around Cape Horn. The supply of food on board became polluted, and to add to their trouble, the ship again leaked so badly that not alone the crew, but also the passengers, were compelled to man the pumps. The task was eventually accomplished and they arrived at Valparaiso, Chile, where the necessary repairs were made, and a fresh supply of provisions were taken on board. They again set sail, arriving in San Francisco Bay the 22nd of July 1849.

Mr. Kuner's skill as an engraver was soon recognized. He

engraved most of the dies for the early gold coins which were cast by the private mints of Moffat & Co. Wass, Molitor & Co. and others who had special license to make coins by order of the National Government. The fifty dollar slug a unique octagon shaped gold coin was one of his many productions, he also engraved the original Great Seal of the State of California.

In 1854 Mr. Kuner returned to Europe via Panama. In August 1854, accompanied by his bride, he returned by the Nicaragua Route, where he then made his permanent home in San Francisco, where he finally departed to the Great Beyond in January 1906. He is survived by five children, Rudolph, Anna, Bertha, Mrs Ida Herner, and Mrs. Martha Gehrcke.

William B. Latham

BY ELIZABETH W. LATHAM

William B. Latham was born in Flushing, Long Island, November 12, 1822. Taught school at the age of seventeen. Graduated from the State Normal School, Albany New York, class of 1841. Took a course in Medical Jurisprudence, studied law, was interested in the *Teachers' Advocate* 1848 published in New York City.

The New York Mining Co. bought the Bark *Strafford,* sailing from New York City, Saturday, February 3, 1849, via Cape Horn, for the new El Dorado, and arriving at San Francisco August 30, 1849. Others in the company, besides Mr. Latham, were Jos W. Winans, Frank B. Austine, C.D. Carter, D. Squire, and several others. Mr. Latham engaged in gold digging, drove ox teams, and finally in the Express & Exchange, business agent for Freeman & Adams Express at Marysville, Notary Public and Real Estate. Practiced law associated with Judge Bryant. Charter member of Yuba Guards (organized 1855), also its secretary. Original member and secretary of Corinthian Lodge #69. Charter member of Washington Chapter #13 R.A.M.

Returned to New York in 1860 and married Phoebe Bell Carpenter, daughter of A.C. Carpenter, draughtsman and shipbuilder. Returned to California and settled in Marysville.

Mrs. W. B. Latham was noted for her charity and church works. In 1872 she, with other ladies, founded what is now known as St. Paul's Episcopal Church in San Francisco. The first meeting and services were held in her house.

Mr. Latham was appointed by Abraham Lincoln a Commissioner of the Board of Enrollment for the Northern District of the State of California, during the Civil War, ranking as Lieutenant. In 1866 he left Marysville and came to San Francisco, where he resided until his death.

Interested in mining, real estate, insurance, farming, rail roads. Took active interest in state and national politics. Among his friends were Judge N. Greene Curtis, Justice Stephen J. Field, Noah Brooks, Gen. G.A. Sutter, Gov. F.F. Low, Senators Geo. C. Perkins, Leland Stanford, Cornelius Cole, Chas. N. Felton, Charles E. DeLong, Chas R. Story, Thos B. Shannon, Timothy Guy Phelps, C. Huntington, Stephen Gage, J.B. Freeman, Judge J.F. Halsey, and John F. Miller.

Mr. Latham died in San Francisco, December 7, 1910.

John Ogilvie

BY MRS. HENRY C. SIERING

 John Ogilvie was born in St. John, New Brunswick in 1823. He was a descendant of the Earl of Avilie, the head of the main branch of Ogilvies in Scotland. When a young man, he moved to New York City and on July 13, 1848 he was married to Miss Martha McIntyre, a young Scotch girl who had shortly before come to New York from Scotland.

During the excitement in California over the discovery of gold, he was one of those who left for the West. He arrived in San Francisco on the 18th of August, 1849, making the trip around the Horn in a sailing vessel, taking six months to get here. A year later his young wife arrived bringing with her an infant son. John Ogilvie engaged in business in San Francisco, and remained here until his death in October, 1902.

George Henry Eggers

BY IDA EGGERS MEYER

 My Father, George Henry Eggers, was one of the California Pioneers who came on the Peruvian brig *Copiapo*, which sailed on the eighth of May, 1849 from the Bay of Panama, after a voyage of ninety-four days, including the time of stopping at the intermediate ports of Acapulco and Monterey for provisions and water. Arrived safely at last in the Bay of San Francisco.

My father, George Henry Eggers, was a native of Germany. He was born in the village of Lagershausen in the Province of Hanover on the fourteenth of April 1821, and lived since his arrival on the twelfth of August, 1849 in California, where he passed away on the 24th of May, 1896 at the age of 76 years, 1 month, and 8 days.

Daniel Joseph Edgar

BY EMILY CATHERINE EDGAR

 Daniel Joseph Edgar was born in Boston, Massachusetts March 21, 1834. His ancestors came from England in 1640 and settled in Massachusetts in a place afterwards named Edgartown in their honor. His early boyhood was spent with his parents in New Orleans, Louisiana, where his father James Edgar was Judge of the Federal Court of the State of Louisiana.

When the gold fever broke out in 1848, he crossed the plains — then a boy barely fourteen years of age, and went directly to the mines, arriving there Sept. 20th, 1849, spending nearly twenty years in the mines of Mariposa and Tuolumne Counties. In 1868 he came to San Francisco to fill the position of "Chief" of the mailing Dept. on the *Times*. After serving two years in that capacity be became "Chief" of the Mailing Department on the *San Francisco Chronicle*, which position he held for twenty-six consecutive years.

On November 17th, 1869 he married Emily Carolyn Graves, daughter of Dr. Philip Graves, a prominent pioneer physician and surgeon of Stockton, California.

He died April 16th, 1902, leaving his widow, two sons and a daughter.

Frederick H. Pratt

BY CARRIE PRATT ELEVELL

Frederick Henry Pratt was born in Saybrook, Conn, April 18th, 1824.

On the 10th of May, 1849, he crossed the Missouri River en route to California. His party travelled by foot and ox-team and, after many fights with Indians and much sickness, arrived in California in September 1849.

Mr. Pratt engaged in mining and commercial pursuits in different parts of California and was postmaster in San Rafael for many years.

He married Miss Josephine Ponce de León and was the father of a large family. He was a good citizen, exceedingly patriotic, and during the Civil War gave generously to the fund sent out by California for the Union Cause.

Mr. Pratt died in Alameda May 15, 1905, and his funeral was conducted by the Society of California Pioneers.

John C. Meussdorfer

BY IRENE H.E. MEUSSDORFFER

 My father, John C. Meussdorffer was born April 9, 1823 in (Kudenbach) Bavaria, Germany. In May 1847 he left his native country for America, arriving in New York July 4, 1847. He followed the hat business in Albany and Buffalo, his superior knowledge and skill in the business brought him a flattering offer from Havana which he accepted.

When rumor brought the exciting tidings of the discovery of gold in California, he resolved to search the new El Dorado by way of the plains. Returning to New Orleans, he took a steamboat up the Mississippi and Missouri Rivers to St Joseph, where he fitted out for his long and then unknown journey overland. His party consisted of nearly thirty men, women, and children, with five teams of oxen and wagons. When crossing Green River, the head team of oxen, after entering the river, started back for the shore, and this compelled my father to swim the whole width of the river to reach the other side.

He left the East February 1849, arriving in the first white settlement September 19, 1849. After their safe arrival in California, the party disbanded, my father going to Placerville then called Hangtown. Here he met with the varying experiences of gold mining, sometimes successful and sometimes not. Thinking to do better he was among the disappointed at Gold Bluff, at Trinity, and Klamath mines.

In 1852 he came to San Francisco and opened a hat store at Kearny and Sacramento streets and was the first to manufacture fur hats and head gear of that description. Twenty dollars each was then the price for stage-drivers' hats and those knights would wear no other than a Meussdorffer hat, traveling many miles to procure the same.

He married my mother, Caroline Pflinger and had three daughters and five sons by this marriage.

F.G. Ernst Janssen

BY CATHERINE KATZENBACH

 Our father, F.G. Ernst Janssen was born at Vechta, in the Grand Duchy of Oldenburg, in Germany, November 7th, 1830. Vechta is a small walled town celebrated for its manufacture of linens. Here he received his early education, later finishing at one of the gymnasia at Osnabruck.

He was eighteen years old when the news of discovery of gold in America reached the young people of Germany. With some of his neighbors, he set sail on the German bark *Talisman*, leaving Bremen March 1849. After having stopped at Valparaiso, South America, the good ship under the guidance of Captain Maier entered the Golden Gate September 12, 1849. Among its passengers were Edward Kruse, A. Eherhartt, Dr. Precht, and Henry Bremermann. These remained life-long friends.

Soon after landing, young Janssen went with others to Hangtown to mine. Later he returned to San Francisco and took up commercial work. Here he met Miss Leontine C.R. Helmke, who had come to visit her brothers, and was married to her December 3, 1855. About 1857 they moved to Oakland and went into business there. In 1868 he returned to business in San Francisco where he remained until his death, February 28, 1895. He was a member of the famous "Vigilante Society." He took pride in the civic growth of Oakland where he kept his home.

His widow and seven children survive him: Carl A. (a member of the California Pioneers who died in 1905), Edward A., Mrs. A.E. Pirrie, Leontine C.R. Janssen, and Catherine Katzenbach.

Thomas R. Dolliver

BY ELLEN R.D. JEWELL

 Born in Massachusetts May 31,1821. When twelve years of age he was apprenticed to a shoemaker, a trade which he followed for twenty-five years.

In 1844 Mr. Dolliver was married to Miss Anna . . . , an English girl. They made their home in Western Mass for a few years until 1848 when they removed to Milwaukee Wisconsin, accompanied by their two older children. Another child, a daughter, was born soon after their arrival and was but a few months old when the news of the discovery of gold in California was unfolded to the world and, like many young men of that time, Mr. Dolliver was determined to try his fortune in the newly discovered gold region of the far west.

A company was formed in Milwaukee, consisting of some thirty-five or forty men. They called themselves "The Milwaukee Rangers." They left St. Joseph, Mo, April 16, 1849, bound for the Land of Gold. Mr. Dolliver was the cook of the party. All arrived at their destination in safety — October 1, 1849. All members of the party were in good health with the exception of Mr. Dolliver who was suffering from malarial fever. He returned East in 1850.

In 1851 he returned to California and settled in Sonora, afterward in East Oakland. In 1860 all the family moved to San Francisco where they have since resided. Mr. Dolliver established the firm of Dolliver & . . . in 1868 located on Sutter or Polk, and on Market Street. He was strictly honorable and upright in all his dealings and conducted a very highly successful business for more than thirty years. One more child was added to his household, a son born in 1862.

His family of four children survived him. He died in Oakland April 5th, 1911. His wife died in San Francisco in 1905. In the portrait gallery of his native town of Marblehead may be seen among others, a portrait of Mr. Dolliver, accompanied by the following inscription: "Walked across the Plains of America in 1849." Mr. Dolliver's surviving children are Mrs. Sarah Church, Mrs. Ellen Jewell, Mrs. Clara . . . and Thomas Sewall Dolliver.

The above lines were written by his daughter, Ellen R.D. Jewell who treasures his memory with much affection.

Joseph McGregor

BY FANNIE MCGREGOR WEBER AND FLORA MCGREGOR EGERT

 A native of Perth, Scotland, born February 28,1814. He arrived in San Francisco in October 1848, coming from Valparaiso, Chile, where he had gone intending to become a resident. Within a few months of his arrival there, the news came of the discovery of gold in California. He then joined the exodus to the land of gold.

He did not go to the mines, but at once established his business in a tent on the Long Wharf (Commercial Street Wharf) later removed to a one-story frame building on Commercial Street, west of Sansome. On the completion of the St. Nicholas Hotel building (S.W. corner of Commercial and Sansome Streets), he removed to that building where he remained permanently. As an adjunct to his business, he established the San Francisco Observatory. A . . . astronomical observatory, the first on the Pacific Coast, other than that maintained by the United States government. The observatory was located on a bluff on the south-eastern slope of Telegraph Hill (this location was the eastern end of Green Street, after streets were laid out). From the cupola of the observatory a time ball dropped at 1:00 PM daily. Joseph McGregor resided in San Francisco continuously until his death on October 28, 1867. He was survived by his wife, four daughters, and four sons.

Nathan Crowell Paddock

BY MARIE BOUCHER

 Nathan Crowell Paddock, born in East Dennis September 7, 1819. When a young man in his teens, went to Boston, securing a position with a wholesale grocery firm, learning the business. When the cry for gold was heard, he came to San Francisco on the steamer *Unicorn*, arriving October 31, 1849. His first venture in business was flour, hay, and grain, he having the first mill known as "The Golden Era." He was twice burnt out in the two big fires which occurred in those early times.

He next retired from business, going into the "Steam Navigation" of which he was elected President. After the railroad was started, he sold out, then he became interested in mines, where he amassed a fortune.

He returned to Boston and in July 27, 1857, he was married to Mary Elizabeth White. He then returned to San Francisco with his bride. Two sons and three daughters were born to them.

On February 2, 1858 he joined the Society of California Pioneers, being a faithful member. He died in Oakland, California March 9, 1890, after a good and well-spent life.

Part Nine:
The History of the
Daughters of California Pioneers

This summary of the history of the Daughters was compiled from the organization's minutes faithfully recorded over the past one hundred years.

The History of the
Daughters of California Pioneers

The year 1900 introduced a new century. It was also the beginning of a new women's organization. The founding members of
the Society of Daughters of California Pioneers were dedicated
ladies who set the stage for one hundred years of community activities in San Francisco. Their history is an example of the role of
women's clubs in the society of that, time and of their concern
with civic problems, during a period when women had no vote.
They acquired influence by writing letters of endorsement or of
protest to governmental authorities. The Daughters also wanted to
educate themselves about environmental issues and California history. It was a time when society conceded only limited importance
to "educated" women.

So it was on Friday, November 23, 1900 at 2 PM that a meeting of spirited ladies was held in the parlor of the old Pioneer Hall
in San Francisco, headquarters for the original men's Pioneer Society established in 1850. Mrs. Mary Burnett opened the meeting
with a few remarks about the objectives of the organization: to
perpetuate the memories of their mothers and fathers and to "pro-
mote social intercourse among the daughters." Membership was
open only to the daughters of members of the Pioneer Societies of
San Francisco and Sacramento; the records would be searched to
ensure that all forty-six applicants were true daughters of the old
pioneers. Mrs. Burnett was elected President pro-tem of the new
society and Miss Grace de Forest, Secretary.

The ladies met again on December 3, 1900 to elect a Board
of Directors, from which officers would be chosen, and to read a

proposed code of bylaws. Their charter was also extended for thirty days. A notice for the next meeting was placed in local newspapers. On December 20, 1900 the bylaws were read and revised. Articles of Incorporation were filed with the state early in the new year to prevent any other organization using the name. All was set for the new organization to function well into the future. The Society of California Pioneers agreed to allow the Daughters the use of their hall for meetings and social events. Among early activities, a funeral committee was selected to attend the funerals of old pioneers as they passed away. An important decision was made to help the Society of California Pioneers with a reception for President McKinley on the occasion of his visit to San Francisco. Unfortunately, the President was assassinated in Buffalo, New York in December of 1901. The Daughters expressed their sorrow by sending a telegram to the widow and by making a contribution to the McKinley Monument Fund.

The first social event was held in Pioneer Hall on March 18, 1901. It was a great success, described as having been "crowded to the doors." With the election of new officers in December, the ladies had successfully completed their first year and were looking forward to 1902. They celebrated their accomplishments with a Promenade concert in Pioneer Hall. A tradition was begun when the Daughters celebrated their founding with a breakfast on the first Saturday in December.

In spite of great harmony and fellowship, the Daughters were not always "ladylike" in their behavior. The minutes of August 4, 1902 describe in considerable detail some heated discussions among the group. For example, the use of "the City of Sacramento" in the bylaws was questioned, a discussion ensued, and a vote was taken as to whether it should remain. The question arose of whether a two-thirds majority vote of the members present could revise the Constitution. Miss de Forest, Secretary, challenged the President by stating it could not. The President stated the Civil Code of California applied to corporations and went ahead with the vote. Miss de Forest still debated the question and was called again to order by the President. Miss de Forest persisted and declared the vote invalid. The President left her chair and stepped in front of the assembled members, declaring as President that she was bound to preserve order. She threatened to bring charges against Miss de Forest at the next Board meeting!

The next Board minutes in September reflect the following:

> Report of the Board of Directors in the case of
> Mrs. S. Morse vs. Miss Grace de Forest for disturbing
> the harmony of the meeting. We, the undersigned
> Board of Directors, find the members guilty as charged.
> We reprimand the member for this misconduct, cau-
> tion her against repeating this offense, demand that she
> conduct herself properly, and strictly obey the rules and
> regulations of the Society.
> Signed,
> Mary Palmer, Chairwoman
> (and other Board members)

Calm reigned once again after this stormy session, and the Daughters continued with their plans to honor their ancestors' memories. To commemorate their efforts, the Daughters ordered gold pins inscribed with a star to be worn on appropriate occasions.

The year 1903 saw the beginning of an ambitious program of education for the Daughters. History, Parliamentary, and Forestry sections, and a Save the Yosemite Valley Committee were formed. The Daughters campaigned to enjoin the Department of the Interior not to change Spanish names on maps of California to

English names. By May, the election of officers was held. Membership had increased to seventy, with ladies coming from Oakland, Stockton, Hayward, Berkeley, Alameda, and San Jose.

In January of 1904 a *Sequoia Gigantea* was planted in Historic Valley in Golden Gate Park. John McLaren, Superintendent of the Park, donated a tree and the Daughters paid forty-five dollars for fifty yards of loam at ninety cents a yard, in which to plant it. Other significant activities were the Daughters' vote to donate a Bear Flag for the California Building at the St. Louis Exposition, to support restoration of El Camino Real, the old Spanish road built by early settlers, and to encourage the selling of flowers on the streets of the city. (Flowers continue to be an integral part of the San Francisco scene to this day.)

In 1905, at the May meeting, another confrontation broke out regarding the election of officers. A Miss Keith moved that a committee be formed to consult an attorney, but was voted down. The minutes reflect, "She continued to discuss the matter, denounced the proceedings, refused to yield the floor or be in order and, amidst the confusion, the Chair declared the meeting adjourned at 5:30 PM." Perhaps her pioneer ancestor's traits of determination and stubbornness had carried down too well!

The minutes from September 1905 through April 1906 are gone. On April 18, 1906, in the earthquake and fire, those minutes, as well as most of San Francisco, perished. We are fortunate, however, to have the leatherbound books from the inception of the Daughters up until the time of the quake. It was a small miracle that the books had been taken to the home of a member to be worked on; that member's home was spared in the fateful event.

The new year of 1906 had begun pleasantly enough with a successful social and literary program, including a talk on famous artists, ancient and modern. On April 16, there was a "fine program and the meeting was well attended." The Daughters did not

Tree planting, Golden Gate Park, January, 1904. Names of those shown in Notes and Sources, page 329.

suspect that this would be the last gathering in the old Pioneer Hall. In less that forty-eight hours, Pioneer Hall, with its magnificent historical collection, was a ruin. Quake and fire took their toll and the old Hall was gone. So were the artifacts that the Daughters had gathered. The Daughters had to start over.

On "Street Cleaning Day" in March of 1907 the Daughters served lunch at the Pioneer Restaurant to the men cleaning the streets of the city. Two hundred men were served pork and beans, bread, and coffee, courtesy of the proprietor who also donated the use of his facilities.

Nominations and elections were held by the Daughters later that spring, and the annual reports were read and placed in the minutes. A particularly poignant entry is this excerpt from the Recording Secretary, Miss Ronnie B. Hutchinson:

May 31, 1906, a call reached us from the Daughters of California Pioneers. Once more the Pioneer Daughters were to meet, after going through an ordeal that showed the weakness and strength of each individual. When we parted at our social meeting on April 16, 1906 the last meeting ever held in old Pioneer Hall in which we had spent so many happy hours, it was without a thought, a premonition of the utter desolation and ruin that would meet our sorrowful eyes when next our lagging footsteps led us that way.

After the misery of the destruction of our homes, filled with the treasure of many years' collecting, we thought of Pioneer Hall, all it meant to us and all it contained, and a fierce pain gripped our hearts. Gone, all gone! The fire had destroyed it all! Gone was our beautiful building — gone were all the historical relics, the portraits of the members, the reminiscences written by the old Pioneers themselves, the Bear flag, old Emperor Norton's regalia, the piano, tinny but loved, the meteor that fell from the sky, the picture of Sutter's Fort where my father and mother were married and all the old pistols, swords and knives. No artist or master workman, no matter how clever, could replace them. Pioneer Building was to be rebuilt, more beautiful than ever. With that consolation we had to be content.

Thus ended the first year after the earthquake and fire of 1906. With their usual vigor, the Daughters met again in September. They were determined to move forward, and when the statue of Father Junipero Serra was dedicated in Golden Gate Park they placed a wreath on it. Their annual luncheon on December 7, 1907, was followed by a reception for the Pioneers that afternoon. Mothers of the Daughters were included at this reception, which was held in Pioneer Hall at 5 Lick Place.

At the January meeting of 1908, Mr. Almarin H. Paul, a member of the Society of California Pioneers, read a paper on the collection and preservation of relics pertaining to the early history of California. He suggested that the Daughters find a temporary home for such relics, and the Park commissioners granted them space in the Park Museum. A joint celebration to commemorate the discovery of gold and the sixtieth anniversary of the Mexican-American Peace Treaty was held.

At the September meeting, the new officers decided to put a bronze tablet on the tree in the park on October 24 and a lovely ceremony was prepared for this. The minutes read:

> A pleasant stroll from the museum, the meeting place, to the site of the old 'Forty-niners Camp' of Midwinter Fair recollection, brought the party to the tree, around which Superintendent MacLaren had thoughtfully placed a bench. Luncheon was enjoyed in close proximity to the tree, after which the company gathered in a semicircle facing the object of interest. The President, Miss Clara Adams, with commissioner, Mrs. Herman Meyer, and Lucy F. Adams stood in a group near the tree. The President spoke as follows: "The *Sequoia Gigantea* was planted in 1904. At the time the society of Daughters of California Pioneers, numbering eighty-one, had entered upon the fourth year of its existence. The tree at the time of planting was about the same age. The fifty feet of loam, in which the tree was planted, had been purchased by the Society for this occasion. The solid links that cannot be broken stand for the chain of history that is our inher-

itance, and as more links may be added as the tree enlarges, so, as time goes on, may our society add to that history a record worthy of our fathers. Last, but not least, bearing the letters D.C.P. — Daughters of California Pioneers — Daughters of the men who helped to give this glorious state to the Union. Theirs the honor, ours the inheritance! May we be worthy of our noble ancestors"

Clara A. Adams, Pres. D.C.P.

Then, as the two members of the committee parted the branches, she placed the tablet upon the young sequoia, passing the chain attached to the inscription plate around the trunk of the tree, and clasped and locked the padlock which joined the ends of the chain together. The singing of "Auld Lang Syne" by the members of the Society as they circled around the tree, closed the ceremonies.

The year of 1909 was remarkable for Pioneer Days, which was held in the Hall on April 17. The Society of Pioneers sent the following communication to the Daughters:

To the Secretary of the Daughters of California Pioneers, San Francisco

Dear Madam:

At the meeting of the members of the Society of California Pioneers held May 1, 1909, the following resolution was adopted:

Resolved: That we old Pioneers extend to the Society of Daughters of California Pioneers our gracious thanks for the grand old 1849 and 1909 feast and musical entertainment given to the Members of

this Society on April 7, 1909, and it is our hearty wish
when they get as old, that their hearts will be younger
in knowing they added to the happiness of the old
men, and that the Secretary be directed to extend to the
Daughters of Pioneers our grateful thanks.

> Respectfully yours,
> John Spear, Secretary

In September of 1909, the Daughters passed a motion to buy
a Mission Bell and place it somewhere along El Camino Real. The
Presidio took precedence, however, over the King's Highway. The
Commanding Officer of the Army refused to allow the bell to be
placed on the original Mission site until after the new buildings
were up, but upon completion of them the Daughters would be
given permission. (We know the bell was beside the entrance to the
Officers Club in the Presidio until the late 1980s. We have recently
tried to locate the bell through various Federal agencies and Army
officers, but to no avail as yet at the time of this publication.)

Expenses for the Annual Breakfast, held in Pioneer Hall, were
reported as follows:

Donnelly and Brannan
Pastry $5.50
3 gallons white wine $2.25
I pint rum $0.60

The Emporium
Pineapple $0.50
Limes $0.50
Sugar $0.50
Ice $0.15

Goldberg-Bowen Company
Bonbons $2.75

As the new year began in September, 1910 the Daughters agreed to help distribute "Panama Pacific Exposition" postcards in October. These were to be mailed to encourage Fair officials to select San Francisco for the site. As it happened, the Fair did come to The City, and was a major cultural event of 1915, celebrating the opening of the Panama Canal. The Fair also showcased the rebuilding of San Francisco, compared to the rising of the Phoenix from the ashes.

In January of 1912 the Sempervirens Club asked the Daughters to endorse the movement to have the California Highway Commission construct a state highway between San Francisco and the California Redwood Park before the opening of the Panama-Pacific Exposition in 1915. (Apparently the endorsement of the Daughters was considered a political advantage, reflecting the growing prestige of the organization.) Additional events of 1912 included the planting of two more trees in Golden Gate Park to honor the Pioneer Mothers and Fathers, as well as the annual basket picnic that took place in the Pioneer Women's log cabin in Historical Valley of the Park.

The Daughters continued their endorsement of political issues during the year by supporting the City Beautiful Campaign in preparation for the coming Exposition, the resolution by the California Club enforcing laws against white slave traffic, and the efforts of the Landmarks League to preserve the adobe building in the Presidio. In October an ambitious study of California history was commenced, including the voyage of Sir Francis Drake, the Spanish governors, discovery of gold, and statehood. In addition, the Daughters supported the movement to have the Federal Government change the name of Goat Island back to its original name of Yerba Buena. The Annual Breakfast was held on December 14, and thus the year ended.

The year of 1913 saw the Daughters dressed in forty-niner costumes for the Pioneer Breakfast in March. These were actually their mothers' or grandmothers' dresses, carefully preserved throughout the years. The usual political issues occupied the Daughters that year as well. The removal of the cemeteries from San Francisco was again protested with a signed petition sent to the State Government in Sacramento. The Daughters tried to obtain a Women's Building at the State Fair. They also felt it their duty to appeal for a national appropriation to fight white slave traffic in California. After a very busy year, the membership had grown to one hundred and one direct descendants of Pioneers. The Daughters had worked hard at furthering the goals that had been set at their original meeting more than a decade before, and were undoubtedly proud of what they had accomplished.

When the Daughters resumed their meetings in September, they were delighted to be presented with a gavel made from a French railroad tie in Panama, presented by Mrs. F.S. Hislop. A new activity was inaugurated that fall by their first celebration of the discovery of gold, held at the St. Francis Hotel with music and refreshments provided. The presentation of a Daughters' President pin to the outgoing President upon the completion of her duties was established.

At the October, 1914 meeting at the St. Francis Hotel, an invitation from the Society of California Pioneers to once again resume meeting in Pioneer Hall was received and accepted by the members. After viewing the drawing for a proposed Mother's Monument, the ladies went on record opposing the nude figure shown. Another item on the agenda was the continuing opposition to removal of the dead from the cemeteries; the Daughters voted to hire and decorate two automobiles for the parade before the election, protesting the removal of the remains. Eventually, of course, the City of San Francisco prohibited the burial of any remains in the city limits, and ordered that all such burials should be in Colma, just south of the City.

During 1914 the Daughters became greatly concerned with the Belgian people suffering the effects of World War I, and arranged to send supplies to these early victims of the War. This humanitarian gesture seemed the appropriate thing to do.

In early 1915 the Daughters voted to participate in the opening day parade of the Panama-Pacific International Exposition. In March they voted to give a memorial fountain to San Francisco honoring the Pioneers, and upon approval of the design and a cost of $3,350, an application was sent to the Mayor at City Hall, requesting a suitable location.

In August the Daughters gave a new flag to be used on the California Building at the Exposition. Their efforts continued to be recognized by the award of a bronze medal for their part in the Exposition and a silver cup for participating in the Midsummer Bal Masque at the Civic Auditorium. A drinking fountain was unveiled as a gift to the City in Union Square on September 11. The Municipal Band played to celebrate this civic gesture, and the Daughters again were in the spotlight as supporters of good causes in California. During this fall period, the Daughters voted to make a presentation to the battleship *California*, but no further mention is made of what this entailed.

In 1917 the Daughters endorsed the preservation of the California Building of the Panama-Pacific Exposition as a State Normal School. They also endorsed keeping Ina Coolbrith as poet laureate of California. They heard of the plans for the new M.H. de Young Museum in Golden Gate Park and visited the Japanese Tea Garden there, as well as the 1904 tree and the log cabin. The Daughters approved of the movement by the Grand Army of the Republic (a Civil War veterans organization) to erect a monument to Abraham Lincoln in the Civic Center. The old pioneers were not forgotten and the Daughters started a *Biography Book* of their fathers.

In early 1918, with the U.S. involved in World War I, the Daughters voted to use the Christmas Tree Festival money for chocolate for the benefit of California soldiers. Other war efforts involved furnishing a room in the building known as the "Outside Inn," maintained as a place for mothers visiting soldiers stationed in San Francisco and wounded soldiers in Letterman Hospital.

In January of 1919 attendance at the meetings was limited due to the Spanish influenza epidemic raging at the time. The Daughters endorsed only one resolution, presented by the Women's Federation convention, for six months pay for discharged soldiers.

At the September meeting a report on the restoration of the California Missions was considered and voted affirmatively, jointly supported by many other organizations in California. By January 1920 a progress report on the missions was received. With three million dollars deemed necessary, the conclusion was that only fifteen missions could be restored. The Recording Secretary made a particular note in the Minutes that the Spanish influenza epidemic was not over and that many members were kept home by illness in their families. She indicated that at times she and the President were both ill but never missed a meeting. The Native Sons of the Golden West invited the Daughters to attend the ceremony of the placing of a tablet on the old Niantic Building. The *Niantic* was originally a ship that was tied to the wharf in the Gold Rush days and turned into a hotel for old forty-niners.

By the fall of 1920 the war had been over for about a year and the minutes of the Daughters reflect increasing interest and awareness in women's and civic issues, spurred by the passage of the amendment to the United States Constitution giving women the right to vote. The Daughters were asked to endorse increased salaries for teachers (twenty dollars a month) as well as for equal policewomen's pay and pension — "the same as the men." At the Daughters' twentieth annual breakfast at the Fairmont Hotel in December, the President noted that there were eight past presidents together at one table.

The Daughters were kept busy during the year of 1921 with important issues: the purchase of the Spring Valley water properties, the recall of police judges, exhibition of old photographs, and lectures on various subjects. The April tea at the Fairmont Hotel was a great social success with many of the eighty-five attendees from other clubs in the City. The Daughters joined the "Save the Redwood League" and the Travelers Aid Society. The fall season began with a September "get together" luncheon. A request from the San Francisco Historical Publicity Motion Picture Company to endorse the historical filming of San Francisco was received prior to the filming. The traditional basket lunch took place in October with a visit to the museum. The year of 1922 closed after a busy schedule.

In January of 1923 another film producing company requested the Daughters' endorsement of a projected film. Their reply to this was the same as before: they would only approve the film if it gave full credit, and no dishonor, to their pioneer fathers and grandfathers! A "home talent day," held on March 18, was broadcast from the Mercantile Trust Company's radio transmitter on top of Telegraph Hill that evening. The Daughters had become quite involved with the new technology of the twentieth century. In May they participated in the Spring Flower and Wild Flower Pageant held at the Fairmont Hotel and won first prize for their floral bouquet, thus adding a handsome cup to their collection.

The 1923-24 year began with a luncheon in October and a Music Week program in November. The Society of California Pioneers invited the Daughters to their Thanksgiving Eve Ball, and in December the Daughters gave magazine subscriptions to the Base Hospital in Palo Alto for their disabled veterans. One action for the year was to advise the Mayor that the fountain in Union Square was not working properly and should be repaired.

In January the Daughters announced their intention of planting a grove of redwood trees on Angel Island in memory of the California Pioneers. They also received a percolator and a merchandise certificate from O'Connor Moffatt's department store as a prize for the Flower Pageant. The meeting of October 20 was a big surprise for the ladies when the 680-foot dirigible *Shenandoah* passed directly over Pioneer Hall on a globe-circling trip! When the twenty-fourth annual breakfast was held in the Red Room of the Fairmont Hotel, ten of the original old pioneers were invited to this event. The following year the Daughters decided to change the name of the Annual Breakfast in December to "Founders' Day," as it has been called ever since.

During early 1925, the Daughters held many talks on such topics as "Early Days in San Francisco," "The Geology of California," Thomas Larkin, John Sutter, and other people and events of historical interest. The Daughters were continuing to honor the memories of the Pioneers, thus fulfilling one of the original goals of the Society.

On September 9, 1925 the Society of California Pioneers celebrated their Diamond Jubilee. This event took place the same day as Admission Day, celebrating the day California became a state. The Daughters were invited to be in the receiving line at the reception held by the Pioneers in Pioneer Hall after the parade. Later they held their own Silver Anniversary in the Fairmont Hotel and their Christmas Jinks shortly after.

During 1926 the bylaws were amended in February to raise the initiation fee to five dollars and the annual dues to three dollars. In March the Daughters heard a talk on the "psychology of dress" and saw the film "Faith Progress in San Francisco" at the White House, a local department store that was owned by art collector Raphael Weill.

A get-together luncheon was held at the Whitcomb Hotel to start the year 1926-27. Another busy year came to a conclusion with Founders' Day breakfast at the Fairmont Hotel. Christmas Jinks included a request that the Daughters wear gowns from their mother or grandmothers. By the time the new year came around the Daughters were once again involved in political issues with a letter to the Board of Supervisors to keep Mt. Davidson as a public park. (The issue remains somewhat of a problem to this day.) By May, the usual nominations and election of officers were held but a sad blow was faced by the Daughters when the newly-elected Vice-President, Ella Lees Leigh, died. A new Vice-President was elected before the summer adjournment. Twice this year the society lost beloved members who had sustained it for many years.

The fall season of 1927-28 began with the Society of California Pioneers' picnic in Fairfax on Admission Day. The Daughters had sent letters of protest to retail merchants of Oakland, Berkeley, and San Francisco for not closing on Admission Day. However, a letter of thanks was sent to Raphael Weill of The White House department store for closing his store on that day.

In the early part of 1928 the Daughters endorsed the movement to preserve the Palace of Fine Arts, an elegant building left over from the Exposition of 1915. It is fortunate that there were enough civic minded organizations interested in keeping the building for the future benefit of all citizens. At the May meeting the Historian donated a bottle of champagne from Mrs. Agatha Jacobs. The historic champagne bottle had arrived to San Francisco on July 5, 1849 aboard the *Niantic* and had been buried with the ship at Sansome and Clay Streets until 1873. The Daughters decided to place the bottle, on loan, in their Pioneer Exhibit at the De Young Museum.

The Society of California Pioneers again invited the Daughters to the Admission Day picnic on September 9. The Daughters wrote to the Retail Merchants Association commending those stores which closed on Admission Day and protesting those which remained open. Founders' Day was celebrated later in the year, with the Christmas Jinks being a costume party. As a finale to the year, the Daughters drafted a letter to Robert Welles Ritchie, author of the book *Hell-Roaring Forty-Niners.* No one was going to insult the Daughters' fathers without a strong protest from the ladies!

The Daughters started the new year of 1929 by sending an air mail letter of congratulations to the new President of the United States, Herbert Hoover; an acknowledgment was later received from him. (Our bylaws today forbid talk of a religious or political nature at our meetings.)

In September of 1929 the Daughters were invited to attend a movie exhibition of wildlife hunting in Alaska. A picnic basket lunch at the Japanese Tea Garden in Golden Gate Park was held. The Daughters endorsed the purchase of China Basin by the City of San Francisco for future recreational activities. (Some seventy years later, the Basin is being developed to reflect those goals.) By November, Founders' Day was held at the Palace Hotel, shortly before Black Friday, November 29 — the Stock Market crash. (The Daughters would be greatly affected by this event, as subsequent minutes reveal.)

During the 1930-31 year the Daughters continued with their usual activities. At the Founders' Day Breakfast, their thirtieth anniversary, the mothers and fathers of the Daughters were the honored guests at the Terrace Room of the Fairmont Hotel. At the Christmas Jinks the participants brought a book or a toy to be donated to an institution. This was a change from the usual exchanging of gifts among the Daughters themselves.

The effects of the Great Depression were highlighted in the January 1931 meeting when the Daughters heard a talk about the Community Chest (a forerunner of the present day United Way). A request for groceries or twenty-five cents was made to those attending the February luncheon at the Green Lantern Restaurant. The only civic matter in the minutes was a letter to the Commandant of the Twelfth Naval District upholding his stand to return the name Yerba Buena to Goat Island. In May the usual elections were held, but sadness again overtook the Daughters with the death of their newly-elected President before installation. A meeting was called to elect a new Vice-President.

The year 1931 was much more subdued as far as social activities were concerned. A few talks were given, with the emphasis on helping the needy as the Depression worsened.

In June thirteen Daughters and their guests were privileged to be guests aboard the *U.S.S. California.* The Daughters had donated a leather guest book to the ship some years before. At the September meeting a talk was given on the Community Chest. At the time of the Thanksgiving social the Daughters were requested to bring groceries for distribution to people hard hit by the Depression.

In February 1932 the Daughters were asked to take clothing for the needy to the nearest firehouse. The philanthropic efforts of the Daughters were admirably tallied, as thirty-six bundles of toys, forty-eight handmade bibs, and fifteen packages of clothing were contributed for the needy.

The new year of 1932-33 began with a luncheon at Lucca's Restaurant, a venerable old Italian restaurant in North Beach. At the meeting a motion was made to formally present the collection of artifacts to the Society of California Pioneers (except for an original program of the First Grand Celebration of Admission Day in San Francisco on October 29, 1850, to be kept in the care of the Daughters' Historian). Donations of groceries were requested for the Thanksgiving basket for the needy. The November social was devoted to sewing for the needy, and the ladies were instructed to bring their thimbles and scissors. The months toward the end of the year included the Founders' Day breakfast and the usual Christmas Jinks. Daughters were again requested to bring a book or toy for homeless children.

In January a report was given on the Daughters' philanthropic work. The February social was a travelogue on "A Trip to the Orient," followed by oriental songs and dance. By May it was reported that members resided in far away places such as Germany, Honduras, and New York. Activities were definitely curtailed due to the Great Depression, but the philanthropic work continued.

The September meeting opened with a luncheon at the City Women's Club on Post Street. The Daughters were again informed about the Community Chest and advised to be prepared to sew at their Thanksgiving Party social and to make a donation for Christmas boxes. By December the Christmas Jinks committee again requested toys for the needy or sick children. In the same month, a request from the editor of the *Pioneer Quarterly* was made asking that new members gather material on the pioneer experiences of their fathers and mothers, this to be published in a later issue of the *Quarterly*.

In January of 1934 the Daughters wrote to Mayor Rossi strongly protesting the movement to keep stores open on Washington's Birthday as well as on Admission Day. They also protested the reopening of the Barbary Coast. This colorful section of the City had been notorious since Gold Rush days with an unsavory reputation for tolerating all vices. By the time World War II arrived, some seven years later, the old Barbary Coast was once again in business to entertain the thousands of servicemen who flooded the City. With the increasing value of real estate today the

Barbary Coast has changed, now gentrified with professional offices and designers' shops for the affluent. (The Daughters of 1934 would be pleased to see their wishes fulfilled at last.)

In April of the same year radio station KGBB announced they would broadcast the Daughters' meetings and programs, daily at 11:00 AM, on their "Milady's Notebook" feature. The Daughters were keeping up with the new technology. They also endorsed the "Buy America" program inaugurated during the Depression to stimulate the economy. The usual May elections were held, and another year ended with an emphasis on philanthropic work through the Federation of Women's Clubs. The Great Depression was lessening but still very much in evidence.

The minutes for 1934-35 are sparse. At the first meeting in October a Daughter reported on the placing of a plaque by the California Historical Society on the site of the first habitation in San Francisco occupied by Captain Richardson in 1835. No mention is made of the Founders' Day Breakfast, but the toys brought to the Christmas Jinks were later given to tubercular children.

In February of 1935 a resolution was passed to recommend that the old United States Mint at Fifth and Mission Streets be preserved as a California Historical Museum. A new Mint had been built on upper Market Street; the Daughters, with their usual concern for historic matters, voiced their opinion on the matter. Fortunately the old Mint was saved (and was open until the Loma Prieta Earthquake in 1989 weakened some of the structure and made it unsafe for visitors; it is now closed to the public).

The year 1935-36 began with a luncheon at the Argonaut Hotel followed by a meeting at Pioneer Hall and a talk on the Community Chest. The Depression was still the biggest concern of the time. The Thanksgiving Social was a literary and musical program. Founders' Day Breakfast in December was held in the Gold Ballroom of the Fairmont Hotel. Voluntary donations of silver (coins) and canned foods were requested for the committees of the Women's Federation, the umbrella organization of women's clubs that distributed charity to the needy.

In January the President announced that she would be broadcasting the aims of the Daughters over radio station KCGC, on January 7. In contrast to the programs of the early days, the February meeting featured a movie of springtime in the California desert. The new technology had changed the types of programs that the Daughters now enjoyed.

Again the year brought emphasis on charitable and civic works, primarily through membership in the City and County Federation of Women's Clubs. Historical preservation was still the primary goal of the Daughters, but the needs created by the Great Depression had broadened their awareness and the scope of their community efforts. The entire United States, as well as the world, was consumed by the great economic crisis, and the Daughters tried to do their part to alleviate the prevailing misery.

At the September 1936 meeting a talk was given on the San Francisco-Oakland Bay Bridge. A prominent columnist, Anita Day Hubbard, was to be approached regarding the Daughters' participation in the opening celebration of the bridge. Miss Hubbard was a guest speaker at the October meeting. At the November meeting a talk was given about the *Kangaroo*, the first ferryboat on the San Francisco-Marin County line in 1852. At Christmas toys or books were collected for tubercular children at the County Hospital.

In January of 1937 the elusive bottle of champagne from the *Niantic* was reported to have been given to the Society of California Pioneers. No further details are given, and the mystery remains unsolved! The Pioneer Society announced in the April newspapers that they had purchased a site on McAllister Street (across from City Hall) for their new building; this was to be their headquarters for many years. In May the Pioneers advised the Daughters that a donation or a monthly rental fee would be required in the future for use of a meeting place in the new building.

1937-38 began with the electrifying news that a formal letter had been received from the Society of California Pioneers, stating that the Daughters could not meet in Pioneer Hall as there was no room for ladies! The Daughters immediately replied, requesting permission to meet in the new building as heirs of the pioneers of 1849. Next came a letter, received in November, from the President of the Society of California Pioneers stating that the Daughters would be adequately looked after. In December another letter was received confirming that the Daughters would have a place in Pioneer Hall. To make amends, the Pioneer Society invited the Daughters to their egg-nog party celebrating the opening of the Hall.

January 28, 1938 was the opening of the new Pioneer Hall, which also celebrated the eighty-ninth anniversary of the discovery of gold in California. In February the Daughters decided to request a special day for their organization at the Golden Gate International Exposition coming in 1939. The fair was going to be a big event in the state (and was to be one of the last joyful events before World War II).

In October the meeting was held in Pioneer Hall. The Ladies' Auxiliary of the Society of California Pioneers (wives of the members of the Pioneer Society) had invited the Daughters to use their room on the first floor for their meetings, and the Daughters accepted. By December the usual Christmas party was held, but no request was made for food and clothing as had been done previously.

February 18, 1939 came with a bang! It was the opening of the long-awaited Golden Gate International Exposition on Treasure Island (long ago Goat Island, subsequently Yerba Buena Island, with an extension of fill called Treasure Island). President's Day for the Daughters was celebrated on the balcony of the Yerba Buena Club, another historic event for the Daughters.

In September the Daughters met at Veneto's Restaurant on Bay Street, another excellent restaurant in North Beach. Later, the Daughters were guests of the California Commission at the California Building on Treasure Island.

The following year, 1940, the Daughters celebrated Lincoln and Washington birthdays, and Valentine's Day. On April 17 the Daughters were invited to a luncheon by the state chairman of the Women's Board of the Golden Gate International Exposition. This was a singular honor as only a few outstanding clubs were invited. June 17, 1940 was designated the Daughters of California Pioneers Day at the Exposition, and this, too, was a great honor for the society.

The October 1940 meeting was held as a picnic lunch in the Redwood Empire Building at the Exposition grounds on Treasure Island. In November there was a Thanksgiving reception. The Founders' Day Breakfast was held at the Alexander Hamilton Hotel, and the Daughters again donated toys and books for the tubercular children at City Hospital.

The spring meetings of 1941 followed the usual routine, with an added discussion concerning the purchasing of Defense Bonds, later changed to "War Bonds." (At this time no one was prepared for the historic events that would make the change inevitable.)

The October social of 1941 was a Halloween party in the Hall. Founders' Day Breakfast took place on December 6 at the Alexander Hamilton Hotel. Just as the Daughters had met a day or so prior to the Great Earthquake, so their Breakfast took place the day before Pearl Harbor, December 7, 1941. President Roosevelt called it "a day of infamy," and so it was. The United States was not at war with Japan.

In January of 1942 the Daughters donated twenty-five dollars to the Red Cross. The usual tributes to Washington, Lincoln and St. Valentine were made during February. At the President's Tea held in the Bellevue Hotel elections for officers took place, and the Daughters voted to buy a $100 Defense Bond for the war effort.

In October the Daughters voted to withdraw from the City and County Federation of Women's Clubs. They also protested to Congressmen and Senators in Washington against painting murals in the Rincon Annex post office as they felt the materials would be better used in the war effort. Although the usual Founders' Day Breakfast was held at the Alexander Hamilton Hotel in December, the war cast a gloom over all activities.

In March of 1942, while World War II was going on, the Daughters held an indoor picnic. At the meeting a letter was received from the Post Office authorities concerning the mural-painting question. The position of the Daughters was upheld and a promise made that nothing would be done until after the war.

Another indoor picnic opened the 1943-44 year in Pioneer Hall. The Daughters bought another $100 war bond and in December gave a cash donation to the tubercular children's ward at the San Francisco Hospital. The October meeting opened with a complimentary luncheon from the President. The Daughters voted to withhold the initiation fee of five dollars for the remainder of the year. No Founders' Day Breakfast was held in December, but donations of ten dollars each were made to the Society of California Pioneers and the *Examiner* fund for Wounded Soldiers.

A new cause to rally around occurred in late summer of 1945. The San Francisco Women's Chamber of Commerce was waging a war of protest to prevent the removal of the cable cars. In October the Daughters appointed a delegate to the Women's Chamber of Commerce and followed this with further protests to the Mayor and to the Board of Supervisors. Thanks to the Daughters and many others who supported their position, the famous San Francisco cable cars are still running. During this year the Daughters contributed ten dollars to the Sister Kenny Foundation, an organization devoted to the cure of polio; Sister Kenny, an Australian nurse, was the sponsor.

In March 1946 the Daughters asked the Board of Supervisors to clean up the famous Lotta's Fountain on Market Street at Kearny and O'Farrell. The fountain is standing today, named for little Lotta Crabtree, darling of the forty-niners. She was a talented little girl who sang for the miners so long ago.

The year 1946-47 was a time of few meetings and no socials. In September the Daughters protested against the old United States Mint being turned into a garage, as they wished it preserved as a historic building. They also protested the sale of Angel Island to private parties and stated it should be kept for either State of Federal use. Fortunately, again, the stand of the Daughters and others was heard. (The island is now a National Monument to the early immigrants to America.)

By October 1947 meetings resumed. The annual reports were read and the previously nominated slate of officers were elected and installed. Membership in the Save the Redwoods League was resumed and donations were given to the Sister Kenny Foundation, the San Francisco Center for the Blind, and the Society of California Pioneers. Once again the Founders' Day Luncheon was held in the Alexander Hamilton Hotel, complimentary to members in good standing. Things were getting back to normal after the War.

The Downtown Association was interested in preserving the Palace of Fine Arts. A delegate of the Daughters went on record stating it should become a working art center. Other interesting activities concerned the Freedom Train, which was visiting the City with a display of artifacts and documents from the time of Columbus through surrender documents of World War II. In October 1948 the Daughters opposed a movement to build a golf course in Golden Gate Park. Recommendations made to the City included the suggestion that the James Lick Monument, at Market and Larkin, be cleaned up and that a walk be built around it. In February of 1949 the Daughters made donations to the Sister Kenny Foundation and the March of Dimes, both organizations involved in the polio epidemic.

The year 1949-1950 began in October at Pioneer Hall. A discussion took place about the centennial anniversary in 1950 for the admission of California to the Union. Dues for Save the Redwoods were paid, but no luncheon was held in December. The question of whether the Daughters could go back on radio with the programs was raised but left answered. In May the United States Navy invited the Daughters to participate in a parade at Hunters Point.

A special meeting was held in August to elect a new Treasurer, as the newly-elected one had died shortly after being installed. At this same meeting the Daughters voted to write to their Congressmen to outlaw Communism in this country.

With the opening of the 1950-51 year the Daughters attended the Centennial Luncheon in the Palace Hotel given by the Federation of Women's Clubs. In October the Daughters, along with the Association of Pioneer Women and the Women's Auxiliary of the Society of California Pioneers, placed a wreath at the base of the Pioneer Monument. This nine-foot bronze statue of a woman, dressed in cape and bonnet with her hands stretched out over two children, is located near Stow Lake in Golden Gate Park. In December the Daughters were present at a ceremony honoring the men who died on the *U.S.S. San Francisco*. The mast and bell of the ship were placed at Observation Point on Ocean Highway near the Golden Gate. The display is still an integral part of the Golden Gate National Park.

An important change was made in the Constitution at this time, in regard to the eligibility for membership in the Daughters. Previously open only to descendants of the men who were members of the Society of California Pioneers, the Daughters voted to extend membership to whomever could show she was a direct descendent of a pioneer (male or female) who had arrived in California prior to January 1, 1850. Thus membership was extended "to descendants of the earliest of the pioneers, from the time of the first Spanish settlers — enriching our membership to represent the full extent of California's history."

The first meeting in 1952 was in February, followed by a St. Patrick's Day event; special invited guests included Mayor Robinson (who sent his regrets) and the four club editors from the newspapers. Nominations in April brought some of the new members to the Board, thus bringing new energy and fresh ideas. The possible purchase of Angel Island by the City was announced and discussed during the fall season. The Daughters voted to pay the Pioneer Society five dollars for the use of the Hall. Donations were made to the March of Dimes for polio research and to the Red Cross, as well as to the committee in charge of restoring Constitution Hall in Philadelphia.

The Daughters wrote to Governor Earl Warren, congratulating him on being appointed Chief Justice of the United States Supreme Court, and to President Eisenhower, commending him for making the appointment, to which he replied the following month. Replies were likewise received from Chief Justice Earl Warren, as well as the Mayor in answer to a protest against changing the name of Lick Place to Crocker Place. The Daughters again supported the "Save the Cable Cars" campaign. Founders' Day luncheon, held at the Fairmont Hotel, featured the Honorable Judge Molinari as guest speaker.

The following year the Daughters wrote to the Secretary of

the State Legislature protesting a movement to abolish the holidays set aside for Lincoln and Washington in February and Veterans Day in November. A letter was sent to Joe Di Maggio, congratulating him on being inducted into the Baseball Hall of Fame and for the honor he brought to the city of San Francisco.

The Daughters were asked to join in the formation of the San Francisco Council of Women's Clubs. The President and Vice President were designated to attend the meeting to determine if they wished to do so. A meeting and luncheon were held at the Marines Memorial Building, and the piano was sold because of the cost of storage fees.

Over the next decade, the Daughters were actively following their historical interests, attending talks about Bay Area counties, Cape Horn and the days of sail, "Fraternal Organizations," "Victor Castro: The Last of the Spanish Grandees," "Vigilantes of San Francisco," book reviews of biographies of early California, "Aviation in the Bay Area," given by Commander Vinton, a talk on San Francisco history by Father Floyd Lotito, and "Human Aspects of Early California Cases," presented by Justice Bray. Excursions included tours of wineries in the Napa Valley and Los Gatos, visits to the Luther Burbank Gardens in Santa Rosa, the Oakland Museum, and the historic state capitol in Benicia, and an outing to Mare Island which included a tour of both the grounds and the cadet training ship, *Golden Bear* of the California Maritime Academy, followed by luncheon at the Officers Club. (Both the ship and Mare Island have since been retired.) Members of the Board began attending the San Francisco Birthday Luncheon held annually on June 29 at the Officers' Club in the Presidio to celebrate the founding of the City in 1776. (Some of us remember seeing "our bell" outside the Club at these occasions.)

Featured speaker at our eighty-fourth Founders' Day Luncheon in December, 1988 was Raymond Clary, historian for Golden Gate

Park, who spoke on the "1894 Midwinter Fair in the Park." An outcome of his talk was to discover that an original kiosk from the Fair had been in storage for many years. The Board subsequently voted to sponsor its repair, paying for the materials and a plaque, while Golden Gate Park workers donated their skill and labor towards its restoration. The final dedication of the kiosk took place several years later (appropriately celebrated with a champagne reception) at the San Francisco History Museum, where it had been installed, once again in view of the public.

Gladys Hansen, City Archivist in the History Room of the Public Library, spoke to us about the 1906 earthquake and fire at a tea on October 6, 1989. Ironically, only a few days later, on October 17, the Loma Prieta earthquake occurred. This destructive earthquake was like a crude illustration of the famous quake, so recently described.

Meanwhile Pioneer Hall on McAllister Street had undergone considerable renovation during the late 1970s. Upon its completion a special luncheon was held to show off the improvements of the building, which included the small auditorium in the basement for showing films to school groups, the comfortably furnished up-to-date library, and the magnificent second-floor gallery used for social gatherings.

At this time the old records of the Daughters were retrieved from basement storage boxes. Like opening a time capsule, many of the early documents pertaining to the founding of our organization were discovered: a roster of charter members, the minutes of meetings, ledgers of membership dues paid by our grandmothers, invitations to early social events, and newspaper articles. One of our members volunteered to sort through and organize the records so as to make them accessible to our present membership. The task was tremendous and entailed dedicated long hours and months of work. An unexpected discovery was a collection of manuscripts written in 1917, comprised of brief biographies of the pioneer fathers of the Daughters — some in beautiful penmanship, but almost illegible! Already, so many years ago, a seed had been planted to assemble the stories of our pioneer ancestors. A newsletter, to appear twice yearly, was initiated to keep members living in faraway places abreast of our discoveries, renewed goals, and projects.

A focus over the next years turned towards genealogy, with events planned around various libraries. At a gathering in the newly refurbished library of Pioneer Hall the librarian showed us the steps for research of the materials available, and a visit was made to the headquarters of the Native Daughters of the Golden West, whose genealogical library and records were explained and opened for our use.

As many of us had belonged to the Daughters through a legacy from our grandmothers, we tended to take our membership for granted. But would the next generations, our children and grandchildren, be able to trace their lineage, or would their only claim to their heritage be family legends and hearsay? Thus longtime members were encouraged to research and compile their family genealogical charts, tracing their roots back to the ancestor who arrived in California before January 1, 1850. As an incentive, they would receive a handsome certificate, to be presented at Founders' Day, when possible.

New applicants for membership in the Daughters were now required to submit a standardized "pedigree chart" showing their pioneer lineage, rather than merely stating the name of the ancestor with an informal outline. It had been several generations since our original membership requirement was that of being an actual daughter of a member of the Society of California Pioneers. The passing of time tends to dilute some of the facts.

While working on our genealogy we soon came to realize the vast resources of family and California history which lay dormant behind each chart. There were stories of adventurous individuals who ventured out to explore a new land. What a wealth of California history was represented among our membership! Thus, the project of this book was born, to gather stories of our ancestors into a collection that would reflect the origin and purpose of our organization. Honoring and remembering our courageous ancestors, while recording their stories for our future generations, would create a legacy for our grandchildren.

By 1993 the City and County of San Francisco announced their intention of purchasing the property of Pioneer Hall on McAllister Street as the site for a new Superior Courthouse. The Society's eventual move was inevitable, as the narrow lot with the three-story building, directly across from City Hall, had been overshadowed by towering structures on either side. However, at the time of the renovation, it had not yet been obvious that the property would so soon have to be vacated. The Society of California Pioneers had occupied this choice location since 1936. Within eight months Pioneer Hall was dismantled. A thorough inventory of the enormous collection of museum artifacts was computerized and packed for storage with the latest methods and archival materials. In the spring of 1994 the Daughters asked the Society to return property that had been stored in the vault of the Hall for a number of years: the silver tea set (given by a Past-President) and the die for our membership pin — but there was no trace of either item.

The Society of California Pioneers moved into their temporary home at One Hawthorne Street in August 1994. There, amid crates, boxes of books, and some of the artifacts, the Daughters held their monthly board meetings. By 1996 the Society was able to purchase a building on the corner of Fourth and Folsom Streets. After considerable structural reconstruction the administrative offices and most of its collections were able to move in March 1998. Construction work continued until completion, into the year 2000.

Pioneer Hall has returned to its old neighborhood of before the 1906 fire and earthquake. Within a few blocks from its original location, the new Pioneer Hall now takes its place in the midst of San Francisco's new cultural center.

We, the Daughters of California Pioneers, find it hard to believe that our organization has been in existence for a hundred years. To compile this book has been to witness a drama on the stage of history, complete with scenes of earthquakes, wars, changing customs, and political points of view; of wonderful expositions, involvement in civic affairs, and supporting the causes we felt important. Now we honor the efforts of our ancestors — the men and women who took part in the formation of California — and are proud to tell their stories. We have followed the original aims and goals of those ladies who met a hundred years ago and feel that we have served them well.

Notes and Sources

Mariano de la Luz Verdugo

Francisco Verdugo was the son of Francisco Verdugo and Inés de Cuéllar. He was in Cuba as early as 1519, where his brother-in-law, Diego Velasquez, was Governor. He served as *alcalde* at Mexico City in 1529 and was at Compostela in Nueva Galicia in 1532. In 1534 he sailed to Spain and returned to Mexico in 1535 with his wife, Isabel Velasquez, his daughter, Francisca, and her husband, Alonso Bazan. He died in 1547.

Francisco Verdugo's brother, Manuel Verdugo, his uncle, Bartolomé de Cueva, and at least one cousin, Juan de Cueva, were listed as in the Indies during the same era. (Peter Boyd-Bowman, *Indice Geo-biographico de Cuarenta Mil Pobladores Espanoles de American en el Siglo XVI* (Bogota, Instituto Caro y Cuervo, 1964), pp. 102, 148.

A *cacique* was a hereditary ruler of an Indian state. This word, brought by the Spaniards, is roughly equivalent to the Aztec term *tlatoani*.

"Conquistadores de la Nueva Espana" in *Diccionario Porrua*, Tomo I, Quarto Edicion (Mexico, D.F., Editorial Porua, 1976), p. 497.

Guillermo S. Fernandez de Recas, *Cacicasgos y Nobiliario Indigena de la Nueva Espana* (Mexico: Instituto Bibliografico Mexicano, 1961), pp. 113-125.

Joseph Donohoe, Lillian Fish and Ione Graff, "Carrillo of Alta California," in *Antepasados*, Vol. I, No. 4, p. 3.

Thomas Workman Temple II, "Genealogical Tables of Spanish and Mexican Families of California" (Ms. in The Bancroft Library, fmF 860,T4), p. 75.

Marie E. Northrop, *Spanish-Mexican Families of Early California: 1769-1850* (New Orleans, Polyanthos, 1976), p. 262.

Hubert Howe Bancroft, *History of California*, 7 volumes (San Francisco, The History Company, 1886-1890), I, p. 662, n. 40; V, p. 762

Rudecinda Lo Buglio, Bartolome T. Sepulveda and Nadine Marcia Vasquez, "Lista de los Individuos que Servieron en los Nuevos Establicimientos," in *Antepasados*, Vol. II, Bicentennial Issue, p. 7.

Bill Mason, "The Garrisons of San Diego Presidio: 1770-1794," in the *Journal of San Diego History*, XXIV, No. 4 (Fall 1978), pp. 402-3, 406 and 409.

Libro de Primero de Matrimonios, Mission San Juan Capistrano, entry 35.

Yorba, Grijalva, Avila

José Antonio Yorba: *Spanish Alta California*, by Alberta Johnston Denis.
Juan Pablo Grijalva: *Dawn of the Dons*, by Tirey L. Ford.
Josef Maria Avila: *Spanish Arcadia*, by Nellie Van de Grift Sanchez.
(All of the above verified in Bancroft's *History of California*.).
Land Grants, Sacramento, Copies in possession of the author.
Missions of California, edited by Davis Dutton.

Pablo Antonio Cota

Antepasados, Volume III. Publication of Los Californianos, 1978-1979. Editor, Rudecinda Lo Buglio.
Diary of Fray Juan Crespi, Missionary Explorer of the Pacific Coast, by Herbert Eugene Bolton.
Libro de Bautismos, Mission San Carlos de Monterey.
Church records of Mission San Luis Obispo.
Libro de Matrimonios I, Mission San Luis Obispo, Entry #50.
Provincial State Papers, California Archives, Sacramento, California.
Church records of the respective Missions.
Libro de Difuntos I, Mission Santa Barbara, entries # 46, 74.

Maria de Los Angeles Cota

Santa Barbara Mission *Book of Bautismos*, Entry #78.
San Carlos Mission *Matromonios*, Entry #654.
Bancroft's *History of California*
Monterey County Spanish Archives, Original File #25.
San Francisco Bulletin, 1877.
San Carlos Church, Monterey, *Difuntos*.

Louis Pombert

The King's Daughters (Filles du Roi). Second edition, published by *Lost In Canada* magazine.
Thwaites, Rueben Gold ed., *Collections of the State Historical Society of Wisconsin*, Volume XII, (Madison, Wisconsin: Democrat Printing Company, State Printer, 1892) pp. 154-169.
Morgan, Dale L., *Jedediah Smith and the Opening of the West* (Lincoln, Nebraska: University of Nebraska Press, 1953), pp.193-258, p. 413.
Departmental State Papers in California Archives. Volume 33, p. 199.
Translations of Mexican records from the Monterey County Recorder's Office, Volume I pp. 17, 28, 223-228.
Bancroft, Hubert Howe, *History of the Pacific States of North America*, California Volume III (San Francisco, Califomia, The History Company, 1890) p. 22.

James Black

Indexes to the Old Parochial Registers of Scotland. Christenings 1801-1820. Carnwath, Scotland.
Family History Library (hereafter FHL), Salt Lake City, UT film #1024971.
Marin Journal, San Rafael (hereafter MJSR) 25 June 1870.
James Black's Bible in Possession of great-great-granddaughter, Charmaine A. Burdell (hereafter CAB).
International Genealogical Index (hereafter IGI).
FHL microfiche March 1992: 4301.

Dorothy Gittinger Mutnick, *Some Alta California Pioneers & Descendants* (hereafter Mutnick) Past Time Publications, Lafayette, CA, Division One Pl-Z; 966.

"The Black Will Case," *San Francisco Evening Bulletin* (hereafter SFEH) 21 March 1874, testimony of Black's daughter, Mrs. Burdell.

MJSR 20 January 1866.

Mutnick, Div. One A-Fig: 368, 369.

Mission San Rafael Arcangel (hereafter MSAR) baptism #2028.

FHL film #909236.

The Courier Press, Petaluma, 24 January 1900.

MSRA marriages FHL files #909235.

James Williamson file, National Home for Disabled Volunteer Soldiers, Dayton, OH.

Society of California Pioneers Library.

Alley, Bowen & Co. *History of Marin County,* 1880 (hereafter Hist.Marin) p. 284.

Mutnick. Div. One Pl-Z: 1180.

Letter, Dr. W. Scott Polland Collection (hereafter WSPC) Bancroft Library U.C.

Hubert H. Bancroft, *Register of Pioneer Inhabitants of California, 1542-1848,* (Dawson Book Shop, L.A., CA 1964) (hereafter Bancroft). McIntosh 724. Black 721.

Permit WSPC.

Mount Olivet Cemetery, San Rafael, Tombstones.

Deposition of James Black in Hanson vs.McCue,Calif. Superior Court 1870, Exhibit 2 #412:108, 110.

Hist.Marin 154.

Jack Mason, *Early Marin,* House of Printing, Petaluma,CA, 1971 :65.

Robert G. Cowan, *Ranchos of California,* Academy Library Guild Fresno, CA 1956, p. 52.

"Marin's Old Days", MJSR 25 January 1923.

G.W. Hendry and J.N. Bowman, *The Spanish.and Mexican Adobe and Other Buildings in the Nine San Francisco Bay Counties, 1776-1850,* Bancroft Library, U.C. Berkeley. Part I Marin Co. 1940, Nicasio 98,99.

Hist. Marin 285.

"Black's Will is Broken", MJSR 9 April. 1874.

"Black Will Case", SFEB 20, 23 March 1874, testimony of Mrs. Mary Joynson and Judge McM. Schafter.

Alley, Bowen & Co. *History of Mendocino County 1880*: 475.

"James Black, Marin Pioneer Cattle Baron", *Independent Journal,* San Rafael. May 16, 1970.

John A. Hawgood, editor, *First and Last Consul Thomas Oliver Larkin.* Pacific Books, Publishers, Palo Alto, CA 1970, Appendix A.

MSRA baptisims. FHL film #909236.

Bancroft: Black 721.

Hist. Marin 206.

Inquest No. I, 23 Aug.1850, death of an Indian Point Reyes, signed James Black.

"The Black Will Case," SFEB 23, 24 March 1874, testimony of U.M. Gordon and Judge McM. Shafter.

MJSR 9 April 1874; 19 March 1874.

SFEB 3 April 1874.

MJSR 18 June 1874.

Bernarda de Villar Lyons and George Lyons

This account is drawn from research and original documents compiled by Teresa Lyons Di Gangi, who was the great-granddaughter of Bernarda and George Lyons through her paternal grandfather Daniel Lyons.

H. H. Bancroft, *History of California,* Vol IV, p. 721.
Illustrated History of Southern California, Published by Lewis Co., Chicago Ill. pg 376.
Lucy Wantworth (daughter of Martin de Villar) Diary notes, November 1933, San Diego Historical Society.
V.E. Smythe, *History of San Diego,* pp. 277 - 278.
Daniel Lyons Family Bible, passed through Marjorie Lyons McLung, Davis,California.
Illustrated History of Southern California, Published by Lewis Co., Chicago Ill. pg. 376.
Joe Stone *San Diego Union Tribune;* "Yesterday in the West", May 29, 1977.
History of San Bernadino and San Diego County. Eliot and Co. 1883, Reprint Riverside Museum, pg, 192.
San Diego Union Tribune June 12, 1872.
W. Davidson, Notes 1931; San Diego Historical Society.

Eli Moore

History of the State of California and Biographical Record of Coast Counties Calif. Prof. J.M. Guinn A.M. (1904), page 1221.
Calif. Historical Society Quarterly Vol. 16,1937.
The California Trail by George R. Stewart (University of Nebraska Press, 1962) p. 187.
History of San Mateo County. Frank M. Stanger in 1938, San Mateo Times.
Frank M. Stanger, *Peninsula Community Book.* (A.W. Sawston, 1946), p. 168.
"The Moore Family of Pescadero", by LaVerne Brazil. Term paper, College of San Mateo, 1948.
"A Pioneer of '47". Statement of Alexander Moore of Pescadero, Bancroft Library. 1878. Call #CD 127.D.

John & Caroline Churchman

Ash Spring School later became Oak Grove School, located in what is now the small town of Graton.

Iroquois Stalker, Watseka, Illinois, Vols. I and III, Winter 1973.
Census of 1850.
New Historical Atlas of Sonoma Co., Illustrated, Thomas H. Thompson and Co. 1877.

Stevenson's Regiment

"To a Distant and Perilous Service: Stevenson's Regiment" by Richard Reinhardt, *American Heritage,* June/July 1979.

Charles Henry Lipp

Bancroft, Hubert Howe. *California Pioneer Register.*. (Baltimore: Regional Publishing Company, 1964) p. 222.

Bancroft, Hubert Howe. *History of California,* Vol. V, 1846-1848. (San Francisco: The History Company, 1886), pp. 419-518.

Clark, Francis D. *Stevenson's Regiment in California, 1847-48.* (New York: George S. Evans & Co., 1882).

Federal Government, Department of Veterans Affairs. (Mexican War and Civil War documentation)

Grand Army of the Republic, Farragut Post No. 12, Ledgers #1 and 2, 1869-1904. Vallejo Naval and Historical Museum.

Haskins, C.V. The *Argonauts of California.* 1890, p. 394.

Lin Northun, conversations. San Pablo Lodge No. 43, I.O.O.F., Vallejo.

Vallejo City Directory, 1870.

Vallejo Evening Chronicle, April 13, 1896, and April 25, 1919.

Russ Family

W. F. Swasey, *The Early Days and Men of California.*.

Bailey Millard, *History of the San Francisco Bay,* Volume III (The American Historical Society, Inc. 1924).

Zoeth Skinner Eldredge, *The Beginnings of San Francisco,* Vol II, (San Francisco, 1912).

Charles Lockwood, *Suddenly San Francisco: The Early Years of an Instant City.*

James Kenny

Katherine Shannon Kenny by Aldine Gorman.

Early Reminiscences of the Mendocino Coast by Kate Gorman (1860-1950).

Mendocino Historical Review. Mendocino Historical Research, Inc. Spring 1974.

Historical and Biographical Record. "James Kenny", pgs. 1476-1477.

Memories of Cuffey's Cove and Early Greenwood 1850-1930. by Flora Buchanan and Yerda Matson Dearing (Greenwood Hobbyists, May 1977).

Lester Hulin

The History of Oregon, by Rev. H.K. Hines D.D. Published by the Lewis Publishing Co. Chicago, 1893.

John Parrott

John Parrott by Barbara Donohue Jostes (Lawton & Alfred Kennedy, San Francisco, 1972).

Dr. Galen Burdell D.D.S.

Extensive Genealogical Research for this section was undertaken by great-grandaughter Charmaine A. Burdell.

Galen Burdell Death Certificate Mass. Archives Vol. XCV p.152 Francis Lamon.

Virgil D. White, *Genealogical Abstracts of Revol. War Pension Files,* pub. 1991 James Gault Vol. II p.1325; John Cunningham Vol. I p.841.

Estate of John Burdell, Simsbury, Hartford Co., Conn. No.403 Farmington Probate Dist.

Family History Library, Salt Lake City, UT, microfilm #0533494 "St. John's Dutch Reformed Church" Canajoharie, Montgomery Co.,NY.

Jack Finney, *Forgotten News-Crime of the Century,* pub. Simon & Schuster Inc. 1985.

R.M. Devens, *Our First Century: One Hundred Great & Memorable Events,* pub. 1877 Chapter LXXIII "Horrible & Mysterious Murder of Dr. Burdell, A Wealthy NY Dentist In His Own Office 1857", p.626-633.

Soc. of Calif. Pioneers, Archives p.154.

Octavius Thorndike Howe, *Argonauts of Forty-nine,* pub. 1923, pp. 75, 76, 204, 205.

San Francisco Chronicle August 23, 1915 "The Peoples Safety Value "How Duxbury Reef Got Its Name."

Calif. Hist. Soc. Library, San Francisco, CA . List of Officers and Members of St. Francis Hook & Ladder Co. No.l.

Petition dated 22 June 1850.

Southern Calif. Hist. Soc. Quar. Winter 1973 p.435 Bradford Luckingham "Benevolence in Emergent San Francisco."

Calif. Hist. Soc. Quar. Vol. XXV (1946) No. 2 (June) p.111, No. 3 (Sept.) p.257.

San Francisco Evening Bulletin. "The Black Will Case", 21, 24 March 1874, Testimony of Mrs. Burdell, 23 March, Testimony of Judge McM. Shafter.

Mercury-San Francisco Dental Soc. Vol. 33 Sept. 1982 No.5. Thomas A. Jacobs D.D.S. "Galen Burdell Pioneer Dentist."

San Francisco Medical Press, April 1864, editor Henry Gibbons M.D. "Death From Chloroform."

Northwestern Bottle Collectors Assn., *The Glassblower,* May 1970. Editor Frank Sternad pp. 10-11 "Dr. G. Burdell."

North Marin County Water District. Point Reyes Water System Improvements, Engineering Report & Draft EIR November 1979. pp. 15,18.

Mary Floyd Williams, *History of the San Francisco Committee of Vigilance,* pub. UC Berkeley 1921, p. 447.

Galen Burdell's membership papers, San Francisco Committee of Vigilantes 1856. Collection of Charmaine A. Burdell.

Grace Canitrot Borel

Fick, Ronald G. *San Francisco Is No More.* Menlo Park, CA 1963 p. 3.
Kahn, Edgar M. *Cable Car Days in San Francisco,* Palo Alto, CA 1949 pp 57-59.
Fick, Ronald G. "The Antoine Borel Family" *La Peninsula: The Journal of the San Mateo Historical Society.*

Jules Francois Bekeart

Frank Bekeart Goldrush Gunsmith, by Phyllis Gernes & Dovanan Lewis, Published by Gold Discovery Park Assoc. Colma, California.

Nathaniel Holland

California State Assembly Journal, 1856.
Letter from W.N. Davis, Jr., Chief of Archives State of California 2/13/07.
History of Bench and Bar of California, Commercial Printing House, 1901.
California Historical Society Quarterly, September 1957.

Whitford Pascoe Harrington

Memorial Book, Society of California Pioneers.
Wagon Trains 1849-1865, by Lois Dove, California State Library 1989.

David Saul Levy

Autobiography of David Saul Levy. California Pioneers Assoc. July 4, 1912.

Milo Jewett Ayer

Descendants of Milo Jewett Ayer who contributed to this account include his great-granddaughter, Dorothy Ayer Powers; Dorothy's daughters: Nancy L. Powers and Laurel Powers Jacobson; Nancy's daughter; Ciarda Ayer Henderson; Laurel's daughters: Alexis T. Jacobson and Brianna E. Jacobson. Nancy is a life member of the Daughters of California Pioneers, a former member of its Board of Directors, and a current member of its Advisory Board of Directors.

Sources of information for this account include various news accounts, Archives of the Society of California Pioneers, and the publication: *The Boston-Newton Company Venture, From Massachusetts to California in 1849,* by Jessie Gould Hannon, University of Nebraska Press, 1969. Ms. Hannon's account brought together companion diaries of the adventure across the continent kept by Charles Gould and David Jackson Staples, two members of the Boston-Newton Joint Stock Association. The Staples journal was previously published in the *California Historical Society Quarterly* in 1943.

James Thomas Lillard, Jr.

It is likely that Lillard traveled with the G. W. Hudspeth party. Lillard describes the leader as the discoverer of the Hudspeth Cutoff. Hudspeth was a neighbor of the Lillards and was in the same regiment as James during the Mexican War. He was a freighter who traveled to California in 1849.

Lillard was recommended for membership in the Sacramento branch of the Society of California Pioneers by I.S. Chiles on June 1, 1869.

C. Haskins, *The Argonauts of California*, p.376. J. T. Lillard is listed as a member of the Sacramento Pioneer Association, p. 374. Lillard is spelled "Lilliard," in this publication.

H.H. Bancroft. *California Pioneer Register and Index.* 1542-1858.

National Archives, Mexican War. Pension Application and Affidavits for James T. Lillard.

History of Northern California (Lewis Publishing Co. 1891).

Sacramento Society of California Pioneers, Sacramento Archives and Museum Collection, File XI41

The Winters Express Saturday, January 12, 1889.

John Mathews

A Brief History of Napa, Sonoma, Lake and Mendocino Counties Prior to 1873, by C.A. Menefee. Publisher: Reporter Publishing House, Napa. 1879: Page 292.

Mexican War records; from the National Archives.

Yuba County Records, *Marriage Certificates.* No 1 From May 1 1851 to 1865 .

Microfilm, Family History Library, Church of Latter Day Saints.

History of Mendocino County California, 1880. Page 604

Samuel J., Reid, Indian Affairs, California. Round Valley Indian Reservation. *List of Employees Fourth Quarter, 1877.* National Archives, San Bruno, CA.

William John Clarke

The Diary of William John Clarke, Illinois to California 1849. Family printed in 1985.

The Heart of the Laggan: The History of Ramoghy and Ray National School, by May McClintock, County Donegal, Ireland, 1990.

Sacramento: An Illustrated History, by Thor Seveson, California Historical Society.

Yolo County History, by William O. Russel, Woodland, California, 1940.

The Illustrated History of Yolo County. Depue and Company, San Francisco, California 1879.

Elias Beard and James Hawley

History of the State of California and Biographical Record of Coast Counties, J.M. Gunn.

Rev. Samuel Gray

Journals of the Forty Niners. Salt Lake to Los Angeles. Diaries and records of S.Young, J. Brown, J. Stoves and others. Edited with historical comments by L.R. Halen, Professor of History, Brigham Young University.

The Far West and the Rockies Historical Series 1820-1875,Vol II, California Room, State Library.

Jefferson James

Chronicle of the Builders, Dr. Wallace Smith, Professor of History, Fresno State University.

History of the James Ranch: First Families of Virginia by Ivabelle Garrison.

Hiram Throop Graves

The Argonauts of California, Fords, Howard & Hulbert, New York, 1890.

Memoirs and Masonic History of the Late Samuel Graves, Frank Eastman & Co., San Francisco, 1882.

Who Was Who in America. Vol. I, 1897-1842. The A.N. Marquis Co., Chicago, Ill.

Ithiel Corbett

History of Milford, Mass. by Adin Ballour, Boston 1882.

History of Chautauga County, by Andrew W. Young.

History of the Daughters of California Pioneers

Page 293, Tree Planting Photograph; Reading from left to right.

First row: Mr. Latham, Mr. Van Dercook

Second row: Mr. Baker, Mrs. J. M. Hutchings, ?, Miss Clara A. Adams, ?, Mrs. Morse, ?, Mrs. Ella Lees Leigh, ?, Mrs. S.S. Palmer, Miss Lucy F. Adams (President of DCP), Miss Eliza D. Keith, Mrs. Henry Tricou.

Half Row (back of second row): ?, Mrs. M. Murphy, ?, Mrs. Limbeau (at right of Mrs. Morse, back), Mrs Keith (at left of Eliza D. Keith, back).

Third Row: Miss Suzie A. Adams, Miss Louise Neppert, Miss Ophelia Levy, Mrs. Gurnett, Mrs. Templeman, Miss Ila Biven, Miss Julia Neppert, ?, ?, ?, Miss Kate McWilliams, Miss Martha Galloway.

Index

About the Artist

Marion Poett Howard Hoekenga, along with her sister, Virginia Howard Siegman, is a lifetime member of the Daughters of California Pioneers. Their father, William Henry Howard, was active in the Society of California Pioneers, and the great grandson of William Davis Merry Howard, San Francisco entrepreneur. W.D.M. Howard was instrumental in the forming of the Society, and was its first president from 1850-53. He came to California in 1839 as a super cargo on the ship *California*, trading in hides. He bought out the Hudson Bay Co. with his business partner Henry Mellus. Together they donated the first fire engine to San Francisco, and Howard was very active in getting the Center Wharf built to aid in loading and unloading cargoes in San Francisco's growing sea trade. He bought the Spanish land grant Rancho San Mateo, and left lasting improvements in both communities.

Marion has studied art as a lifelong pursuit. After graduating from University of California, Santa Cruz with a degree in history, she moved to a ranch in northeastern Nevada. The artist continued to paint and draw ranch scenes and high desert subjects. She also drew most of the nineteenth century buildings in the near-by mining town of Eureka, and sold works that were commissioned. She now lives in Boulder City, Nevada and continues to draw and paint landscapes of the low desert. Doing the sketches for this book brings together the two interests Marion enjoys most— art and history.

DAUGHTERS OF HISTORY has been typeset in Monotype Centaur, a face designed by Bruce Rogers for the Metropolitan Museum in 1914, modeled on letters cut by the fifteenth-century printer Nicolas Jenson. The italic type, originally named Arrighi, was designed by Frederic Warde in 1925, who modeled his letters on those of Ludovico degli Arrighi, a Renaissance scribe. The text of the book was designed by John Strohmeier. It has been printed and bound by Vaughan Printing of Nashville, Tennessee. The paper is Frazier Mills Offset Antique.

CARIBBEA
Cl